February 12–13, 2018
Tempe, AZ, USA

Association for Computing Machinery

Advancing Computing as a Science & Profession

I0013427

HotMobile'18

Proceedings of the 19th International Workshop on
Mobile Computing Systems & Applications

Sponsored by:
ACM SIGMOBILE

Supported by:
Intel, Samsung, Cisco Meraki, & Google

Association for
Computing Machinery

Advancing Computing as a Science & Profession

The Association for Computing Machinery
2 Penn Plaza, Suite 701
New York, New York 10121-0701

ISBN: 978-1-4503-5630-5 (Digital)

ISBN: 978-1-4503-5870-5 (Print)

Additional copies may be ordered prepaid from:

ACM Order Department
PO Box 30777
New York, NY 10087-0777, USA

Phone: 1-800-342-6626 (USA and Canada)
+1-212-626-0500 (Global)
Fax: +1-212-944-1318
E-mail: acmhelp@acm.org
Hours of Operation: 8:30 am – 4:30 pm ET

Welcome to ACM HotMobile 2018

We are delighted to welcome you to the nineteenth edition of the International Workshop on Mobile Computing Systems and Applications – *HotMobile '18*. This year continues the tradition of selective, highly interactive workshops that discuss the latest ideas in mobile systems and applications, along with new breakthroughs in underlying technologies. In addition to the technical program and keynote speakers, the program is designed to continue the HotMobile tradition of engaging the audience in deep technical discussions and debates of controversial approaches.

The selection of full papers to this workshop was highly competitive. Out of 65 submissions, the technical program committee accepted 19 for publication and presentation, resulting in an acceptance rate of 29%. An in-person PC meeting was held at the Stony Brook University to make final acceptance decisions. The PC members demonstrated a strong commitment to the selection process, not only by submitting high-quality reviews, but by traveling to New York from locations all over the world, including Singapore, Germany, and France. Accompanying full papers are a set of posters and demonstrations of exciting early stage research from the community. Collectively our program spans a rich range of topics including mobile DNA analysis, virtual reality, self-driving cars, new sensing technologies, and the Web. We feel this reflects the strong health, vibrancy and breadth of the mobile computing field.

Putting together ACM HotMobile 2018 has been a collaborative effort involving many within our community. First, we would like to thank the authors whose ideas and effort provide the heart of the workshop. We are also indebted to diligence and energy of the program committee, organizing committee and steering committee. We greatly thank ACM SIGMOBILE for sponsorship of this event, in addition to a large number of generous corporate supporters, including Samsung, Intel, Cisco Meraki, and Google. We sincerely hope that HotMobile '18 is an engaging and stimulating meeting of the mobile community, and provides ample opportunities for discussion and debate with a wide range of academics and industrial practitioners.

Minkyong Kim
HotMobile '18 General Chair
Samsung

Aruna Balasubramanian
HotMobile '18 Program Chair
Stony Brook University

Table of Contents

Session: Applications using New Hardware
Session Chair: Sharad Agarwal *(Microsoft Research)*

Session: Augmentation
Session Chair: Haito Zheng *(University of Chicago)*

Session: New Applications of Inertial Sensing and Beyond
Session Chair: Jacob Sorber *(Clemson University)*

Keynote Address

Session: Web

Session Chair: Mark Corner *(UMass Amherst)*

Session: Cameras

Session Chair: Ardalan Amiri Sani *(University of California, Irvine)*

Invited Talk

Session: Performance and Experimentation

Session Chair: Mirco Musolesi *(University College London)*

HotMobile 2018 Workshop Organizers

General Chair:	Minkyong Kim *(Samsung Electronics, USA)*
Program Chair:	Aruna Balasubramanian *(Stony Brook, NY, USA)*
Apps Chair:	Kevin Boos *(Rice University, TX, USA)*
Local Chair:	Robert LiKamWa *(Arizona State University, USA)*
Student Travel Grant Chair:	Kyungmin Lee *(Facebook, USA)*
Demos & Posters Chairs:	Eduardo Cuervo *(Microsoft Research- Redmond, USA)* Chunyi Peng *(Purdue University, USA)*
Sponsorship Chair:	Ardalan Amiri Sani *(University of California – Irvine, USA)*
Publication Chair:	Shubham Jain *(Old Dominion University, USA)*
Registration Chair:	Songkuk Kim *(Yonsei University)*
Publicity Chairs:	Iqbal Mohomed *(Samsung Research America)* JeongGil Ko *(Ajou University, Sth. Korea)*
Web Chair:	Mateusz Mikusz *(Lancaster University, UK)*
Steering Committee:	Nigel Davies, Chair *(Lancaster University, UK)* Ramón Cáceres *(Google, USA)* Mahadev Satyanarayanan *(Carnegie Mellon University, USA)* Roy Want *(Google, USA)* David Chu *(Google, USA)* Prabal Dutta *(University of Michigan, USA)* Elizabeth Belding *(University of California – Santa Barbara, USA)* Nic Lane *(University of Oxford and Nokia Bell Lab, UK)*

Program Committee: Fadel Adib *(Massachusetts Institute of Technology, USA)*
Sharad Agarwal *(Microsoft Research, USA)*
Elizabeth Belding *(University of California – Santa Barbara, USA)*
Kate Ching-Ju Lin *(National Chiao Tung University, Taiwan)*
Samir Das *(Stony Brook University, USA)*
Monia (Manya) Ghobadi *(Microsoft Research, USA)*
Ben Greenstein *(Google, USA)*
Inseok Hwang *(IBM Research, USA)*
Robin Kravets *(University of Illinois at Urbana Champaign, USA)*
Nic Lane *(University of Oxford and Nokia Bell Lab, UK)*
Sung-Ju Lee *(KAIST, South Korea)*
Youngki Lee *(Singapore Management University, Singapore)*
Robert LiKamWa *(Arizona State University, USA)*
Joerg Ott *(Technische Universität München, Germany)*
Giovanni Pau *(UPMC – Sorbonne University, Paris, France)*
Jacob Sorber *(Clemson University, USA)*
Narseo Vallina Rodriguez *(IMDEA Networks and ICSI, UC Berkeley, USA)*
Jun Wang *(Huawei R&D, USA)*
Mi Zhang *(Michigan State University, USA)*
Ying Zhang *(Facebook, USA)*
Xia Zhou *(Dartmouth College, USA)*

HotMobile 2018 Sponsor & Supporters

Sponsor:

Gold Supporters:

       SAMSUNG

Sapphire Supporter: cisco Meraki

Bronze Supporter: Google

Applications and Challenges of Real-time Mobile DNA Analysis

Steven Y. Ko
Computer Science and Engineering
University at Buffalo
stevko@buffalo.edu

Lauren Sassoubre
Civil, Structural, and
Environmental Engineering
University at Buffalo
lsassoub@buffalo.edu

Jaroslaw Zola
Computer Science and Engineering
Biomedical Informatics
University at Buffalo
jzola@buffalo.edu

ABSTRACT

The DNA sequencing is the process of identifying the exact order of nucleotides within a given DNA molecule. The new portable and relatively inexpensive DNA sequencers, such as Oxford Nanopore MinION, have the potential to move DNA sequencing outside of laboratory, leading to faster and more accessible DNA-based diagnostics. However, portable DNA sequencing and analysis are challenging for mobile systems, owing to high data throughput and computationally intensive processing performed in environments with unreliable connectivity and power.

In this paper, we provide an analysis of the challenges that mobile systems must address to maximize the potential of portable DNA sequencing, and *in situ* DNA analysis. We explain the DNA sequencing process and highlight the main differences between traditional and portable DNA sequencing in the context of the actual and envisioned applications. We look at the identified challenges from the perspective of both algorithms and systems design, showing the need for careful co-design.

CCS CONCEPTS

• **Human-centered computing** → *Ubiquitous and mobile computing*;

KEYWORDS

Real-time mobile DNA analysis, mobile DNA sequencing, MinION

ACM Reference Format:
Steven Y. Ko, Lauren Sassoubre, and Jaroslaw Zola. 2018. Applications and Challenges of Real-time Mobile DNA Analysis. In *HotMobile '18: 19th International Workshop on Mobile Computing Systems & Applications, February 12–13, 2018, Tempe , AZ, USA.* ACM, New York, NY, USA, 6 pages. https://doi.org/10.1145/3177102.3177114

1 INTRODUCTION

DNA, a polymer made from four basic nucleotides (abbreviated by A, C, G, T), is the main carrier of genetic information. The DNA sequencing is the process in which this information is extracted by converting physical DNA molecules into signals that describe the

exact order and type of the constituent nucleotides. The ability to sequence DNA has revolutionized molecular biology, biomedicine and life sciences in general. Among many applications, some we review in Section 2, it is recognized as a critical method for diagnosing and improving human health (e.g. dissecting genetic mechanisms of cancer [15]), identifying pathogens and protecting public health (e.g. detecting and tracking spread of infectious diseases [6]) or understanding our environment (e.g. impact of microorganisms on water, air and soil [14]).

The end-to-end DNA sequencing and analysis involves a combination of laboratory and bioinformatics steps (see Section 3). In a traditional setup, these steps are performed at massive scales by highly trained personnel using expensive benchtop DNA sequencers and supporting computational servers. Consequently, the process has been confined to high-end laboratories, limiting the access and extending the time it takes from sample collection to interpretable results.

The recently introduced portable DNA sequencers, specifically Oxford Nanopore Tech. (ONT) MinION [16] (see Fig. 1), are changing this situation. Compared to the traditional DNA sequencers, these devices are relatively inexpensive and truly mobile: smaller than a cell phone, USB powered, and designed to be easily operable "in the field." Moreover, they use biochemical principles (i.e. nanopore-based single molecule sequencing [11]) that enable near real-time streaming of raw signals as soon as DNA molecules are "sensed," usually within minutes from the process initiation. As a result, portable DNA sequencing emerges as a rapid *in situ* diagnostic tool, especially when DNA samples are difficult or impossible to preserve or transport. Examples include the DNA surveillance of Ebola [13] and Zika [5] during the recent outbreaks, deployments in the Arctic [3] and Antarctic [8], in rainforests of Ecuador [12] and even in the International Space Station [2].

Figure 1: Illumina MiniSeq (left), vs. portable MinION (middle) and forthcoming SmidgION (right). Pictures not to scale. The approximate size in centimeters is marked for reference. The current price of MinION is $1,000 compared to $50K for an entry-level benchtop sequencer.

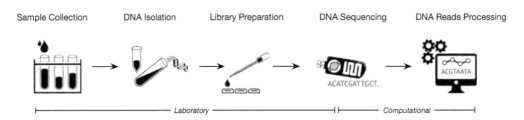

Figure 2: Major steps in a DNA sequencing workflow.

However, portable DNA sequencing and analysis are challenging for mobile systems. This is because the underlying computations, as well as data and communication intensive operations, have to be balanced to ensure the desired quality of the analysis while running in real-time, typically in the energy and bandwidth constrained environments. Currently, mobile DNA sequencing is driven by the existing bioinformatics tools designed primarily for desktop systems, and organized into mobile workflows in an *ad hoc* manner. While these solutions have been successful in the initial trials, they cannot be expected to scale if the underlying problems of processing speed, energy efficiency and resilience are not addressed. As the technology behind portable DNA sequencing matures and becomes more accessible, it is reasonable to assume that it will be adopted by individual consumers. Consequently, the underlying algorithms and software will have to operate in a wide range of conditions and workloads, and under varying resources, while remaining easy to use.

In this paper, we discuss the challenges that mobile systems must address to maximize the potential of portable DNA sequencing, and *in situ* DNA processing. We look at the identified challenges from the perspective of both algorithms and systems design, and argue for careful co-design and functionality separation. The paper is written from the systems perspective, for readers with no prior background in genomics or bioinformatics. Its slightly extended version is available from https://arxiv.org/abs/1711.07370.

2 SEQUENCING APPLICATIONS

We begin with a discussion of general applications that highlight the enabling nature of the portable DNA sequencing.

Sequencing When Time is Critical: Rapid diagnosis of infectious diseases is critical for protecting human health [6]. The DNA sequencing can be used to identify an infectious agent, assess its responsiveness to vaccines or antibiotics, and prescribe the best treatment. In some diseases, starting the right treatment within hours is vital [1, 7], and when responding to epidemics, real-time genomic surveillance increases situational awareness (e.g. by tracking evolution rate and transmission patterns), helping with planning and resource allocation [5, 13]. Importantly, the same principles apply in detection and mitigation of biological threats [18]. However, the current culture-based laboratory methods for identifying pathogens take days, and in fact some pathogens are difficult or impossible to grow in culture.

Because emerging portable DNA sequencers are free from these limitations, they offer a significant advantage when time is critical. One excellent example is the response to the recent Ebola epidemics,

where a mobile laboratory using MinIONs, transported in a standard airplane bag, was deployed in Guinea [13]. Despite logistic difficulties, such as lack of continuous electric power and poor Internet connectivity, the laboratory became operational within two days, was generating results within 24 hours from receiving a sample, and provided valuable insights into disease dynamics.

Sequencing When Location is Critical: The samples we know the least about, and would like to study by DNA sequencing, are usually located far from established sequencing facilities. This is especially true for metagenomic studies in which communities of microbial organisms are sampled directly from their native environments [14]. However, many types of samples cannot be transported due to the legal (e.g. export barriers), or practical considerations (e.g. cost effectiveness). Furthermore, sequencing in laboratory is too constrained to study rapidly changing environments.

Portable DNA sequencers reached the level where they can be operated in some of the most demanding environments. For example, in one recent study, a battery-only powered laboratory, consisting of MinIONs and an *ad hoc* cluster of two laptops without Internet connection, was harnessed for *in situ* analysis of microorganisms found in the depths of South Wales Coalfield [4]. Although the entire process was far from simple, the study demonstrated that DNA sequencing in remote locations is currently feasible. Other studies [2, 8] serve as a further proof of principle.

Future: With the continuing improvements to the sequencing technology, and simplification and automation of DNA extraction and preparation protocols (see next section), we may expect that portable DNA analysis will become a ubiquitous tool. Rapid medical diagnostics, forensics, agriculture, and general exploration of microbial diversity on Earth and in the outer space, are just some domains that will benefit. However, the most exciting opportunities are in consumer genomics. ONT has been promoting the idea of Internet of Living Things (IoLT) [19], where anyone will be able to sequence anything anywhere, opening endless possibilities for DNA-driven discoveries. Yet, because even short DNA sequencing runs can easily deliver gigabytes of data, which may require hours to analyze, the success of IoLT will depend on the ability of mobile and cloud computing to provide adequate support.

3 PORTABLE VS. BENCHTOP

In order to understand computational challenges in portable DNA sequencing, it helps to first look at the end-to-end DNA sequencing process, and how this process differs between the current benchtop sequencing platforms and the emerging portable sequencers.

Table 1: General characteristics of different steps in DNA sequencing.

	Library Preparation		DNA Sequencing		DNA Reads Processing	
	MinION	Illumina	MinION	Illumina	MinION	Illumina
Time Scale	Minutes-hours	Hours-days	Real-time, Minutes-hours	Days-weeks	Real-time, Minutes-hours	Batch-mode, Minutes-days
Equipment	Basic, portable laboratory equipment (e.g. pipettes, centrifuge)		Small portable USB device	Benchtop machine	Laptop to data center	
Energy	1-2W		1W	Up to 10KW	No data available, sustained high load	
Software	N/A		Proprietary firmware, drivers and control software		Usually open source, complex string and statistical algorithms	
Advantages	Fast and easy protocol	Protocols for very low DNA mass	Inexpensive, portable, real-time, long reads	Low cost per base, low error rate	Streaming and interactive sequencing	Many tested workflows available
Challenges	High mass of input DNA	Time and labor intensive	High error rate, high cost per base	Short reads, expensive device	High error rate	Short read length, high data volume

3.1 How DNA is Studied

A typical DNA sequencing workflow involves both laboratory and computational steps (see Fig. 2 and Tab. 1). While the specifics of the protocols executed in every step may vary, the main steps remain the same irrespective of the DNA sequencing platform.

Sample Collection: The first step is to obtain the material from which DNA will be extracted. The choice and quantity of material to sample are dictated by the particular application. Sample types include patient's blood (e.g. in epidemiology), feces (e.g. when studying gut microbial flora), water or soil (e.g. when tracking biological contaminants), etc. The samples are preserved, e.g. by freezing or adding a chemical buffer, to minimize degradation or contamination until they can be further processed. As we mentioned earlier, sometimes samples may be impossible to adequately preserve, necessitating immediate processing.

DNA Isolation: In this step, the collected samples are subjected to chemical, mechanical or thermal processing to extract and purify the DNA molecules. DNA extractions performed in a laboratory with the standard commercially available kits take from minutes to hours, and in addition to the basic tools like pipettes, involve heating/cooling and specialized equipment, e.g. a centrifuge. Thus, this step requires access to power supply, or the use of improvised substitute solutions.

Library Preparation: The purified DNA is further processed, to make it compatible with the sensing machinery of the sequencer. This usually involves basic biochemical processing that nevertheless may require complex protocols. The step becomes nuanced when DNA has to be biochemically barcoded or amplified as required in some applications. Overall, the entire library preparation takes from several minutes to several days, and usually does not require additional equipment beyond the portable laboratory tools.

DNA Sequencing: Once the DNA library is ready, the actual sequencing can be performed. Currently, several sequencing platforms are available, e.g. Illumina, PacBio, Ion Torrent or Oxford Nanopore. They differ in how DNA is detected and read, which translates into differences in: sequencing speed and throughput (i.e. the number of nucleotides detected per unit of time), length of the output reads (i.e. how long DNA fragments sequencer can sense), and error rate (i.e. how many incorrectly detected nucleotides one may expect in the output). These differences are crucial, since they

directly affect the downstream processing and analysis. The current sequencers are controlled by computers, which also receive and store output data. With the exception of the MinION, they are not portable, taking days to complete a single sequencing run in laboratory. Finally, the sequencing process involves additional consumable resources, such as biochemical reagents and flow cells – devices in which the actual DNA sequencing happens.

DNA Reads Processing: This final step is purely computational. Its goal is to first convert signal produced by a sequencer into DNA reads, and then analyze these reads for insights. Because of the volatility of DNA, and the technical limitations of the sequencing platforms, DNA is hard to sequence as a single large molecule (e.g. a chromosome). Instead, it is sequenced in fragments that the sequencer is able to sense. The raw signal produced for each detected DNA fragment is run through base calling algorithms to generate DNA reads – the actual strings where detected nucleotides are represented by corresponding letters, commonly referred to as bases (**A**denine, **C**ytosine, **G**uanine, **T**thymine).

The collected DNA reads are the input to bioinformatics analysis. Here different workflows can be applied, depending on how samples had been prepared for sequencing, and what are the questions of interest. For example, *de novo* DNA assembly aims at reconstructing genome from input reads, while metagenomic analysis uses DNA reads to detect, classify, and functionally annotate microorganisms present in the sequenced samples. However, irrespective of the applied analysis, the common denominator is the reliance on compute and memory intensive string, combinatorial and statistical algorithms, ranging from massive graphs construction and traversal, through clustering, to large databases querying. Consequently, this step requires access to non-trivial computational resources, often exceeding capabilities of a single laptop or even a desktop computer.

3.2 Comparison

To compare portable and benchtop sequencing we concentrate on the MinION, currently the only portable sequencer, and Illumina platform, the dominating benchtop solution. We make our comparison in the context of *Library Preparation*, *DNA Sequencing*, and *DNA Reads Processing*, since these steps vary between platforms. Table 1 summarizes our comparison.

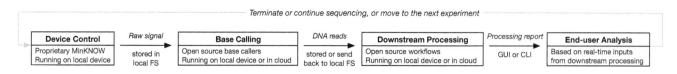

Figure 3: Current MinION software workflow.

Library Preparation: The attractiveness of MinION is in rapid sequencing protocol that can be executed in the field. The protocol takes roughly 10 min, and can be automated by using portable hands-off sample preparation hardware [17]. However, compared to standard protocols, it has limitations: it usually leads to lower quality sequencing output (i.e. with higher error rates), and it requires significant amount of input DNA (∼240 ng). In comparison, protocols for the Illumina platform, while much more complex and labor intensive (most take hours), can be performed with an order of magnitude less DNA, without impacting sequencing quality.

DNA Sequencing: The MinION is based on the idea of nanopore sequencing, where DNA molecules pass through organic nanoscale sensors in a flow cell [11]. This approach has three main advantages: first, it permits portable and easy to use design with a minimal power consumption, second, it enables real-time sequencing – the signal gathered by hundreds of nanopores in a sequencer becomes immediately available for downstream processing, third, it can produce long reads (current average is ∼7K bases compared to ∼250 bases for Illumina). All this comes at the price of high error rate (10%-30% compared to ∼0.1% for Illumina), which may lead to poor sequencing yield and complicates downstream analysis. Finally, because of the lower throughput, the cost of sequencing a single base is relatively higher (if we exclude upfront investments). This is in part because the MinION flow cells last for at most 48h of continuous sequencing.

DNA Reads Processing: The DNA reads produced in real-time by MinION allow for flexible approach to bioinformatics analysis, with the emphasis on streaming and one-pass strategies run outside of data centers. This makes "interactive" sequencing possible: the process can be terminated as soon as enough reads have been collected to answer question at hand. Long reads simplify tasks such as querying of databases or DNA assembly, but the high error rate makes other tasks (e.g. variants detection) challenging, or requires more input reads to resolve uncertainties. In contrast, the Illumina platform is high-throughput and high-volume oriented. The data from a single batch run is typically processed by well established, and to some extent standardized, workflows executed in a data center close to the sequencing facility. Low error rate combined with high DNA reads volume, makes tasks such as variants detection possible. However, short reads force complex algorithms on other tasks, e.g. assembly.

4 MOBILE COMPUTING PERSPECTIVE

We are now ready to highlight some of the open problems in portable DNA analysis as pertaining to mobile computing. To help understand the problems, we first provide the overview of the state of the art in mobile DNA analysis software. Then we discuss the limitations and open problems. While we base our discussion on the

current MinION platform, we believe that the points we make are equally applicable to the future generation of portable sequencers.

4.1 Current Software Overview

Figure 3 shows the MinION software architecture. The first component is MinKNOW – the proprietary control and signal acquisition software. MinKNOW is responsible for the configuration and supervision, including initiation and termination, of sequencing runs. It also receives and stores DNA signals generated by the ASIC in the sequencer's flow cell.

The second component is base calling software. Here multiple options are available [20], including execution on the host device or delegation to a specialized cloud service (e.g. Metrichor [10]). The current basecallers are very compute intensive, e.g. they typically involve Recurrent Neural Nets (RNNs), and are often recommended to run in the cloud.

The final software component consists of the application specific bioinformatics tools selected by end-users. Here, bioinformatics and computational biology keep delivering many open source solutions to choose from. Usually, these tools are organized into a pipeline of their own, and may involve multiple processing stages (e.g. preprocessing to remove low-quality data, querying a database to find sequences matching given DNA reads, building a tree of genetic relationships, etc.). Depending on the complexity, this DNA analytics may be deployed on the host machine, but more frequently it will be running in the cloud.

4.2 Limitations

The software architecture discussed above has been already used with success to showcase the promise of portable DNA sequencing. However, the approaches thus far focused on manual and *ad hoc* organization of the existing tools to run in a mobile setup, without addressing many important concerns, including a systematic approach to energy, data and network management. While this is a great first step, this strategy has too many limitations to be sustainable in a long term.

Energy Management: Energy is one of the most critical resources in mobile environments. It is especially important for mobile DNA analysis, because a sequencer is directly attached to, and draws energy from, a host device. Then, computational tasks at different stages of the sequencing workflow may run for tens of minutes to hours. Yet, the current software tools do not have any mechanisms to consider energy as a managed resource. In fact, bioinformatics software tools are routinely designed under the assumption that they will be executing either on computational servers or in data centers, with abundant main memory and storage, parallel execution capabilities, and stable power supply.

Data Management: DNA sequencer generates large volumes of data, which flows through various processing stages. For example, a 48h continuous run may produce over 200 GB of output, scattered across millions of files. Furthermore, if a cloud backend is used for the analysis, data is moved back and forth between a mobile device and the backend.

Currently, data is managed independently by each software component. This puts an unnecessary burden on software designers since they need to implement not only core functionality (e.g. a base calling algorithm) but also data management logic (e.g. data transfers, ensuring interoperability with other software, etc.). It also hinders rapid deployment of new data management mechanisms, as they have to be integrated into multiple and disjoint software elements.

Network Management: Some of the most promising and anticipated applications of mobile sequencing are *in situ* scenarios, where DNA has to be completely handled at a remote location. Here, network connectivity could be sporadic and bandwidth could highly fluctuate. However, the current software is not designed to be adaptive to changing network conditions. It assumes either no network connectivity, and hence runs locally, or depends on full network connectivity, and hence the always-on availability of a cloud service. Moreover, the decision to run locally or remotely is left to the end user, who must decide before executing the experiment.

Consumables Management: A flow cell is the workhorse of a sequencer. It is a consumable that can be used to analyze only a limited number of DNA samples, and within a limited time. Moreover, a flow cell degrades over time, and that translates into progressively lower sequencing throughput and growing error rate. Hence, in truly mobile setups it is necessary to manage flow cells as a scarce resource. While this problem has been recognized, currently no systematic solution exists that would offer the necessary functionality.

4.3 Open Problems and Our Approach

The majority of the limitations we identified above, are cross-cutting issues that involve multiple software components. For example, all software components should have some form of data, energy, and network management – in order to implement a new solution that addresses a limitation for any one of these, we need to work with multiple components and apply the solution across all of them. This is time consuming and error prone, and thus hinders rapid innovation.

To address this challenge, we envision a new software architecture that identifies all necessary functions and separates them into different software components with clean interfaces to ensure interoperability. Specifically, we propose the architecture based on three elements: the data management layer, the DNA analytics layer, and the workflow manager. This architectural separation has the benefit of allowing different components to innovate independently from other components. It also has an advantage of simplifying software development, by allowing each component to focus on its core functionality. It also accommodates the existing software, especially growing set of bioinformatics tools.

Data Management Layer: The goal of having a separate data management layer is to free other software components from the burden of managing data on their own. Thus, the data management layer should provide all functionality related to DNA analysis data. This includes 1) an interface for other components to read and store data, including the backward compatibility support for the POSIX interface that the existing tools use for flat files, 2) efficient algorithms and mechanisms for data management, including discovery, monitoring and delivery, and 3) integration with cloud services for processing delegation and data backup.

Interesting questions arise for the design of a data management layer in all three aspects. First, for the clean slate interface design, the primary question is what kind of abstractions make the most sense for DNA analysis. As mentioned earlier, there are mainly three types of data – raw signals generated by a sequencer, DNA reads (strings), and analysis results (e.g. stored as data tables). Thus, perhaps the most natural interface design is to have an abstraction for each data type. That would allow other components to easily search, access, and when needed join data without dealing with low-level details such as file management.

Second, once we design the interface, the underlying implementation can freely employ various data management mechanisms. For example, it is well-known that DNA has much inherent redundancy due to its small alphabet (four letters) and because it is repetitive. Thus, compression strategies can help reduce the volume of data to manage. However, it is an open question as to how best to compress this data in a mobile setting, considering the trade-offs between computing cost, computing precision and constrained storage. The existing general as well as DNA-specific strategies, which take into account DNA quality and properties of known genomes, may work well, but it remains to be seen which strategy is practical in a mobile setup.

Lastly, DNA sequencing and analysis data needs to be moved back and forth between a mobile device and a cloud service. As discussed earlier, base calling requires extensive RNNs and it is recommended to run it in the cloud. Similarly, some DNA analyses are computationally intensive and require access to large reference databases. Thus, the data management layer needs mechanisms to optimize data transfer. Here again, the existing techniques, such as similarity detection and dynamic chunking, may or may not work well.

DNA Analytics Layer: Ideally, the DNA analytics layer should have multiple sub-components, each implementing one algorithm relevant to DNA reads processing. The goal of this layer is to allow algorithm designers to focus on algorithms and their implementations without worrying about other orthogonal issues, such as data or energy management.

Interesting questions arise if we consider that DNA processing can leverage both mobile devices and cloud services at the same time. This provides an opportunity to revisit current solutions and redesign them such that they become amenable to running in both domains, or in either one of the domains. In fact, we can envision a programming model to simplify implementation of such strategies. The model could provide primitives to encapsulate alternative realizations of the same DNA processing task as small migratable entities, allowing them to move across mobile and cloud domains or run in parallel if necessary. It could be further extended to account for the fact that certain DNA processing problems can be answered with different quality, trading specificity or sensitivity for computational, memory or energy performance. For instance, one of the most general questions a user may wish to ask is *"what's in my pot"* [9], which is to report all known organisms whose DNAs have been found in a sample. The question can be answered by classifying detected organisms at the species level (i.e. fine-grained assignment) or just at the family level (i.e. coarse-grained assignment). The fine-grained assignment will typically require large reference databases and compute intensive sequence comparison. However, the process can be accelerated by using alternative strategies with lower precision (e.g., with data sketching and clever indexing). By implementing such multiple strategies, we could open more flexible execution paths. For example, in cases where resources are scarce, "approximate" tasks could provide less precise but potentially useful information, while waiting until resources are sufficient for a detailed answer.

One additional advantage of having task-based analytics layer is the ability to easily deploy workflows with stream processing and speculative execution capabilities (the techniques known to improve resource utilization). We note that while many of the existing algorithms, especially involving querying of reference databases, can be cast into this model with little or no effort, some other (e.g. construction of DNA assembly graphs, clustering, etc.) would require additional research and reformulation.

Workflow Manager: The goal of the workflow manager is to orchestrate all aspects of the DNA sequencing and analysis workflow, taking into account multiple static and dynamic factors that a user might encounter during a sequencing experiment. Many of the limitations that we discussed earlier fall into this category. Energy consumption, network connectivity, bandwidth variation, flow cell degradation, etc. all contribute to dynamically changing conditions of an experiment. Hence, the workflow manager should carefully monitor these variables and continuously make decisions on what the best course of actions is. This leads to several design questions. For example, how to monitor an experiment including not only the basic properties of a mobile device, e.g. how much energy is left or what the current network condition is, but also status of a flow cell and the quality of reads it is producing. Currently, very limited resources are available regarding flow cell monitoring, which we believe is an interesting research opportunity.

Once we have monitoring capabilities, the second question is how best to utilize available resources to get a desired outcome. This is especially important since a user conducting a DNA analysis in the field often has to make critical decisions based on limited information. For example, suppose a user is conducting DNA analysis in a remote area where there is no network connectivity. The user might wonder if she has enough energy to finish pending DNA analysis on her laptop and use the resulting data to adjust her experiment (e.g. collect more samples, etc.), or if she should move to an area where there is network connectivity to offload the analysis to a cloud and then continue the experiment. The workflow manager should either assist users to make well-informed decisions, or be intelligent enough to make decisions on its own, without requiring any user intervention. In cases where DNA analysis algorithms are amenable for partitioning or migrating across different domains, the workflow manager could make fine-grained decisions of moving various computational tasks across domains directly.

5 FINAL REMARKS

The proposed architecture is our attempt to introduce a more systematic and scalable approach to mobile DNA analytics, by tapping into concepts known from mobile computing. One potential caveat is that the proposed architecture would require reimplementation of some of the existing bioinformatics tools to fully leverage facilities in the DNA analytics layer. However, we believe this is feasible considering that portable sequencers are relatively new technology, with almost no algorithms designed for mobile systems. Currently, our team uses the latest release of MinION to investigate the questions we pose in this paper in the context of environmental DNA analysis.

REFERENCES

[1] M.D. Cao, D. Ganesamoorthy, A.G. Elliott, H. Zhang, M.A. Cooper, and L.J. Coin. Streaming algorithms for identification of pathogens and antibiotic resistance potential from real-time MinION sequencing. *GigaScience*, 5(1), 2016.

[2] S.L. Castro-Wallace, C.Y. Chiu, K.K. John, et al. Nanopore DNA sequencing and genome assembly on the International Space Station. *bioRxiv*, 2016. doi: 10.1101/077651.

[3] A. Edwards, A.R. Debbonaire, B. Sattler, L.AJ Mur, and A.J. Hodson. Extreme metagenomics using nanopore DNA sequencing: A field report from Svalbard, 78 N. *bioRxiv*, 2017. doi:10.1101/073965.

[4] A. Edwards, A. Soares, S. Rassner, , P. Green, J. Felix, and A. Mitchell. Deep sequencing: Intra-terrestrial metagenomics illustrates the potential of off-grid nanopore DNA sequencing. *bioRxiv*, 2017. doi:10.1101/133413.

[5] N.R. Faria, E.C. Sabino, M.R.T. Nunes, L.C.J. Alcantara, N.J. Loman, and O.G. Pybus. Mobile real-time surveillance of Zika virus in Brazil. *Genome Medicine*, 8(1), 2016.

[6] J.L. Gardy and N.J. Loman. Towards a genomics-informed, real-time, global pathogen surveillance system. *Nature Reviews Genetics*, page nrg.2017.88, 2017.

[7] F.C. Hewitt, S.L. Guertin, K.L. Ternus, K. Schulte, and D. R. Kadavy. Toward rapid sequenced-based detection and characterization of causative agents of Bacteremia. *bioRxiv*, 2017. doi:10.1101/162735.

[8] S.S. Johnson, E. Zaikova, D.S. Goerlitz, Y. Bai, and S. W. Tighe. Real-time DNA sequencing in the Antarctic Dry Valleys using the Oxford Nanopore sequencer. *Journal of Biomolecular Techniques*, 28(1), 2017.

[9] S. Juul, F. Izquierdo, A. Hurst, X. Dai, A. Wright, E. Kulesha, R. Pettett, and Turner. D. J. What's in my pot? Real-time species identification on the MinION. *bioRxiv*, 2015. doi:10.1101/030742.

[10] Metrichor Ltd. Metrichor, an Oxford Nanopore Company. https://metrichor.com/, 2017.

[11] H. Lu, F. Giordano, and Z. Ning. Oxford Nanopore MinION sequencing and genome assembly. *Genomics, Proteomics & Bioinformatics*, 14(5), 2016.

[12] A. Pomerantz, N. Penafiel, A. Arteaga, L. Bustamante, F. Pichardo, L.A. Coloma, C.L. Barrio-Amoros, D. Salazar-Valenzuela, and S. Prost. Real-time DNA barcoding in a remote rainforest using nanopore sequencing. *bioRxiv*, 2017. doi:10.1101/189159.

[13] J. Quick, N.J. Loman, S. Duraffour, et al. Real-time, portable genome sequencing for Ebola surveillance. *Nature*, 530(7589), 2016.

[14] C. Quince, A.W. Walker, J.T. Simpson, N. J. Loman, and N. Segata. Shotgun metagenomics, from sampling to analysis. *Nature Biotechnology*, 35(9), 2017.

[15] M.R. Stratton, P.J. Campbell, and P.A. Futreal. The cancer genome. *Nature*, 458(7239), 2009.

[16] Oxford Nanopore Technologies. Oxford Nanopore. https://nanoporetech.com, 2017.

[17] Oxford Nanopore Technologies. Voltrax. https://nanoporetech.com/products/voltrax, 2017.

[18] M.C. Walter, K. Zwirglmaier, P. Vette, S. A. Holowachuk, K. Stoecker, G. H. Genzel, and M. H. Antwerpen. MinION as part of a biomedical rapidly deployable laboratory. *Journal of Biotechnology*, 250, 2017.

[19] E. Waltz. Portable DNA sequencer MinION helps build the Internet of Living Things. *IEEE Spectrum*, 2017.

[20] R.R. Wick, L.M. Judd, and K.E. Holt. Comparison of Oxford Nanopore basecalling tools. https://github.com/rrwick/Basecalling-comparison, 2017.

Creating the Perfect Illusion : What will it take to Create Life-Like Virtual Reality Headsets?

Eduardo Cuervo
Microsoft Research
cuervo@microsoft.com

Krishna Chintalapudi
Microsoft Research
krchinta@microsoft.com

Manikanta Kotaru
Stanford University
mkotaru@stanford.edu

ABSTRACT

As Virtual Reality (VR) Head Mounted Displays (HMD) push the boundaries of technology, in this paper, we try and answer the question, "What would it take to make the visual experience of a VR-HMD Life-Like, i.e., indistinguishable from physical reality?" Based on the limits of human perception, we first try and establish the specifications for a Life-Like HMD. We then examine crucial technological trends and speculate on the feasibility of Life-Like VR headsets in the near future. Our study indicates that while display technology will be capable of Life-Like VR, rendering computation is likely to be the key bottleneck. Life-Like VR solutions will likely involve frames rendered on a separate machine and then transmitted to the HMD. Can we transmit Life-Like VR frames wirelessly to the HMD and make the HMD cable-free? We find that current wireless and compression technology may not be sufficient to accommodate the bandwidth and latency requirements. We outline research directions towards achieving Life-Like VR.

KEYWORDS

Virtual reality, Computer Graphics, Mobile devices, Video compression, wireless networking

ACM Reference Format:
Eduardo Cuervo, Krishna Chintalapudi, and Manikanta Kotaru. 2018. Creating the Perfect Illusion : What will it take to Create Life-Like Virtual Reality Headsets?. In *Proceedings of 19th International Workshop on Mobile Computing Systems and Applications (HotMobile'18)*. ACM, New York, NY, USA, 6 pages. https://doi.org/10.1145/3177102.3177115

1 INTRODUCTION

The ultimate goal of VR Head Mounted Displays (HMD) is to provide an experience of virtual worlds that are indistinguishable from physical reality – deemed *Life-Like VR* in this paper. Today's HMDs such as Oculus Rift [42], HTC Vive [23] etc. remain far from providing this perfect illusion [10]. In order to achieve Life-Like VR, displays must match the limits of human visual perception specifically w.r.t to display properties such as resolution, field of view and frame refresh rates. In this paper we ask the question, *"What will be the specifications of a HMD that provides a Life-Like VR experience and what is the path to such a device being built?"*

Based on the limits of human visual perception, we first show that Life-Like VR headsets will require 6 − 10× higher pixel densities and 10 − 20× higher frame rates of that of existing commercially available VR headsets. We then ask, "Will it be possible to create Life-Like headsets in the near future, given this gap in specifications to be bridged?" We examine various technological trends such as pixel densities, frame rates, computational power of GPUs etc. Our analysis indicates that while displays are likely to achieve Life-Like specifications by 2025, the computational capacity of GPUs will remain a bottleneck and not be able to render at the high frame-rates required for achieving a Life-Like VR experience.

We discuss various approximation techniques that can be used to bridge the computational gap and the open research challenges. Offloading computation to a powerful computer (not part of the headset) will provide better quality experience than a standalone headset. However, this means that the rendered frames need to be transmitted to the HMD using cables connected to the headset. In order to allow unrestricted mobility and avoid tripping hazards, a key requirement for HMDs is to be cable-free. We then ask the question, "What is the path to making the Life-Like VR headsets cable-free?" We find that the required data rates will be so high that existing as well as upcoming wireless standards (802.11ad, 802.11ay) will find it hard or even impossible to transmit rendered video to the headset. We examine techniques to understand the path to reducing this extremely high data rates that will have "acceptable" degradation to the Life-Like video quality and discuss open research challenges.

In summary, we make the following contributions,

- Drawing on fundamentals of human perception, we posit that a Life-Like VR-HMD will require 6 − 10× higher pixel density and 20 − 30× higher frame rate compared to current day VR-HMDs.
- We analyze various technological trends we show that the key bottleneck to realizing Life-Like VR will be the significantly high demand on rendering computation.
- We show that the wireless bandwidth needed to transfer rendered Life-Like VR frames from a rendering machine to the HMD will be extremely high and no wireless standard in horizon will be able to accommodate it.
- Finally, we outline possible solutions and research directions that might help in realizing Life-Like untethered VR.

2 SPECIFICATIONS FOR LIFE-LIKE VR

In this section we try to establish the specifications of a Like-Like VR headset based on the limits of human perception.

Field of view (FOV). A Life-Like VR headset's FOV should ideally be same as that of the human eye i.e. $210°$ horizontally and $135°$ vertically [4] as depicted in Figure 1. For stereoscopic vision there

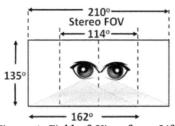

Figure 1: Field of View for a Life-Like VR-HMD

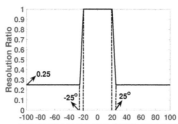

Figure 2: The foveation function

Display Property	Value
Field of View	$210^o \times 135^o$
Angular Pixel Density	>60 pixels/degree
Frame Rate	>1800 Hz
Dynamic Range	$1 : 10^9$
Colors	10 Million
Latency	> 7-20 ms

Figure 3: Specification for a Life-Like VR-HMD

is an overlap of 114° degrees between the two eyes in the center. Thus, each individual eye has a view of 162° ($\frac{210}{2} + \frac{114}{2}$).

Angular Pixel Density (APD) 20/20 vision allows a person to resolve two contours separated by 1 arc-minute (1.75mm at a distance of 20 feet) or 60 pixels/degree of angle subtended at the eye [43]. This ability to distinguish between two closely placed lines or contours is called *Resolution acuity*. Most people with corrected vision have better than 20/20 vision and human visual acuity ranges between 0.3-1 arc-minutes or (60-200 pixels/degree) [9].

Another important measure of acuity is *detection acuity* – the ability to detect tiny objects in the scene e.g. small spots. Detection acuity of the human eye far exceeds resolution acuity, especially in the periphery and in high contrast scenes. It has been measured that it is possible to detect a fine black line subtending only 0.5 arc-seconds [39] against an illuminated white background. In order to accommodate such a high level of detection acuity, the display intuitively should have a pixel density of 7200 pixels/degree. However, detection acuity works by averaging over large spatial extents and a lower acuity may suffice.

Today, HMDs typically offer a pixel density 10 pixels/degree and up to 13 pixels (e.g. Vive Pro [24]) – about 6× lower than the basic 20/20 vision standard. Thus, there is an immense gap between current day VR-HMDs and what the human eye is capable of. In the absence of user studies that establish what pixel densities will provide a Life-Like experience, based on the above discussion we speculate that *Life-Like VR will require somewhere between 60-120 pixels/degree (resolution of 1-0.5 arc-minutes).*

Foveal and Peripheral Vision. Broadly human vision can be classified into *foveal* and *peripheral* vision. Foveal, around center of the eye (fovea), has high resolution acuity (Section 2) and is able to discern finer details in the scene. Peripheral vision extends far from the center and while it cannot discern fine details, it can detect and help the eye focus its attention on important parts of the scene.

A VR-HMD with built-in eye tracking capabilities, e.g. the Fove VR Devkit [17], could potentially use lesser resolutions away from the person's center of the eye. Guided by user studies, [31] proposed a *foveation function* that does not "significantly" affect the users' perception. Figure 2 [19] depicts resolution as a function of angular separation (eccentricity) from the center of the eye. Resolution is 100% between -20° to 20°, then it is linearly reduced to 25% within 5° and finally kept constant at 25% elsewhere. For a $210^o \times 135^o$ FOV, foveation reduces the overall number of pixels by 70%.

Frame Rate (Refresh Rate) While most current day VR headsets support frame rates of 90Hz, some commercial gaming monitors support frame rates of 240Hz (Foris FG2421 [16]) and 480Hz (Zisworks [47]). Nvidia recently debuted a working version of a 1700Hz display [26]. Why are such high frame rates essential for VR? While objects in the real world move continuously, in a video, pixels corresponding to moving objects will jump from a location to another in discrete steps across frames. This affects human visual perception due to two characteristics of the human eye.

Eye's Tracking Movements : As we follow objects with our gaze, human eyes reflexively tend to predict and track relative movement at high angular speeds in order to maintain gaze on the object. With *smooth pursuit movements* [33], the eye keeps a moving stimulus in view of the *fovea* – the area of the retina with the highest resolution acuity. These movements are continuous and can be as fast as 30 degrees/second [8]. When objects in view move faster, eyes try and follow them with *saccades*, which are extremely rapid changes in the eye viewpoint, in jumps from one position to another, as fast as 180 degrees/second or higher. Finally, the eyes move involuntarily to track objects if the head moves through the vestibulo-ocular reflex [33], matching the yaw and pitch angular velocities of the head of approximately 17 degrees/second [30].

Eye's Continuous Integration of Visual Stimuli : Processing in human eyes is not a discrete but a continuous analogue process where photo-receptors continuously accumulate light energy falling on them, which is in turn continuously processed by the brain to draw inferences about the world. When pixels corresponding to an object remain stationary in the video frame for a complete refresh cycle while the eyes move in anticipation of motion, they accumulate light energy from different parts of the image rather than the intended moving object. This causes a smearing and strobing effect called *judder*, reducing the eye's ability to detect objects clearly and inducing *simulator sickness* [3].

To avoid the above effects, frame rate of the HMD must be fast enough to avoid any abrupt discontinuous jumps in pixels corresponding to a moving object. Consider the eyes following an object in view, moving smoothly at an angular velocity of up to $30^o/sec$ (corresponding to vestibulo-ocular reflex and smooth pursuit movements). For an HMD with resolution of 60 pixels per degree, the pixels corresponding to this object will displace by 1800 pixels each second. In other words, a frame rate of about 1800Hz would ensure that there are no discontinuous pixel jumps. Note, that given eye's ability to follow objects at speeds up to $180^o/sec$ (due to saccades), higher frame rates may be required for a Life-Like experience. In the absence user studies, in this paper, we conservatively assume that frame rates of at least 1800Hz are required for a Life-Like experience.

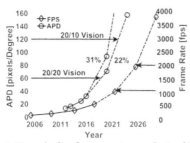

Figure 4: Trends for frame rates and pixel/degree.

Dynamic Range, Colors and Bits Per Pixel

Human eyes have a fantastic ability to *adapt* to lighting conditions, allowing us to see dim stars in low starlight as well as objects in bright sunny conditions – a contrast range (ratio of minimum to maximum intensities) of up to $1:10^9$. Further, the eye can discern about 10 million colors. These two factors in combination require a wider color space than the one offered by the standard 24-bit RGB space. It is for this reason that modern displays, especially OLED technology, provide high dynamic range color (HDR), often represented using a 96 bits per pixel floating point representation. [6]

3 TRENDS AND PATH TO LIFE-LIKE VR

Based on Section 2, Figure 3 summarizes the specs for a Life-Like VR HMD. In this section, we ask the question, "is it likely that Life-Like VR HMDs will be technologically feasible in the near future?" We try to answer this question by examining various relevant technological trends for both displays and GPUs.

Field of View (FOV). VR headset with a Life-Like FOV of $210^o \times 130^o$ is already available today (StarVR [38]). At a slightly lower FOV (200 degrees horizontally) but higher resolution, the Pimax 8K also aims to cover most of the human visible field of view [32]

Angular Pixel Density (APD). Today, the availability, specification and prices of displays for screens under 10 inches is driven by smartphones and tablets. Since VR is an upcoming technology with much smaller adoption, displays in VR headsets lag behind those of smartphone screens even though the underlying LCD/OLED technology is fundamentally the same. VR manufacturers today are forced to either rely on displays designed for smartphones (GearVR) or rely on smaller batches of specialized displays relying in slightly older technology (Vive, Rift). As VR gains popularity and the adoption gap between smartphones and VR headsets become narrower, the technological lag currently affecting VR displays will become narrower or disappear. Consequently, in this analysis of the evolution of screen pixel densities, we include all screens under the 10 inch form factor i.e. smartphones, tablets and VR-HMDs.

Table 2 provides the progression of highest pixels-per-inch (PPI) of commercial displays seen since 2012. In Table 2, we also provide the equivalent APD if this display technology were to be used in a 210° Field of View. In order to compute the equivalent APD, we use as reference the StarVR [38] HMD, that offers a pixel density of 533 PPI and a corresponding APD of 15.8 pixels/degree (2560 pixels over 162°). Further, we provide the percentage increase in APD per year during the last interval. The trend indicates between 22-31% increase in PPI per year. Figure 4 speculates the PPI based on the maximum and minimum growth trends that displays with 60 pixels/degree (20/20 vision) will be available by 2018 and 120

pixels/degree (20/10 vision) between 2021-2023. Indeed a display with PPI 2250 (APD of 67 pixels/degree) has been announced by Samsung to be released in 2018 [27]. We speculate it will take roughly two-three years for these announced displays to materialize in commercial devices and so VR-HMD displays with Life-Like pixel densities will probably appear between 2021-2025.

Table 1: Trends in Pixel Densities

Year	Max PPI	Equiv. APD	Increase/Year	Device
2012	440	13		LG [22]
2013	538	16	22.7%	LG [35]
2015	806	24	22.4%	XperiaZ5 [37]
2016	1058	31	31.3%	SEL [46]

Frame Rate. Framerates for LCD/OLED displays in the gaming industry have doubled steadily almost every 4 years over the last 12 years as depicted in Table 3. Since inherent switching times of OLEDs are under 0.1ms, the frame rate is fundamentally limited by speed of the digital circuits that control the OLEDs. Given this trend, it is reasonable to expect displays like the 1800Hz prototype presented by Nvidia [26] to be commercially available before 2025. In Figure 4 we speculate that we will see commercial monitors with frame rates of around 1000Hz by 2021 and 1800Hz before 2025. Commercial VR HMDs will likely see these frames rates two-three years later, depending on the adoption gap between VR headsets and smartphones at the time. This means that by 2028 VR-HMDs will probably start having refresh rates that offer a Life-Like experience.

Table 2: Trends in Frame Rates

Year	Max Frame Rate (fps)	Device
2005	60	Laptops
2009	120	Samsung 2233RZ
2013	240	Foris FG2421
2017	480	Zisworks [47]

Computation Capability for Rendering. In VR, the frames to be displayed are typically computed by a powerful computer based on physics, geometry and other logic related to the virtual scene. A higher pixel density implies that computation needs to be performed for a larger number of pixels and in a finer detail. A higher frame rate implies that the computation for each frame needs to be performed faster. Even though displays might have the pixel density and refresh rates that are required for a Life-Like experience, the computers generating these frames must be able to keep up.

VR headsets today, typically use powerful GPUs to perform the computations required for rendering in VR. Table 3 depicts the trend in increase in GPU computational power with the progress of years. As seen from Table 3, GPU computational power in GFlops has been increasing at an average of 34% per annum. These increases have been primarily due to improvements in the fabrication processes over the years from 40nm to 12nm technology. IEEE's International Roadmap for Devices and Systems (IRDS) [25], predicts improvements in the fabrication processes up to 5nm over the next four years. The IRDS foresees complications in shrinking beyond 5 nm, and focuses on alternative devices such as neuromorphic circuits, quantum "'qubits'", spintronics, and others [25]. Relying on process shrinking and related incremental improvements thereafter, we speculate that the average growth in computational capacities at 34% to continue until 2025 resulting in about 140TFlops.

In Table 3 GTX780 , is comparable to what Vive and Oculus consider VR-ready, the GTX 970. Both operating at about 4TFlops [1] are capable of rendering 2.6 Million Pixels (2160 × 1200) at a frame rate of 90Hz. A VR HMD with $210^o \times 135^o$ FOV ($162^o \times 135^o$ per eye [2]) with APD of 60 pixels/degree operating at 90Hz refresh rate will have to render 157 Million Pixels ($162 \times 135 \times 60 \times 60 \times 2$) and will require the equivalent of about 244TFlops. If we allow for the VR-HMD to make use of foveation technology, then this requirement will drop to about 73TFlops. If GPUs are able to render at the equivalent of 140TFlops by 2025, then it will be possible to have VR-HMDs that operate offer 20/20 vision at 180Hz refresh rate. Note that this refresh rate is still 10× less than the minimum of 1800Hz required to avoid judder completely (Section 2).

Table 3: Trends in GPU Computational Power

Date	GFlops	Fab	Rate of Increase	Device
2010-03	1345	40nm		GTX480
2010-10	1581	40nm	27%/yr	GTX580
2012-12	3090	28nm	65%/yr	GTX680
2013-05	3977	28nm	24%/yr	GTX780
2014-07	4612	28nm	11%/yr	GTX980
2016-05	8228	16nm	39%yr	GTX1080
2017-12	13800	12nm	41%yr	Titan V

Summary. We summarize our analysis of trends as follows,

- We speculate that between 2025-2028, display technology will be Life-Like offering $210^o \times 135^o$ FOV, APDs of 60 pixels/degree (20/20 vision) and refresh rates of up to 1800 Hz.
- We also speculate that GPU technology will lag behind and will only be able to render 180 frames/sec at that resolution. This implies that intermediate frames will have to be generated using cheap approximate techniques such as image-based rendering (Section 4).

4 UNTETHERING THE HMD

As we saw in Section 3, the key bottleneck in VR is the computation involved in rendering frames. Given space, power and heat dissipation constraints, mobile GPUs suitable for standalone HMDs are typically 6 − 10× less capable, than state-of-the-art GPUs found in desktop/gaming PCs or server class machines. For example, mobile GPUs today operate between 500GFlops (Adreno) - 1500GFlops (Tegra X2) while the best desktop GPUs operate at 13000GFlops. Similarly, graphics intensive content is often ported to mobile devices 7-10 years after debuting on full-sized devices (e.g. Doom 3, GTA Vice City, and Skyrim). Consequently, most high-end HMDs today, rely on a powerful GPU enabled PC (separate from the HMD) to render frames. These frames are then transmitted to the HMD via cables that connect the HMD to the PC. However, these cables are undesirable since they not only restrain free-motion but also might result in a hazard. In this section we explore the question "What is the path to un-tethering Life-Like VR-HMDs?"

---

[1]Graphics performance depends on many more factors other than Flops, including number of shading units, bandwidth, amount of memory and scene complexity. We used Flops because we consider it is a simple yet effective predictor of GPU growth.

Bandwidth Needed for Loss-less Wireless Transmission of Life-Like Rendered Video A straightforward way to un-tether an HMD is through wireless transmission of rendered frames. A few virtual reality systems and headset manufacturers today, use wireless connectivity to un-tether the HMD [1, 41]. Will it be possible to transmit a Life-Like rendered video wirelessly in the future?

As depicted in Figure 1 in a Life-Like, a stereo HMD with $210^o \times 135^o$, each eye individually has a $162^o \times 135^o$ field of view. For an APD of 60 pixels per degree, with 96 bits per pixel and 1800 frames/sec refresh rate the raw bit rate required to transmit frames is approximately 27 Tbps ($2 \times 162 \times 135 \times 60 \times 60 \times 96 \times 1800$). If the HMD includes foveation, the resulting bit-rate will be about 8Tbps. The state of the art hardware accelerated loss-less compression (DSC Display Stream Compression) [44] provides a compression ratio of 3:1, reducing this data rate to about 2.7 Tbps.

Current and Future Wireless Standards. 60GHz wireless standards promise the highest wireless bandwidths for wireless transfer. IEEE 802.11ad (WiGig) [21] prototypes today provide around 3 Gbps and promise up to 7Gbps in the future. The Wireless HD standard (UltraGig) [45] was created for HDMI cable replacement and products today provide data rates up to 4 Gbps while promising a theoretical of 25 Gbps. The 802.11ay standard in the making aims to provide a peak theoretical bandwidth of 176 Gbps. All these rates are at least an order of magnitude less than the required 2.7BP's. This indicates that *there is no wireless standard in the horizon capable of accommodating lossless Life-Like VR video data rates.*

Free-space Optics. Optical transceivers transmit data at extremely high data rates over optical fibers in data centers. Ranovus [34] has a commercially available 200Gbps optical transceiver and often multiple transceivers are combined to provide an aggregate bandwidth of several Tbps. High bandwidth free-space-optics (FSO) based communication systems have been considered for stationary links [14, 20] where the transmitter and receiver are at fixed locations. Recently, a FSO system [15] has been proposed which allows for the transceivers to have micro-motions, for example, tiny movements of a building. However, to the best of our knowledge no FSO system exists that can maintain a robust communication link when the transceiver is subject to large and quick motions such as those caused by head and body motions on a VR-HMD.

Partial Computation at HMD. As described in Section 3 GPUs will only be able to compute at an order of magnitude lesser frame rate than the Life-Like requirement of 1800Hz and consequently, the remaining frames will be generated using computationally cheap approximation *image-based rendering* (IBR) [29] techniques such as timewarp and spacewarp [5]. One way to reduce the bandwidth dramatically is transmit only the rendered frames and let a mobile GPU in the HMD generate the remaining frames through local render [13] or IBR [36]. This can reduce the bandwidth requirement by at-least an order of magnitude to about 270Gbps. While this is a significant improvement, this is still much higher than what any wireless standard in the horizon can hope to provide. Further there could be more sophisticated schemes to partition computation between the HMD and the rendering machine that allows fewer frames to be transmitted, thus alleviating the bandwidth bottleneck.

Lossy Compression and Latency Constraints. State-of-the-art lossy compression schemes like H.265 or VP9 can provide an average compression ratio of 200:1 - 1000:1 [40], but may provide much higher compression at very high framerates where temporal locality is stronger. However, these schemes were designed for displays that are located farther from the human eye than an HMD. When used on a stereo VR display that is located close to the human eye, they can cause discomfort, especially when one or more visible artifacts are present in one eye and not in the other, inducing double vision, as we noticed during studies for previous VR systems we built [7, 12]. There is no user study to date that we know of that studies the effect of various compression levels on VR.

Latency constraints : In response to humans actions such as head movements, the VR system must render frames and transmit to the HMD. VR and neuroscience experts have found through through user studies that a latency greater than 20ms causes motion sickness and discomfort, and have projected that it may be necessary to reduce it to 15ms or even 7ms to fully eliminate them [2]. Thus, this end-to-end latency of up to 20ms must include various latencies such as, HMD tracking latency [28], transmission latency of new HMD pose to the rendering machine, rendering computation latency on the GPU, latency of compression of the video frames, latency of transmission of the compressed frames to HMD, decompression latency at HMD and finally display latency of the frames.

In a typical VR-HMD today, at a refresh rate of 90Hz, a newly rendered and transmitted frame will have to wait up to 11ms before it is displayed. Further, rendering frames, having a variable cost, often takes close to the time given by the refresh rate (in this case 11 ms). Including other latencies, the end-to-end latency often exceeds the prescribed 20ms. As a result, HMDs employ IBR techniques to hide latency [5] and minimize motion sickness. Unfortunately, these techniques are only effective to hide small amounts of latency, producing increasingly distracting artifacts as latency grows. This also means that even hardware-accelerated compression such as H.265 or VP9 may not be suitable given their relatively high compression and decompression latencies.

As the refresh rates of displays increase to 1800Hz and computational capacity of GPUs increase to 180Hz, both rendering and display latencies will reduce, leaving more time (up to 15ms) for compression and decompression. This opens up the possibility for lossy compression schemes that provide near Life-Like quality within the latency constrains of VR while reducing the bandwidth requirements for transmitting frames enough to meet the capabilities of wireless radios. For example, a compression scheme that provides a lossy compression of 10:1, coupled with partial computation at HMD can reduce the bandwidth requirement to 27Gbps which will be accommodated by the upcoming 802.11ay standard.

Standalone Headsets. Given that mobile GPU performance lags behind desktop GPUs by a factor of $6 - 10\times$, it is not immediately clear, whether Life-Like standalone VR-HMDs will be feasible by the time displays are. In this section we consider power consumption, and ask the question, "will power consumption be a bottleneck if mobile GPUs are powerful enough to render Life-Like VR?"

For a typical VR-HMD, the battery should last long enough (at least 3 hours to be able to experience full-length VR movies, gaming sessions [18], but perhaps more as line of business applications in VR become common). The energy density of a Li-Ion battery has been doubling once every 20 years [11] and is unlikely to increase significantly in the next few decade unless there is a disruptive breakthrough. Table 4 depicts the improvement in power

efficiency of GPUs with time. As seen from Table 4, in the last 6 years GPU power efficiency in GFlops/Watt has increased by a factor of 8.5×. However, in the same time as seen from Table 3, the computational power increased by a factor of 6×. This indicates that GPUs power efficiency is increasing faster than their computational power, growth difference that may grow more pronounced as it becomes harder to shrink the fabrication process of GPUs. Thus, we believe that it is unlikely that GPUs power consumption will be a bottleneck for mobile GPUs.

Table 4: Trends in Gigaflops per watt

Date	GFlops/watt	Device
2010-03	5.4	GTX480
2010-10	6.5	GTX580
2012-12	15.8	GTX680
2013-05	15.9	GTX780
2014-07	27.9	GTX980
2016-05	45.7	GTX1080
2017-12	55.2	Titan V

Summary We now summarize our findings in this section,

- Wireless transmission of loss-less Life-Like VR frames with foveation will require about 2.7Tbps - no wireless standard in the horizon will be able accommodate this data rate.
- Partial rendering at the HMD coupled with the invention of "near-Life-Like" lossy compression techniques have the potential of alleviating the bandwidth bottleneck and making it accessible to standards such as 802.11ay.
- Since GPU power efficiency is growing faster than their computational capacity, power consumption is unlikely to become the key bottleneck for standalone VR-HMDs.

5 RESEARCH CHALLENGES REALIZING LIFE-LIKE UNTETHERED VR

Based on our study, we see two key bottlenecks in realizing Life-Like untethered VR. First GPUs will fall short of rendering computational capacity. Second, wireless bandwidth will be insufficient to transmit Life-Like rendered VR frames to the HMD. In this section we outline some of the research directions to overcome these bottlenecks.

User study based foveation research. Foveation is a relatively new concept and not yet fully understood, especially at high resolutions, framerates, and FOVs. Research to understanding foveation, guided by user studies, will help answer the crucial question of "How can foveation be effectively used to reduce computational and wireless transfer overheads for Life-Like VR?"

Novel computation sharing mechanisms between HMD and rendering machine. We believe that significant amount of research is required to develop novel techniques where the HMD can share the burden on rendering frames with the rendering machine to not only help make the VR experience Life-Like but also help in reducing the bandwidth required for wireless transfer.

Novel near Life-Like compression techniques ratified by user studies. There is very little understanding of the effects of lossy compression techniques on VR users. We believe that there is a significant open research questions in terms of designing compression techniques that can provide significant compression gains while preserving Life-Like quality of the rendered frames.

High bandwidth Wireless technologies Given that even the upcoming wireless standards such as 802.11ay fall an order of magnitude shy of the bandwidth required to transfer Life-Like VR, the need of the hour is to invent new wireless technologies that can accommodate these high data rates. This might involve developing FSO based wireless communication techniques or novel wireless communication over hitherto unexplored higher frequency spectrum that allow for higher data rates.

Due the development and commercialization of high bandwidth FSO transceivers, and the availability of more spectrum for communication is infrared spectrum compared to radio waves spectrum, we believe that it will be an interesting and useful research direction to develop FSO based communication systems for mobile transceivers like virtual reality headsets.

User study based high framerate low-persistence perception research. Judder and low persistence at high framerates are still not well understood. As the framerate of displays increases, a key question to answer would be "What combination of frame rates and persistence will be sufficient to achieve uncompromising Life-Like VR?" This question can be answered through careful user studies and the development of experimentation techniques.

6 CONCLUSION

In this paper, guided by aspects of human vision we determined what would be the specifications of a VR headset that is indistinguishable from physical reality – Life-Like VR. We then examined the trends in various technologies to determine the bottlenecks in the path to Life-Like VR. We find GPU computational capacity to be the key bottleneck. We then considered the possibility of making VR headsets cable-free and find that none of the existing standards are poised to accommodate the extremely high bandwidth of transferring Life-Like rendered VR frames. Finally, we present open research challenges in the path to realizing Life-Like VR.

REFERENCES

[1] ABARI, O., BHARADIA, D., DUFFIELD, A., AND KATABI, D. Enabling high-quality untethered virtual reality. In *NSDI* (2017).

[2] ABRASH, M. Latency, the sine qua non of ar and vr. http://blogs.valvesoftware.com/abrash/latency-the-sine-qua-non-of-ar-and-vr/.

[3] ABRASH, M. Down the vr rabbit hole: Fixing judder. http://blogs.valvesoftware.com/abrash/down-the-vr-rabbit-hole-fixing-judder/, July 2013.

[4] ANDERSEN, S. R. The history of the ophthalmological society of copenhagen 1900–50. *Acta Ophthalmologica 80*, s234 (2002), 6–17.

[5] BEELER, D., HUTCHINS, E., AND PEDRIANA, P. Asynchronous spacewarp. https://developer.oculus.com/blog/asynchronous-spacewarp/.

[6] BOITARD, R., ET AL. Evaluation of color encodings for high dynamic range pixels. In *Proceedings Human Vision and Electronic Imaging* (2015).

[7] BOOS, K., CHU, D., AND CUERVO, E. Flashback: Immersive virtual reality on mobile devices via rendering memoization. In *Proceedings of the 14th Annual International Conference on Mobile Systems, Applications, and Services* (2016), ACM, pp. 291–304.

[8] BRITANNICA. Sensory reception: Human vision: Structure and function of the human eye, 1987.

[9] CARNEY, T., AND KLIEN, S. Resolution acuity is better than vernier acuity. *Vision Research 37*, 5 (1997), 525–539.

[10] CUERVO, E. Beyond reality: Head-mounted displays for mobile systems researchers. *GetMobile: Mobile Computing and Communications 21*, 2 (2017), 9–15.

[11] CUERVO, E., BALASUBRAMANIAN, A., CHO, D.-K., WOLMAN, A., SAROIU, S., CHANDRA, R., AND BAHL, P. Maui: Making smartphones last longer with code offload. In *MobiSys 2010* (2010).

[12] CUERVO, E., AND CHU, D. Poster: Mobile virtual reality for head-mounted displays with interactive streaming video and likelihood-based foveation. In *Proceedings of the 14th Annual International Conference on Mobile Systems, Applications, and Services Companion* (2016), ACM, pp. 130–130.

[13] CUERVO, E., ET AL. Kahawai: High-quality mobile gaming using gpu offload. In *MobiSys* (May 2015).

[14] CUI, Y., XIAO, S., WANG, X., YANG, Z., YAN, S., ZHU, C., LI, X.-Y., AND GE, N. Diamond: Nesting the data center network with wireless rings in 3-d space. *IEEE/ACM Transactions on Networking* (2017).

[15] CURRAN, M., RAHMAN, M. S., GUPTA, H., ZHENG, K., LONGTIN, J., DAS, S. R., AND MOHAMED, T. Fsonet: A wireless backhaul for multi-gigabit picocells using steerable free space optics. In *Proceedings of the 23rd Annual International Conference on Mobile Computing and Networking* (New York, NY, USA, 2017), MobiCom '17, ACM, pp. 154–166.

[16] EIZO. Focus on the foris fg2421. http://gaming.eizo.com/news/the-gaming-monitor-weve-all-been-waiting-for/, June 2014.

[17] FOVE-VR. Fove 0 eye tracking vr devkit. https://www.getfove.com/.

[18] GIANTBOMB. How long is your average gaming session? https://www.giantbomb.com/forums/general-discussion-30/how-long-is-your-average-gaming-session-1438129/.

[19] GUENTER, B., FINCH, M., DRUCKER, S., TAN, D., AND SNYDER, J. Foveated 3d graphics. *ACM Trans. Graph. 31*, 6 (Nov. 2012), 164:1–164:10.

[20] HAMEDAZIMI, ET AL. Firefly: A reconfigurable wireless data center fabric using free-space optics. In *ACM SIGCOMM Computer Communication Review* (2014), vol. 44, ACM, pp. 319–330.

[21] HANSEN, C. J. Wigig: Multi-gigabit wireless communications in the 60 ghz band. *IEEE Wireless Communications 18*, 6 (2011).

[22] HRUSKA, J. Lg new 440 ppi display is way too much of a good thing. https://www.extremetech.com/computing/130051-lgs-new-440-ppi-display-is-way-too-much-of-a-good-thing, May 2012.

[23] HTC. Htc vive. https://www.htcvive.com/us/, Apr. 2016.

[24] HTC / VALVE. Vive pro. https://www.vive.com/us/product/vive-pro/.

[25] IEEE. International roadmap for devices and systems 2016, more moore white paper. https://irds.ieee.org/images/files/pdf/2016_MM.pdf.

[26] LANG, B. Nvidia demonstrates experimental zero latency display running at 1,700hz. https://www.roadtovr.com/nvidia-demonstrates-experimental-zero-latency-display-running-at-17000hz/.

[27] LARSEN, R. Review: Samsung 2233rz: First 120hz and 3d-monitor. http://www.flatpanelshd.com/review.php?subaction=showfull&id=1239184512, May 2009.

[28] LAVALLE, S. M., YERSHOVA, A., KATSEV, M., AND ANTONOV, M. Head tracking for the oculus rift. In *Robotics and Automation (ICRA), 2014 IEEE International Conference on* (2014), IEEE, pp. 187–194.

[29] MARK, W. R., MCMILLAN, L., AND BISHOP, G. Post-rendering 3d warping. In *Proceedings of the 1997 Symposium on Interactive 3D Graphics* (New York, NY, USA, 1997), I3D '97, ACM, pp. 7–ff.

[30] MOORE, S. T., HIRASAKI, E., RAPHAN, T., AND COHEN, B. The human vestibulo-ocular reflex during linear locomotion. *Annals of the New York Academy of Sciences 942*, 1 (2001), 139–147.

[31] PATNEY, A., SALVI, M., KIM, J., KAPLANYAN, A., WYMAN, C., BENTY, N., LUEBKE, D., AND LEFOHN, A. Towards foveated rendering for gaze-tracked virtual reality. *ACM Transactions on Graphics (TOG) 35*, 6 (2016), 179.

[32] PIMAXTECHNOLOGY. Pimax 8k. https://www.pimaxvr.com/en/8k/.

[33] PURVES, D., AUGUSTINE, G., FITZPATRICK, D., ET AL. Neuroscience. 2nd edition. https://www.ncbi.nlm.nih.gov/books/NBK10991/, 2001. Types of Eye Movements and Their Functions.

[34] RANOVUS. Ranovus announces availability of worlds first 200g cfp2 direct detect optical transceiver to enable 38.4 terabits per data center interconnect rack.

[35] REED, B. Lg new 440 ppi display is way too much of a good thing. http://bgr.com/2013/08/21/lg-display-538-ppi/, May 2012.

[36] REINERT, B., KOPF, J., RITSCHEL, T., CUERVO, E., CHU, D., AND SEIDEL, H.-P. Proxy-guided image-based rendering for mobile devices. *Computer Graphics Forum 35*, 7 (2016), 353–362.

[37] SONY. Xperia z5 premium. https://www.sonymobile.com/global-en/products/phones/xperia-z5-premium/.

[38] STARVR. Starvr. https://www.starvr.com/, July 2013.

[39] STRASBURGER, H., RENTSCHLER, I., AND JÜTTNER, M. Peripheral vision and pattern recognition: A review. *Journal of vision 11*, 5 (2011), 13–13.

[40] SULLIVAN, G., AND OHM, J.-R. Meeting report of the 13th meeting of the joint collaborative team on video coding (jct-vc). http://phenix.it-sudparis.eu/jct/doc_end_user/current_document.php?id=7746.

[41] TPCAST. Tpcast vive. https://www.tpcastvr.com/.

[42] HTTPS://WWW.OCULUS.COM/EN-US/RIFT/. Oculus rift, Mar. 2016.

[43] VISUAL FUNCTIONS COMMITTEE. *Visual acuity measurement standard.* May 2015.

[44] WALLS, F., AND MACINNIS, S. Vesa display stream compression. http://www.vesa.org/wp-content/uploads/2014/04/VESA_DSC-ETP200.pdf.

[45] WIRELESSHD. Wirelesshd. https://www.wirelesshd.com/.

[46] YOKOYAMA, K., ET AL. Ultra-high-resolution 1058-ppi oled displays with 2.78-in size using caac-igzo fets with tandem oled device and single oled device. *Journal of the Society for Information Display 24*, 3 (2016), 159–167.

[47] ZISWORKS. Zisworks zws 480hz: Engineering sample purchase. http://www.zisworks.com/shop.html, 2017 Aug.

Exploring Eye Adaptation in Head-Mounted Display for Energy Efficient Smartphone Virtual Reality

Zhisheng Yan
Georgia State University

Chen Song
SUNY at Buffalo

Feng Lin
University of Colorado Denver

Wenyao Xu
SUNY at Buffalo

ABSTRACT

Smartphone virtual reality (VR) can offer immersive experience while being affordable and easy to use. To enhance the VR experience under limited smartphone computation and battery resources, solutions have been proposed for efficient rendering and content delivery. However, efforts towards optimizing the distinct head-mounted display (HMD) are unfortunately limited. This paper unveils the opportunity of optimizing smartphone VR by leveraging human vision in HMD. In particular, we shift the default fixed full brightness in VR video/game Apps to a dark adaptation based dynamically scaled brightness. By exploiting the time-varying sensitivity of human eyes in dark HMD, we can reduce VR display energy while maintaining brightness perception. The proposed system, Strix, is empowered by a dark adaptation model trained from classic experimental data, a varying trend of perceptual full brightness derived from the dark adaptation model, and a smooth brightness transition scheme balancing energy and experience. Experimental results show that Strix can achieve 25% system energy reduction without negatively impacting brightness perception.

CCS CONCEPTS

• **Information systems → Mobile information processing systems**;

KEYWORDS

Energy; head-mounted display; smartphone; virtual reality

ACM Reference Format:
Zhisheng Yan, Chen Song, Feng Lin, and Wenyao Xu. 2018. Exploring Eye Adaptation in Head-Mounted Display for Energy Efficient Smartphone Virtual Reality. In *HotMobile '18: 19th International Workshop on Mobile Computing Systems & Applications, February 12–13, 2018, Tempe , AZ, USA.* ACM, New York, NY, USA, 6 pages. https://doi.org/10.1145/3177102.3177121

1 INTRODUCTION

The market of Virtual Reality (VR) is boosting exponentially. The first quarter of 2017 has witnessed a 70% increase in global shipment of VR units over the same period in 2016 [8]. Among different types

of VR, smartphone VR has accounted for an impressive 67% of the global shipment [8]. Unlike a tethered VR headset wired to a desktop (e.g., Oculus Rift), in smartphone VR (e.g., Google Cardboard), a smartphone is inserted into a head-mounted display (HMD) in order to render and display the VR content. Although smartphone VR enjoys the mobility since no extra wire is needed, such systems have limited battery and processing resources.

Despite the efforts on improving graphic rendering [3, 15] and content delivery [16, 21] in VR, studies on optimizing smartphone VR display is still limited. Unfortunately, HMD happens to be the most distinct component within VR systems. It has shown unique effects on human vision that one would never experience on regular mobile displays, such as binocular vision rivalry [25], misjudgment of distance [18], and vergence-accommodation conflict [14]. How can we harness the unique visual effects in HMD and design efficient smartphone VR systems remains unclear. In this paper, we take an exploratory step and unveil the opportunity of leveraging HMD vision for smartphone VR optimization. We focus on *eye adaptation* within HMD and utilize this special effect to optimize the display energy in smartphone VR.

In particular, modern smartphones apply a fixed full brightness by default to guarantee a satisfactory viewing experience in video or game Apps. According to our measurement, the display under such a setting can consume a significant percentage (47%~51%) of system power in smartphone VR (Section 2). On the other hand, users wearing HMDs watch the VR content in a dark environment without seeing any ambient light. Human eyes will then experience a physiological effect, called *dark adaptation*, where the sensitivity of eyes is gradually increasing as one spends more time in the dark. Consequently, a lowered screen brightness in HMD could produce the same brightness perception that one would have achieved under the full brightness in normal lighting. Hence, the objective of this paper is to replace the default fixed full brightness by a dark adaptation based dynamically scaled brightness in order to minimize smartphone VR energy. The ultimate goal is to shift the mobile displays that has entertained users for decades to a new HMD vision based display specifically designed for smartphone VR.

Achieving the objective is non-trivial and requires us to overcome two daunting challenges. First, eye adaptation was discovered by studying the luminance threshold of light source that can trigger eyes' response. How to formally model such an effect and map the luminance threshold to the brightness level in operating system (OS) that can support HMD viewing is not yet clear. Second, dynamic brightness dimming, if operated inappropriately, can easily incur the annoying flicker effect. While an extremely high scaling frequency (the number of brightness change per unit time) may result in a smooth viewing [12], it may also diminish the energy saving. This is because frequent and consecutive dimming requests may not be completed in time due to the hardware response time of each dimming [17]. These dimming requests would be postponed one by one, which slows down the brightness dimming.

To tackle these challenges, we present *Strix*, an energy-efficient smartphone VR display system that exploits the dark adaptation to dynamically scale the screen brightness while preserving the viewing quality. Based on a classic physiological study, we train a dark adaptation model using nonlinear regression. Furthermore, by utilizing Weber's Law and a luminance measurement study, we map the adaptation trend of luminance threshold to *perceptual full brightness* in HMD, i.e., the time-varying lowered brightness that can produce a full-brightness perception in smartphone VR. Moreover, we identify the optimal scaling frequency in Strix by considering both flicker perception and display energy.

We have prototyped Strix on commercial off-the-shelf smartphone VR systems. Strix can support any legacy VR Apps and balance energy saving and viewing experience based on an adjustable user knob. We validate Strix designs under various practical settings including VR App type, display type, and VR session duration. The results show that Strix can save an average of 25% system energy with a comparable experience to conventional full-brightness VR display.

To summarize, the contributions of this paper include:

- A HMD vision driven energy-efficient smartphone VR display that exploits eye adaptation (Section 3).
- A set of designs that guide the brightness scaling, including a dark adaptation model specifically for HMD and a smooth transition scheme (Section 3).
- A practical demo of using HMD vision to save display energy while maintaining user experience (Section 4).

2 BACKGROUND AND MOTIVATION

2.1 Smartphone VR Display Power

Smartphone VR is entirely powered by mobile battery. Due to the larger content size and more intensive processing, it is expected to be even more power-hungry than regular smartphone systems. Display is usually the most energy-consuming component (up to 67%) in regular video/game Apps [5, 27]. Considering the added rendering and/or networking power for VR content, the percentage of display power may be reduced in smartphone VR. Therefore, we measure the display power in smartphone VR and confirm its persistent significance.

Figure 1 shows the system power of a 300-second session with display on and off for both VR video (remote) and VR game (local). We use LG Optimus G Pro in an office WiFi network. Details on measurement setup for VR can be found in Section 4. By differential measurement [11], we can obtain the display power of 1754 mW and 1704 mW, which are equivalent to 47% and 51% of system power, in VR video and VR gaming, respectively. This indicates that despite the slightly decreasing percentage, display power is still one of the dominant energy source in smartphone VR. Hence, it is *desirable* to minimize the HMD display power.

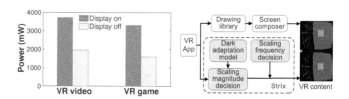

Figure 1: VR display power is still significant.

Figure 2: Architecture of Strix.

Despite the distinct mechanism of Liquid crystal display (LCD) and organic light-emitting diode (OLED), one common energy-saving approach for both displays is to uniformly dim the screen brightness [9, 11]. This can be achieved by decreasing the backlight level of LCD [27] or scaling the supply voltage of OLED [22]. In order not to limit our designs to LCD or OLED, we herein focus on this approach and collectively term it as *brightness scaling*.

2.2 Dark Adaptation

Human eyes can sense an extremely large range of light levels with the brightest and darkest perceivable light level being a factor of 10^9 apart [4]. However, at any given moment, one can only differentiate light sources with a contrast ratio of 10^3 [4]. The wider perceivable range is achieved by *eye adaptation*, where human eyes dynamically adapt their definition of what is bright. In a dark environment, human eyes perform *dark adaptation*, i.e., dynamically decreasing the definition of what is bright (increasing eye sensitivity). For example, when a user using the smartphone at full brightness steps into a dark room from a normal lighted room, her eyes will usually be uncomfortable because the screen is too shining considering her increased eye sensitivity.

Dark adaptation is a classic physiological effect and there is a wealth of studies on it. The dark adaptation experiments aimed at finding the minimum luminance of a light source that triggers a visual sensation. Such a *luminance threshold*, can be found by continuously increasing the luminance of the light source until the subject reports its presence. By measuring this threshold after the subject has stayed in the dark room for different periods of time, studies have found that luminance threshold gradually decreases as the time spent in the dark increases [20]. For example, the luminance threshold can decrease three orders of magnitude in 20 minutes [20]. This provides us an opportunity to reduce the brightness in smartphone VR while preserving the brightness perception. Thereby, it is *feasible* to exploit eye adaptation to reduce HMD energy.

3 STRIX DESIGN

Figure 2 shows the architecture of the proposed system, Strix. Strix runs within a VR App in parallel to the regular VR rendering. When the VR content is rendered/decoded, Strix will determine whether or not the smartphone brightness should be scaled at the upcoming moment and how much it should be scaled. The final display will then generate a combined perception of the rendered frame and the scaled screen brightness. Specifically, Strix leverages a dark adaptation model that we build upon classic physiological data. Since classic dark adaptation focuses on the luminance threshold

Table 1: Model Parameters

θ_1	θ_2	θ_3	θ_4	θ_5	θ_6	θ_7
-1.97	1.39	1.61	-0.23	8.7	0.18	19.43
RMSE: 0.1296, R^2: 0.99, PCC: 0.9965, rho: 0.9982						

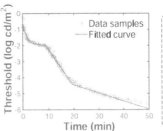 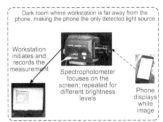

Figure 3: Dark adaptation curve of human eyes. **Figure 4: Measurement of screen luminance.**

that can trigger a sensation, Strix also converts the trained model to obtain the luminance that is perceived as full brightness level and accordingly determines the scaling magnitude. Moreover, Strix applies an optimal scaling frequency to strike a tradeoff between flicker perception and energy saving. In the following, we will describe each Strix module in detail.

3.1 Modeling Dark Adaptation

Although there is a wealth of physiological studies identifying the phenomena of dark adaptation [4, 20], no explicit model is available. We explore the data of an existing dark adaptation experiment and employ a data-driven method to obtain a mathematical model using the data. Figure 3 plots the data samples of the luminance threshold (blue dots) obtained in the dark adaptation experiment in [20] via the methodology described in Section 2.2. It can be seen that the luminance threshold decreases with time, indicating that the eye sensitivity increases.

As shown in the figure, there are three phases in the dark adaptation curve. In less than 10 minutes, the luminance threshold decreases exponentially with time. After staying in the dark for around 10 to 20 minutes or 20 to 50 minutes, the luminance threshold decreases linearly. However, the two linear functions vary with a different slope. Hence, we propose to model the dark adaptation as a piecewise function.

$$\Delta_{\min} = \theta_1 + \theta_2 e^{-t/\theta_3} + I(t, \theta_5)\theta_4(t - \theta_5) + I(t, \theta_7)\theta_6(t - \theta_7) \quad (1)$$

where $\Delta_{\min}$ is the luminance threshold that triggers a eye response, $\vec{\theta} = \{\theta_1, \theta_2, \cdots\}$ are the model parameters, t is the time the user spends in the dark, and $I(t, \theta_i)$ is an indicator function that implies which phase the user is currently staying at. The indicator function can be expressed as follows.

$$I(t, \theta_i) = \begin{cases} 0 & t - \theta_i \leq 0 \\ t - \theta_i & t - \theta_i > 0 \end{cases} \quad (2)$$

We use nonlinear regression with maximum likelihood estimation to determine the model parameters. Table 1 summarizes the trained parameters and the evaluation of goodness of model fit. The proposed model obtains a small root-mean-square error (RMSE) with respect to the range of luminance threshold and close-to-one values for R-squared, Pearson correlation (PCC) and Spearman rank correlation (rho). This validates that the model captures the data samples accurately, which can also be visualized by the fitted curve (red line) in Figure 3.

Note that human eyes may still be exposed to some low-intensity light source (compared to normal ambient light) during the dark adaptation, e.g., the low brightness screen in VR viewing. The impacts of such light exposure during the course of dark adaptation is not yet clear [2]. In this paper, we exclude the impacts of this content illumination. More details are discussed in Section 5.

3.2 Deriving Perceptual Full Brightness

As we discussed, due to the dark adaptation, the OS brightness level for HMD that can produce a sensation of full brightness as in normal lighting is decreased. We term such a brightness level as *perceptual full brightness*. Since the model in (1) only captures the trend of luminance threshold, we now seek the perceptual full brightness for smartphone VR.

According to Weber's Law, perceived change in luminance is proportional to the initial luminance and such a ratio is a constant [7]. In other words, the perceived change between the luminance triggering an eye response and the luminance producing the full-brightness sensation should be identical under normal lighting and VR HMD. Formally, we can express the relationship as,

$$\frac{Lum(B_{full}) - \Delta_{\min}(0)}{\Delta_{\min}(0)} = \frac{Lum(B_{full,prcpt}(t)) - \Delta_{\min}(t)}{\Delta_{\min}(t)} \quad (3)$$

where B_{full} and $B_{full,prcpt}(t)$ is the full brightness (100%) in normal lighting and the perceptual full brightness in HMD. Note that B_{full} is a constant value while $B_{full,prcpt}(t)$ is a time-varying value. Furthermore, $Lum()$ maps the brightness level ([0,100%]) in operating system to the luminance (cd/m^2), $\Delta_{\min}(t)$ is the luminance threshold ($\log_{10}$ cd/m^2) after spending time t in a dark HMD, and $\Delta_{\min}(0)$ represents the luminance threshold just before one steps into the dark, i.e., in a normal lighting condition. Thus we have,

$$Lum(B_{full,prcpt}(t)) = \frac{Lum(B_{full})\Delta_{\min}(t)}{\Delta_{\min}(0)} \quad (4)$$

where $\Delta_{\min}(t)$ and $\Delta_{\min}(0)$ can be obtained from model (1).

To obtain perceptual full brightness $B_{full,prcpt}(t)$, it is necessary to know the relationship between luminance and brightness, i.e., $Lum(B)$. We obtain this relationship using real-world measurement. Figure 4 depicts the measurement setup. Similar as the luminance measurement in classic dark adaptation experiment [20], we display a white image on the smartphone screen as the single light source and configure the screen at multiple brightness levels. For each level, we use a Photo Research SpectraScan PR-715 spectrophotometer to measure the radiance, i.e., the light energy per unit solid angle per unit projected area, at different wavelengths. We then derive the luminance (cd/m^2) of a given brightness level by integrating the radiance at all wavelengths [24].

$$Lum = \int C * v(\lambda) * Rad(\lambda) d\lambda \quad (5)$$

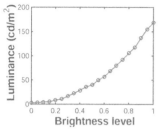

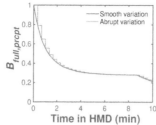

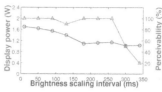

Figure 7: Scaling frequency impacts both power and experience.

Figure 8: Experimental setup for VR session energy measurement.

Figure 5: Luminance of various brightness levels for LG G Pro.

Figure 6: Variation of perceptual full brightness using different approaches.

where $C = 683$ is a constant converting watt to lumens, $v(\lambda)$ is the relative spectral sensitivity function representing different sensitivity of human vision on different wavelengths, and $Rad(\lambda)$ is the measured radiance at a wavelength λ.

Figure 5 exemplifies an observed power law model between the luminance and the brightness. This can be explained by the gamma correction within the display hardware [9]. Using nonlinear regression, we obtain a model,

$$Lum(B) = a * B^b, 0 \leq B \leq 100\% \qquad (6)$$

where B is the brightness, and a and b are the training outputs dependent on smartphones. By replacing the value of $Lum(B_{full,prcpt}(t))$ into (6), we can dynamically derive the perceptual full brightness $B_{full,prcpt}(t)$ as t changes.

3.3 Deciding Brightness Scaling Frequency

We have derived the time-varying perceptual full brightness in HMD. Since the derived $B_{full,prcpt}(t)$ is a continuous value, it is equally important to determine a scaling frequency when following the decaying trend. Figure 6 shows the scaling trend using different scaling frequency. Using a low scaling frequency can lead to abrupt and sudden brightness change, incurring flicker effect. On the other hand, although adopting an extremely high scaling frequency (greater than flicker fusion threshold [12]) can make the brightness transition smooth and nearly continuous, it is not always beneficial. The reason is that smartphones have a hardware limit on the maximum scaling frequency since the display panel suffers a nonnegligible response time after every OS request for brightness scaling. If we use a frequency higher than the hardware limit and send the display much more requests than it can handle, the display will need to buffer and process these requests one by one. This would slow down the decrease of brightness and reduce the energy saving.

We have confirmed this effect. We dynamically scale the brightness with a set of scaling intervals from 10 ms to 350 ms following the variation of perceptual full brightness. We invite 10 users to interact with a VR game (see Section 4 on user study setup) and ask them if they perceive any flicker effect or abrupt change in brightness. We also measure the display power during these 120-second VR sessions (see Section 4) for measurement setup). Figure 7 shows the display power and the percentage of users perceiving flicker (perceivability). As expected, a smaller scaling interval generates

a finer grained sequence of brightness setting and thus more scaling requests. Under a given hardware limit, it takes more time to drop to a low brightness level and thereby consume more power. When the scaling interval is large enough, the display can exploit the full potential of dark-adaptation based brightness scaling and achieve a steady energy saving. However, if the scaling interval is too large, the brightness change and flicker can be perceived by human eyes, degrading the user experience. Since both curves tend to be steady, we can safely choose the optimal scaling interval as 180 ms to balance the energy saving and user experience.

4 EVALUATIONS

Experimental setup. To evaluate Strix, we have implemented two most popular types of VR Apps. We first build a VR game, *Treasure Hunt*, by using Google VR SDK/NDK. We also implement a VR player to play a 360 degree video, *Balloon*, by extending Google ExoPlayer with Rajawali 3D engine. We achieve brightness scaling through Android's WindowManager API. A Handler is created for brightness control. We also synchronize brightness scaling with video and audio codec to support pause, rewind, etc.

Since there is no existing brightness scaling algorithms that explore VR vision, we compare Strix with the following benchmark systems: (a) *Full*: the default system with full brightness. (b) *Instant*: instantly setting a low brightness based on session duration and Figure 6 when a session starts, e.g., $B = 0.4$ for a 2-min session. This mimics the user behavior that directly selects a low brightness before the session. (c) *Linear*: linearly decreasing the brightness to the possible perceptual full brightness instead of using the trend in (1).

We first evaluate Strix by *Mean Opinion Score (MOS)*. We assess the subjective perception of Strix by a user study with 18 participants (age from 19 to 41, 12 males and 6 females, normal/corrected vision, 10 of them also in the study in Section 3.3). The participants are instructed to interact with the VR Apps freely in a large open space just as they would in a real-world home/office setting. We ask them to rate their satisfaction of brightness during the VR viewing. They are told that the highest score indicates comfortable/bright illumination and no brightness changes while lower scores imply more uncomfortable/darker illumination and more noticeable brightness changes. They are not informed about the possible brightness scaling strategies or the difference among the benchmark systems. To remove user memory bias, the four systems are shown to the users in a random order (but recorded by the administrator) under a given device/App/duration combination, as suggested in ITU single-stimulus protocol [19]. Before each test,

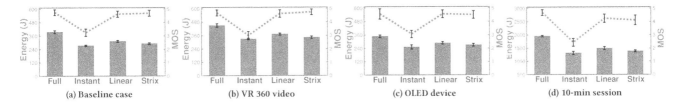

Figure 9: Strix achieves promising energy saving and satisfactory VR experience in various settings.

we ensure that users have used normal viewing for 5 minutes and their eyes have adequately adapted from darkness to the normal lighting [4].

Another evaluation metric is *Session energy*. We measure total energy consumption of the device during a VR session. Considering that the user head-moving pattern cannot be repeated in multiple trials and that wiring a power meter to the smartphone within a HMD is difficult, we adopt the methodology in [13] for repeatable and easy measurement. The system first saves the head movement data automatically during the user study. In the energy measurement, we feed such user interaction trajectory to the VR rendering module and use it to replace the actual sensor reading. That way, the system can automatically switch the VR views without involving HMD or users. Figure 8 shows the energy measurement setup using Monsoon power meter.

Baseline case. We first perform the system-level evaluation on a LG G Pro phone and a Homido V2 VR headset for a 120-second VR game session. Figure 9a shows that Strix substantially reduces system energy while achieving comparable VR experience to the default Full system using fixed brightness. On average, Strix consume 27% less system energy, or 52% less display energy, than Full. This implies that dark adaptation indeed exists in HMD. Furthermore, by applying a proper scaling frequency, we can remove the potential flicker effect in brightness scaling. In contrast, although Linear can also save energy thanks to the same dark adaptation based scaling, it consumes 8% more system energy, or 22% more display energy than Strix. The reason is that Linear does not consider the delicate and exact trend of dark adaptation. Assuming in Figure 6, if we plot a linear brightness-decreasing curve from 1.0 at the beginning down to 0.2 at 10th minute, there would be a significant gap between the scaled brightness for Linear and Strix. This makes it fail to exploit the full potential of dark adaptation, leading to a degraded energy efficiency. It is important to note that the theoretical energy saving of Strix over Linear by using two brightness decreasing curves is noticeably more than the measurement results. We suspect this is due to the insufficient number of measurement trials, which fails to average the energy measurements. Moreover, directly applying a lower brightness using Instant results in a slightly lower energy. Nevertheless, the user experience is far from desirable since the user has to view a very dark ($B = 0.4$ in this case) content at the beginning of session without adequate eye adaptation.

Impacts of App types. We then evaluate Strix in a VR 360 video session. Figure 9b shows that Strix again saves a large amount of energy, i.e., 23% less system energy than Full and 51% less display energy, without sacrificing the user experience. As VR video is a networked system where the content are delivered to the smartphone

player from a remote server, it incurs additional video transport and decoding energy, which increases the total system energy. Therefore, even though we observe a similar amount of display energy saving on VR video, its percentage of energy saving on the device is slightly degraded compared to VR game.

Impacts of display type. Instead of the LCD phone in the baseline case, we further use a Samsung Note 4 with OLED display to evaluate the VR game. Figure 9c demonstrates that all the benchmark systems achieve a lower energy compared to Figure 9a. This is due to the different energy efficiency in two types of display. Brightness scaling on OLED is equivalent to displaying dark content. Since OLED is generally more power efficient when displaying dark pixels, Note 4 consume less energy even though it has a larger screen size. Moreover, despite the lower energy consumption, we can still observe a 22% energy reduction. This result indicates the wide applicability of Strix on various smartphones.

Impacts of session duration. We repeat the baseline case with an extended duration (600 seconds). Instant will now apply the 20% brightness when the session starts while Linear will decrease the brightness to 20% linearly. Figure 9d shows that although all systems consume much more energy due to the extended session, the energy savings of Strix remain unchanged. We also observe a MOS drop for the 600-sec session. In Instant, the VR content would be shown at 20% brightness at the beginning, which is unacceptable for almost every user. Therefore, the average MOS is only 2.4. Since the brightness in Linear and Strix decreases gradually, the negative impact of 20% brightness is less obvious. However, if a longer session is initiated and the brightness decreases based on Figure 6 without any restriction, the MOS may degrade continuously. We discuss a solution in Section 5.

5 DISCUSSION AND FUTURE WORK

Brightness lower bound. To address the negative effects caused by continuously decreasing brightness in a long VR session, we can introduce a brightness lower bound below which the brightness will never drop. This can serve as a user knob to balance energy saving and user experience.

Model improvement. A future direction is to use crowd sensing to collect a more diverse dataset to improve the general dark adaptation model. For example, users with different age and gender may present distinct dark adaptation curves. We may have the chance to further save energy for some insensitive users. The intensity and duration of pre-adapting light (e.g., outdoor or indoor) also matters. We can use light sensor to detect the pre-HMD status and optimize the adaptation. A deep study of how much impact these factors would bring on the dark adaptation model and which of these factors play a dominant role on dark adaptation is needed to further calibrate the current model.

Eye fatigue. While the users do not express feeling of tiredness or strain during our preliminary 2-minute user study, the long-term effect of vision health when using Strix needs further investigation. It is critical to guarantee that under regular VR viewing duration the brightness scaling would not introduce abnormal eye fatigue and impact vision health.

Content illumination. Strix focuses on ambient illumination for brightness scaling, which is identical to default smartphone auto brightness using light sensor. A full-scale study is needed to understand whether or not the content illumination on the screen will impact the dark adaptation and how much the impact is. Similarly, in addition to the brightness scaling done in Strix, we can also compensate the pixel luminance and then scale the brightness one more time. This approach considers content illumination and hence can introduce extra energy-saving space. In addition, since we have full control for individual pixel on OLED, it is expected that we can manipulate regions of content to save energy while preserving/enhancing the content contrast.

Overhead. The computation of brightness change is minimal by using (4) and (6). Strix can be implemented on smartphones with negligible overhead. However, if advanced pixel-level processing is used to further reduce energy, it opens a challenge of striking a tradeoff between display energy saving and energy overhead.

6 RELATED WORK

Display energy reduction for LCD [17, 27] aimed to dim LCD backlight. In contrast, pixel-level control for OLED were proposed based on usability [9, 23] and fidelity [6]. A joint display and transport energy optimization was presented in [26]. These schemes are complementary to Strix since Strix drops the perceptual full brightness. Combining them with Strix is expected to achieve more energy savings.

To improve smartphone VR, FlashBack [3] rendered and cached VR images locally to provide low-latency and high-framerate experience. Furion [15] separated the rendering of background and foreground onto cloud and smartphone, respectively, to enable high-quality smartphone VR. Qian et al. [21] predicted the head movement in VR video and only downloaded some viewports to save the network bandwidth. Abari et al. [1] used mmWave to deliver huge VR data in order to remove the wire in desktop-based VR. FocusVR [28] rendered a smaller VR view to improve OLED efficiency in smartphone VR. In this paper, we steer to a new direction in exploring the physiological effects of dark adaptation to optimize general display efficiency.

7 CONCLUSION

In this paper, we take a important step in exploiting HMD vision to optimize smartphone VR. We present Strix, a brightness scaling system to utilize the full potential of dark adaptation and ensure the smooth brightness perception. Real-world evaluations show that Strix achieves substantial (25% on average) energy reduction without degrading user viewing. We believe the success of Strix can enable a suite of future works studying other HMD vision effects, e.g., binocular vision rivalry, to optimize smartphone VR.

8 ACKNOWLEDGEMENTS

The authors thank Bernd Girod, Stanford University, for his invaluable advice and support of spectrophotometer. We also thank Haricharan Lakshman, Dolby Lab, and Matt Yu, Stanford University for their useful assistance.

REFERENCES

[1] O. Abari, D. Bharadia, A. Duffield, and D. Katabi. 2016. Cutting the Cord in Virtual Reality. In *ACM Workshop on Hot Topics in Networks (HotNets)*.

[2] L. Allen and K. Dallenbach. 1938. The effect of light-flashes during the course of dark adaptation. *The American Journal of Physiology* 51 (July 1938), 540–548.

[3] K. Boos, D. Chu, and E. Cuervo. 2016. FlashBack: Immersive Virtual Reality on Mobile Devices via Rendering Memoization. In *MobiSys*.

[4] Encyclopedia Britannica. 1987. Sensory Reception: Human Vision: Structure and Function of the Human Eye. 27 (1987).

[5] A. Carroll and G. Heiser. 2010. An analysis of power consumption in a smartphone. In *USENIX annual technical conference (USENIXATC)*.

[6] X. Chen, Y. Chen, and C. J. Xue. 2015. DaTuM: dynamic tone mapping technique for OLED display power saving based on video classification. In *ACM/EDAC/IEEE Design Automation Conference (DAC)*.

[7] Tom N Cornsweet and HM Pinsker. 1965. Luminance discrimination of brief flashes under various conditions of adaptation. *The Journal of Physiology* 176 (March 1965), 294–310.

[8] International Data Corporation. https://goo.gl/GhMTqA. Worldwide Quarterly Augmented and Virtual Reality Headset Tracker.

[9] M. Dong and L. Zhong. 2011. Chameleon: a color-adaptive web browser for mobile OLED displays. In *MobiSys*.

[10] Mian Dong and Lin Zhong. 2012. Chameleon: A Color-Adaptive Web Browser for Mobile OLED Displays. *IEEE Trans. Mobile Comput.* 11 (May 2012), 724–738.

[11] M. Dong and L. Zhong. 2012. Power Modeling and Optimization for OLED Displays. *IEEE Trans. Mobile Comput.* 11 (Sept. 2012), 1587–1599.

[12] A. Iranli, Wonbok Lee, and M. Pedram. 2006. HVS-Aware Dynamic Backlight Scaling in TFT-LCDs. *IEEE Trans. VLSI Syst.* 14 (Oct. 2006), 1103–1116.

[13] N. Jiang, V. Swaminathan, and S. Wei. 2017. Power Evaluation of 360 VR Video Streaming on Head Mounted Display Devices. In *NOSSDAV*.

[14] GA Koulieris, B. Bui, M. Banks, and G. Drettakis. 2017. Accommodation and Comfort in Head-Mounted Displays. *ACM Transactions on Graphics* 36 (July 2017), 11.

[15] Z. Lai, Y. C. Hu, Y. Cui, L. Sun, and N. Dai. 2017. Furion: Engineering High-Quality Immersive Virtual Reality on Today's Mobile Devices. In *MobiCom*.

[16] K. Lee, D. Chu, E. Cuervo, J. Kopf, Y. Degtyarev, S. Grizan, A. Wolman, and J. Flinn. 2015. Outatime: Using speculation to enable low-latency continuous interaction for mobile cloud gaming. In *MobiSys*.

[17] C.-H. Lin, P.-C. Hsiu, and C.-K. Hsieh. 2014. Dynamic Backlight Scaling Optimization: A Cloud-Based Energy-Saving Service for Mobile Streaming Applications. *IEEE Trans. Comput.* 63 (Feb. 2014), 335–348.

[18] R. Messing and F. Durgin. 2005. Distance perception and the visual horizon in head-mounted displays. *ACM Transactions on Applied Perception* 2 (July 2005), 234–250.

[19] ITU methodology for the subjective assessment of the quality of television pictures. 2012. ITU-R BT.500-13. (2012).

[20] E. N. Pugh. 1975. Rushton's paradox: rod dark adaptation after flash photolysis. *The Journal of Physiology* 248 (June 1975), 413–431.

[21] F. Qian, L. Ji, B. Han, and V. Gopalakrishnan. 2016. Optimizing 360 video delivery over cellular networks. In *ACM Workshop on All Things Cellular: Operations, Applications and Challenges*.

[22] D. Shin, Y. Kim, N. Chang, and M. Pedram. 2013. Dynamic driver supply voltage scaling for organic light emitting diode displays. *IEEE Trans. Comput.-Aided Design Integr. Circuits Syst.* 32 (July 2013), 1017–1030.

[23] K. W. Tan, T. Okoshi, A. Misra, and R. K. Balan. 2013. FOCUS: a usable & effective approach to OLED display power management. In *UniComp*.

[24] Thorlabs. Radiometric vs. Photometric Units. (https://www.thorlabs.de/catalogPages/506.pdf).

[25] M. Winterbottom, R. Patterson, B. Pierce, J. Gaska, and S. Hadley. 2015. Visibility of monocular symbology in transparent head-mounted display applications. In *Proc. of SPIE 9470*.

[26] Z. Yan and C. W. Chen. 2016. RnB: rate and brightness adaptation for rate-distortion-energy tradeoff in HTTP adaptive streaming over mobile devices. In *MobiCom*.

[27] Z. Yan, Q. Liu, T. Zhang, and C. W. Chen. 2015. Exploring QoE for Power Efficiency: A Field Study on Mobile Videos with LCD Displays. In *ACM International Conference on Multimedia (MM)*.

[28] T Kiat Wee, E Cuervo, RK Balan 2016. FocusVR: Effective & Usable VR Display Power Management. In *MobiSys Companion*.

Augmenting Self-Driving with Remote Control: Challenges and Directions

Lei Kang
University of Wisconsin-Madison
lkang@cs.wisc.edu

Wei Zhao
University of Wisconsin-Madison
wzhao@cs.wisc.edu

Bozhao Qi
University of Wisconsin-Madison
bozhao@cs.wisc.edu

Suman Banerjee
University of Wisconsin-Madison
suman@cs.wisc.edu

ABSTRACT

Self-driving or autonomous vehicle systems are being designed over the world with increasing success in recent years. In spite of many advances so far, it is unlikely that such systems are going to ever achieve perfect accuracy under all conditions. In particular, occasional failures are anticipated when such vehicles encounter situations not observed before, or conflicting information is available to the system from the environment. Under such infrequent failure scenarios, the research community has so far, considered two alternatives — to return control to the driver in the vehicle, which has its own challenges and limitations, or to attempt to safely "park" the vehicle out of harm's way. In this paper, we argue that a viable third alternative exists — on failure of the self-driving function in the vehicle, the system could return control to a *remote* human driver located in response centers distributed across the world. This remote human driver will augment the self-driving system in vehicles, only when failures occur, which may be due to bad weather, malfunction, contradiction in sensory inputs, and other such conditions. Of course, a remote driving extension is fraught with many challenges, including the need for some Quality of Service guarantees, both in latency and throughput, in connectivity between the vehicles on the road and the response center, so that the remote drivers can react efficiently to the road conditions. To understand some of the challenges, we have set up real-time streaming testbed and evaluate frame latency with different parameter settings under today's LTE and Wi-Fi networks. While additional optimization techniques can be applied to further reduce streaming latency, we recognize that significant new design of the communication infrastructure is both necessary and possible.

HotMobile '18, February 12–13, 2018, Tempe , AZ, USA
© 2018 Association for Computing Machinery.
ACM ISBN 978-1-4503-5630-5/18/02...$15.00
https://doi.org/10.1145/3177102.3177104

KEYWORDS

Self-Driving Car, Remote Control, Live Streaming

ACM Reference Format:
Lei Kang, Wei Zhao, Bozhao Qi, and Suman Banerjee. 2018. Augmenting Self-Driving with Remote Control: Challenges and Directions. In *HotMobile '18: 19th International Workshop on Mobile Computing Systems & Applications, February 12–13, 2018, Tempe , AZ, USA*. ACM, New York, NY, USA, 6 pages. https://doi.org/10.1145/3177102.3177104

1 INTRODUCTION

A self-driving vehicle is one that is capable of sensing its environment and navigating itself without human input [23]. It uses a variety of techniques to sense its surroundings, such as LIDAR, RADAR, odometry, and computer vision. It uses these different sensor inputs to understand its environment, recognize various road conditions, traffic lights, road signs, lane boundaries, and track surrounding vehicles. The potential benefits of self-driving vehicles include increased safety, increased mobility and lower costs. It is estimated that self-driving vehicles can reduce 90% of the accidents and prevent up to $190 billion in damages and health-costs annually [11].

Many commercial and academic endeavors are putting significant resources for the development and tests of such self-driving systems [3, 14, 22]. For example, Google started its self-driving project in 2009, and has spent more than $1 billion in building and testing fully self-driving vehicles [12]. While legal and political challenges remain in its widespread adoption, there are also some technical bottlenecks on the way of developing completely reliable self-driving systems.

All self-driving systems make decisions based on the perception of the environment and predefined traffic rules. However, there has been occasional failures of these systems when they have encountered scenarios that were hitherto unseen. For instance, based on the situation in a construction zone, human drivers would realize that it is permissible to cross over a double yellow line by following the appropriately placed cones (which otherwise is illegal to cross in the US), while a self-driving vehicle may not be able to do so, and therefore be unable to move forward. Similarly in poor weather conditions or due to traffic light malfunctions, the cues from different sensors may contradict each other leading to confusion in decision making.

In general, the road rules are complex and may conflict with each other, i.e., the system has to understand when to follow cones and ignore lane markers, and when to obey a road worker and disobey traffic signs. We observe that the real world situations are so diverse and unpredictable, that there are always situations that cannot be matched with predefined rules and may occasionally cause self-driving system failures.

Hence, we propose to use *specially designated remote human operators to augment self-driving system when it fails to perceive or handle current situations.* It is well established that human drivers, especially experts, are capable of making good judgement calls in face of contradictory or inadequate inputs, that sometimes limit a learning system that has yet to encounter a scenario before. While it is tempting to return control (during the failure of the self-driving function) to a local human driver situated in the vehicle, it is foreseeable a future of driverless cabs carrying only underage or licenseless passengers. Hence, we propose to engage remote human drivers as a safety backup when the self-driving function fails. We expect that remote drivers can multiplex and manage a large group of vehicles making scalability feasible. To make such a remote response center with human drivers practical, many challenges and new research questions arise. For example, how the networking infrastructure and protocol should be designed to accommodate such safety and latency critical applications? Also, how the sensory data is processed and sent to the remote center? It brings up many human computer interaction and security issues as well.

As a start, we conduct feasibility study on a real-time streaming testbed and evaluate the impact of today's network latencies on streaming the vehicular environment through audio-visual methods. We illustrate that In today's LTE networks, it is usually possible to accomplish a two-way communication latency of around 100 milliseconds when streaming frames of various resolutions by using standard video compression algorithms [13], which is within the range of tolerant latency for racing games in previous studies [15]. To keep the latency of communication between the remote human drivers and the vehicles bounded, we anticipate that multiple remote response centers be created — based on the maximum end-to-end latency that can be accomplished in such future network designs. Each remote response center then is likely to only manage, control, and provide remote driving augmentation to vehicles within some vicinity. It is also possible that this function will be practical in denser areas with many vehicles, where such system failures are more likely to occur. In the rest of the paper, we explore various issues in realizing these goals and discuss both opportunities and challenges in this direction.

2 REMOTE CONTROL AS BACKUP

In this section, we illustrate how self-driving system works and under what conditions it may fail, e.g., the computer system cannot understand the semantic meanings of road/traffic

Figure 1: A fully self-driving system may fail to recognize the semantic meaning of "local traffic" and crossing double yellow line is allowed.

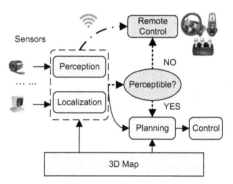

Figure 2: High-level architecture of self-driving system with remote control.

conditions. We posit that remote control system and human operator can augment self-driving systems in such conditions.

2.1 How Self-Driving System Works

A self-driving system consists of several modules that are responsible for perception, localization, planning and control [16]. A high-level architecture of self-driving system is illustrated in Fig. 2. Perception refers to the ability to collect information and extract relevant knowledge from the environment, such as where obstacles are located, detection of road signs/marking, and categorizing data by their semantic meanings. Localization refers to the ability to determine the vehicle's position with respect to the environment. Planning refers to the process of making purposeful decisions in order to achieve higher order goals, typically to bring the vehicle from one location to another while avoiding obstacles and optimizing over designed heuristics. Finally, the control module is used to execute the planned actions. Similar to human drivers, self-driving vehicle follows predefined traffic rules, such as drive within lane, do not cross double yellow line (except left turns), stop at the red traffic light (except right turns in certain cases) etc. The perception module identifies lane boundaries and traffic lights, and the the planning module makes decision based on predefined rules.

Table 1: Possible Self-Driving System Failures

Possible Failures	Examples
Perception failure at night and/or under challenging weather conditions	Unreliable camera at night (even with headlight); [1] Low visibility due to fog; [2] Lane markers are covered by snow.
Confusing or malfunctioning traffic lights/signs	Flashing yellow left turn light with sign instruction; [3] Malfunctioning traffic light turns to both red and green. [4]
Confusing detour due to misplaced cones or complex instructions	Instruction requires extra knowledge (e.g., local traffic only); the detour arranged by traffic barrels or cones is not clear (e.g., misplaced by road workers).
Complex and/or confusing parking Signs	Unclear, confusing, and handwriting road signs; [5] Parking is allowed only under certain dates and permits; Parking lots for particular vehicles, i.e., electronic or small vehicles;
Collision or system/hardware failures	Self-driving vehicle gets involved with collisions [22]; The LIDAR or other sensors fail.

2.2 Where Self-Driving System May Fail

A self-driving system may fail under complex road/traffic conditions caused by road constructions, traffic light malfunctions, randomly placed traffic cones, customized traffic signs, and many other conditions that can hardly imagine (examples in Table 1). One of such examples is illustrated in Fig. 1, the road is closed and only local traffic is allowed. The self-driving system could fail to understand the semantics of construction signs, i.e., the self-driving system cannot understand what "local traffic" means. Also, the system may fail to detour around the road construction zone, i.e., it has to understand when the self-driving vehicle is authorized to cross double yellow line or road boundaries. Also, the system may fail to detour around the road construction zone, i.e., it has to understand when the self-driving vehicle is authorized to cross double yellow line or road boundaries. The detour can also be arranged with traffic barrels which are placed by road workers. Since there is no specific rules to place traffic barrels, it is hard to find a general logic to learn where the detour is. It also has to identify road workers who is instructing the vehicles going through the road work zone. To verify a system with such capability, one has to navigate the system to drive through various road construction zones. In this case, a human operator can understand that the road is closed for "through traffic", and use external tools and knowledges to decide if the original route belongs to "local traffic". While it is possible to use map update and algorithm to handle this particular case, there are also other conditions that are so complex that a computer system may fail to handle and it takes years to realize various conditions and implement corresponding solutions. Some of the possible failures are summarized in Table 1.

2.3 Why Remote Control

Remote control systems can act as an economic and safe backup of self-driving systems. One human operator can manage multiple self-driving vehicles and take actions upon request. It could also replace the human drivers prepared to take over the control after system failures [22]. A high level architecture is illustrated in Fig. 2. Suppose a road lane is closed due to road work, a self-driving system can simply detect that the current lane is blocked, while it may fail to understand the semantic meansing of the road signs. The remote human operator can take over the control if the self-driving system fails. Every detour is different and a fully self-driving system has to be trained and tested over millions (or even more) of such cases before it can be claimed as capable of fully self-driving. Remote control augmented self-driving systems could be more reliably handle such situations. Remote control will consume data for live streaming, but we argue that remote control is used only when self-driving system fails. In the example illustrated in Fig. 1, the live streaming and remote control is used only when the vehicle is taking the detour. It rises open questions such as how many camera feeds and what are the video quality requirements in this application scenario.

3 CHALLENGES AND ISSUES

The remote control system can be a safe backup of self-driving systems, but there are also challenges that should be addressed along the way. We discuss possible research issues and directions in this section.

3.1 Network Infrastructure and Protocol Design

To bound the latency between the remote human drivers and the vehicles, we anticipate that network infrastructures and communication protocol will be designed. In such a network, multiple remote response centers are created and each provides remote driving augmentation to vehicles within some vicinity based on network latency and bandwidth. The remote response center should be selected and/or switched based on the maximum end-to-end latency. In denser areas with many

---

[1] https://www.youtube.com/watch?v=uYav3_7miIc
[2] https://www.youtube.com/watch?v=fc0yYJ8-Dyo
[3] https://www.youtube.com/watch?v=56UDZLlj2q8
[4] https://www.youtube.com/watch?v=femUe6bds0U
[5] https://www.youtube.com/watch?v=cZfj9yL3cWk&t=108s

vehicles or during road constructions, this function will be more practical as system failures are more likely to occur. Given there are different wireless communication protocols, it rises open questions about how to ensure QoS under different network protocols. For example, how to optimize the transmission and ensure QoS under current LTE networks [6]? how to design 5G networks to ensure low latency and high bandwidth vehicle-related traffics [25]?

3.2 Perception Module Design

Similar to human drivers, self-driving vehicles make decisions by matching the contextual information with corresponding traffic rules. The self-driving system fails when the road/traffic condition is unrecognizable or multiple conflicting rules are derived. With remote control, the self-driving system can classify the road conditions into binary conditions: perceptible or not. To this end, the self-driving system can cache the 3D map of the road, traffic signs/lights and surrounding buildings [22], it can detect if it is perceptible by comparing perceived 3D map with cached version. By filtering out the moving objects, the two versions should be fairly similar. If the perception module detects road blockage or road signs that was not cached, then it tries to understand the situation, and transfers the control to remote human operator if it fails.

3.3 Real-Time Streaming

To provide sufficient information for the remote human operator to control the vehicle, the video streams and external contexts, such as extra camera feeds from the vehicle itself and other surrounding vehicles, should be sent to the server in real time. The question is what kind of data and in what format should be transmitted to the server? Suppose both the self-driving system and the server cache the 3D map of the surrounding infrastructures, only the differences can be transmitted to the server and the server can reconstruct the real-time conditions based on the differences. Also, optimization techniques can be used to compress and reduce the data volumes. The data size would be smaller if only the boundary of the objects are transmitted.

3.4 HCI for Remote Control

Remote control is different from control within the vehicle as it suffers various levels of latencies. The remote human operator may see delayed views and the vehicle also receives delayed control messages. There are many open questions like what kind of control is required from the human operator and what is the safe speed under current latency and remote operator's reaction time. The self-driving system can calculate several possible detours or alternative plans, and the remote human operator can pick the most appropriate one. In the cases where the self-driving system cannot understand the environment, a human operator can take over the full control of the vehicle. Self-driving system can also assist remote control. For example, while the vehicle is controlled by the remote human operator, the collision avoidance module of

the self-driving system still works to ensure the vehicle will not get involved with any accidents. The reaction time of the remote operator, the latency of the networks and the vehicular speed should also be well studied to ensure the vehicle is at a safe speed.

3.5 Online Sharing and Learning

If one self-driving system fails, the scenario should be shared and used to train the system so that the self-driving system can better model or handle similar cases. It is also possible to store the road information in the cloud and the self-driving systems update with unusual conditions, e.g., lane closed for road construction, so that the vehicles passing by this road segments can be updated. Also, after the human operator makes a decision, e.g., detour around the blocked lane, other self-driving vehicles passing the same road segment should be able to follow the same detour automatically through online sharing and learning. In such cases, only one or few self-driving vehicles need to be controlled by remote human operators, and the rest self-driving vehicles can use updated road information and recorded decisions to pass through without further human inputs.

4 FEASIBILITY STUDY

In this section, we evaluate the feasibility of real-time video streaming over today's wireless networks used by vehicles, i.e., LTE [17] and Wi-Fi [19]. We present a case study with three levels of resolutions, while choosing the best resolution and bitrate is an open question and further study is required.

4.1 Real Time Streaming

As illustrated in Fig. 3a, we use a customized Android app to compress the raw video frames (in YUV420 format) and send to remote server in real time. The video is compressed by using video compression standard H.264 or MPEG-4 [13]. In H.264, there are two types of frames, I-frame and P-frame. An I-frame, or Intra-coded picture, is a complete image. P-frame (Predicted picture) hold only the part that changes between frames. In other non-real time applications, it can also use both previous and forward frames to generate B-frame (Bidirectional predicted picture) to better compress the frame.

We borrow video parameter settings from popular VoIP applications, i.e., Skype [26] and Google Hangout [24]. In our setup, we conduct case study with three resolutions of 320x240, 640x480 and 1280x960, with bitrate 0.5Mbps, 1Mbps and 4Mbps, respectively. We use UDP to send the compressed frames with a frame rate of 10 over LTE and Wi-Fi networks. The I-frame interval is 1 second, i.e., there is one I-frame every 10 frames. The compression ratio ranges from 5% to 15% for different frames. The server decompresses the video frame by using GStreamer pipeline [5] and sends back the timestamp associated with the frame. The Android app records the two-way latency and frame sizes into sqlite database.

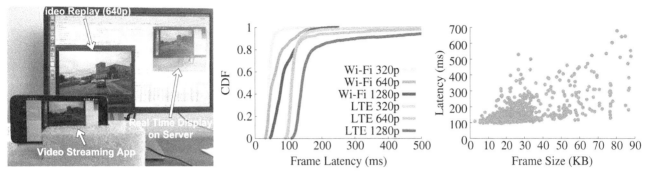

(a) Real time streaming.   (b) The two-way latency of video (c) Latency of different frame sizes.
frames.

Figure 3: Latency measurement of real-time streaming in Wi-Fi and LTE networks. Frame loss rate is from 0.5% to 2% in different networks and resolutions (and bitrates) settings.

4.2 Video Frame Latency

We measure the two-way latency of the compressed video frames in both LTE and Wi-Fi networks. The measurements in Wi-Fi network is used to compare with LTE for protocol overhead. The road experiments are conducted in LTE networks. In both networks, we use the same remote UDP server with a global IP address. For the measurements in LTE networks, we fix the Android phone (Nexus 5X) in vehicle mount holder to record front views. We drive the vehicle for three 5min trips to record two-way frame latency, frame size and loss rate of different resolutions. For the measurements in Wi-Fi network, we use the Android phone to stream a prerecorded video through a single 802.11n Wi-Fi access point. The server is 3 miles away from the streaming location. The two-way latency in both networks is shown in Fig. 3b. The median latency in LTE and Wi-Fi networks are around 100ms and 50ms, respectively. One reason for higher latency in LTE networks is the protocol overhead. Since we use only one Wi-Fi access point, the overhead of handoff is excluded. With carefully designed handoff and scheduling algorithm [19], we believe Wi-Fi is a good candidate for vehicle connectivity in urban area.

4.3 Frame Size and Optimization

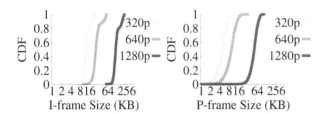

Figure 4: The size compressed frames, with compression ratio 5%-20% of original YUV420 format.

The frame size distributions of I-frames and P-frames are illustrated in Fig. 4. The median size of I-frames is 2-4 times larger than that of P-frames. This is because the video encoder fails to predict the next frame and the difference

between actual frame and predicted frame is much higher than expected. We observe that large frame size may cause long tail latency, as illustrated in Fig. 3c. Some optimization techniques can be used to further reduce the size of the frames. The I-frame interval can be adjusted according to vehicle dynamics. At high speed or during turns, the I-frame interval can be increased as the it is hard to predict next frame in such cases. When the vehicle is waiting at red light, the frame rate or resolution can be reduced since the human operator cannot drive the vehicle anyway. Further, a 3D map of road and infrastructures can be built and cached at both the self-driving system and the server, only the differences (i.e., dynamic objects such as vehicles and pedestrians) are transmitted to the server. Such optimizations can reduce the peak size of the frames to potentially avoid long tail latency.

5 RELATED WORK

5.1 Self-Driving Systems

Corporations like Waymo, Mercedes-Benz and AutoX are trying to develop fully self-driving vehicles [3, 14, 22]. Waymo uses LIDAR as the primary input for object detection [22]. AutoX proposes camera-first self-driving solution to reduce the cost to build a self-driving vehicle [3]. [4] presents a sensory-fusion perception framework that combines LIDAR point cloud and RGB images as input and predicts oriented 3D bounding boxes. [9] describes the architecture and implementation of an autonomous vehicle designed to navigate using locally perceived information in preference to potentially inaccurate or incomplete map data. [7] presents networked self-driving vehicles to coordinate and form an edge computing platform. We believe remote control system can act the safe backup for such self-driving systems.

5.2 Low Latency Networks

Reducing network latency is an active area of research. [18] investigates the causes of latency inflation in the Internet and proposes a grand challenge for the networking research community: a speed-of-light Internet. [1, 25] propose various architectures and techniques for high capacity and low latency 5th generation mobile networks. [20] discusses the requirements of system design for real-time streaming. [19] presents a Wi-Fi based roadside hotspot network to operate at vehicular speeds with meter-sized picocells. [8] uses speculation to predict future frames to reduce latency for mobile cloud gaming. [10] measures the performance of Skype over today's LTE networks and illustrate the inefficiencies of Skype protocols. [6] develops a passive measurement tool to study the inefficiency in today's LTE networks. [2] presents the features to improve quality of service in LTE networks. [21] presents the inefficiencies of current VoLTE architectures. All these work can inspire the design of remote control systems for self-driving vehicles.

6 DISCUSSION

6.1 Multiple Camera Feeds

We evaluate only single camera feed, while it is necessary to stream multiple camera feeds from both the vehilce itself and surrounding vehicles. Streaming multiple camera feeds will increase the data volume and further optimization techniques are required.

6.2 Video Resolution, Bitrate and Quality

In this paper, we present a case study with three levels of resolutions, while choosing the best resolution and bitrate for this application is still an open question. Different video bitrates provide different video qualities for various resolutions. The question is what is the minimum requirements and parameter settings to provide enough quality for remote operator to be fully aware of the surrounding situations. We expect that a live streaming protocol should adjust video bitrate according to network bandwidth and provide the best-effort video quality.

7 CONCLUSION

We propose to use remote control when the self-driving system fails to understand the environment or cannot match the road information with predefined traffic rules. It raises many open questions to design a remote control system and infrastructure. We present case studies in this work and advocate further research into the challenging issues for augmenting self-driving with remote control.

ACKNOWLEDGMENTS

We would like to acknowledge the anonymous reviewers and our shepherd Dr. Giovanni Pau for his detailed comments, guidance and inspiration. This research project is supported in part by the US National Science Foundation through awards CNS-1345293, CNS-14055667, CNS-1525586, CNS-1555426, CNS-1629833, CNS-1647152 and CNS-1719336.

REFERENCES

[1] Mamta Agiwal, Abhishek Roy, and Navrati Saxena. 2016. Next generation 5G wireless networks: A comprehensive survey. *IEEE Communications Surveys & Tutorials* (2016).

[2] Najah Abu Ali, Abd-Elhamid M Taha, and Hossam S Hassanein. 2013. Quality of service in 3GPP R12 LTE-advanced. *IEEE Communications Magazine* (2013).

[3] AutoX. 2016. Camera-first AI brings self-driving cars out of the lab and into the real world. https://www.autox.ai/. (2016).

[4] Xiaozhi Chen, Huimin Ma, Ji Wan, Bo Li, and Tian Xia. 2017. Multi-View 3D Object Detection Network for Autonomous Driving. In *IEEE CVPR*.

[5] GStreamer. [n. d.]. https://gstreamer.freedesktop.org/. ([n. d.]).

[6] Junxian Huang, Feng Qian, Yihua Guo, Yuanyuan Zhou, Qiang Xu, Z Morley Mao, Subhabrata Sen, and Oliver Spatscheck. 2013. An in-depth study of LTE: effect of network protocol and application behavior on performance. In *ACM SIGCOMM*. ACM.

[7] Eun-Kyu Lee, Mario Gerla, Giovanni Pau, Uichin Lee, and Jae-Han Lim. 2016. Internet of Vehicles: From intelligent grid to autonomous cars and vehicular fogs. *International Journal of Distributed Sensor Networks* (2016).

[8] Kyungmin Lee, David Chu, Eduardo Cuervo, Johannes Kopf, Yury Degtyarev, Sergey Grizan, Alec Wolman, and Jason Flinn. 2015. Outatime: Using speculation to enable low-latency continuous interaction for mobile cloud gaming. In *MobiSys*. ACM.

[9] John Leonard, Jonathan How, Seth Teller, Mitch Berger, Stefan Campbell, Gaston Fiore, Luke Fletcher, Emilio Frazzoli, Albert Huang, Sertac Karaman, et al. 2008. A perception-driven autonomous urban vehicle. *Journal of Field Robotics* (2008).

[10] Li Li, Ke Xu, Dan Wang, Chunyi Peng, Kai Zheng, Haiyang Wang, Rashid Mijumbi, and Xiangxiang Wang. 2017. A measurement study on Skype voice and video calls in LTE networks on high speed rails. In *IWQoS*. IEEE.

[11] Todd Litman. 2014. Autonomous vehicle implementation predictions. *Report* (2014).

[12] Daily Mail. [n. d.]. http://www.dailymail.co.uk/sciencetech/article-4889594/Google-s-spent-1-1-BILLION-self-driving-cars.html. ([n. d.]).

[13] Detlev Marpe, Thomas Wiegand, and Gary J Sullivan. 2006. The H.264/MPEG4 advanced video coding standard and its applications. *IEEE communications magazine* (2006).

[14] Autonomous Mercedes-Benz Research & Development. [n. d.]. http://mbrdna.com/divisions/autonomous-driving/. ([n. d.]).

[15] Lothar Pantel and Lars C Wolf. 2002. On the impact of delay on real-time multiplayer games. In *Proceedings of the 12th international workshop on Network and operating systems support for digital audio and video*. ACM, 23–29.

[16] Scott Drew Pendleton, Hans Andersen, Xinxin Du, Xiaotong Shen, Malika Meghjani, You Hong Eng, Daniela Rus, and Marcelo H Ang. 2017. Perception, Planning, Control, and Coordination for Autonomous Vehicles. *Machines* (2017).

[17] Hanbyul Seo, Ki-Dong Lee, Shinpei Yasukawa, Ying Peng, and Philippe Sartori. 2016. LTE evolution for vehicle-to-everything services. *IEEE Communications Magazine* (2016).

[18] Ankit Singla, Balakrishnan Chandrasekaran, P Godfrey, and Bruce Maggs. 2014. The internet at the speed of light. In *HotNets*. ACM.

[19] Zhenyu Song, Longfei Shangguan, and Kyle Jamieson. 2017. Wi-Fi Goes to Town: Rapid Picocell Switching for WirelessTransit Networks. In *ACM SIGCOMM Computer Communication Review*. ACM.

[20] Michael Stonebraker, Uur Çetintemel, and Stan Zdonik. 2005. The 8 requirements of real-time stream processing. *ACM SIGMOD* (2005).

[21] Guan-Hua Tu, Chi-Yu Li, Chunyi Peng, Zengwen Yuan, Yuanjie Li, Xiaohu Zhao, and Songwu Lu. 2016. VoLTE*: A Lightweight Voice Solution to 4G LTE Networks. In *HotMobile*. ACM.

[22] Waymo. 2016. On the road to fully self-driving, Waymo safety report. https://storage.googleapis.com/sdc-prod/v1/safety-report/waymo-safety-report-2017-10.pdf. (2016).

[23] Wikipedia. [n. d.]. https://en.wikipedia.org/wiki/Autonomous_car. ([n. d.]).

[24] Chenguang Yu, Yang Xu, Bo Liu, and Yong Liu. 2014. Can you SEE me now? A measurement study of mobile video calls. In *INFOCOM, 2014 Proceedings IEEE*. IEEE.

[25] Shunqing Zhang, Xiuqiang Xu, Yiqun Wu, and Lei Lu. 2014. 5G: Towards energy-efficient, low-latency and high-reliable communications networks. In *ICCS*. IEEE.

[26] Xinggong Zhang, Yang Xu, Hao Hu, Yong Liu, Zongming Guo, and Yao Wang. 2012. Profiling skype video calls: Rate control and video quality. In *INFOCOM, 2012 Proceedings IEEE*. IEEE.

CARS: Collaborative Augmented Reality for Socialization

Wenxiao Zhang
Hong Kong University of Science and Technology
Hong Kong SAR, China
wzhangal@cse.ust.hk

Bo Han
AT&T Labs Research
Bedminster, New Jersey
bohan@research.att.com

Pan Hui
University of Helsinki
Hong Kong University of Science and Technology
panhui@cse.ust.hk

Vijay Gopalakrishnan
AT&T Labs Research
Bedminster, New Jersey
gvijay@research.att.com

Eric Zavesky
AT&T Labs Research
Bedminster, New Jersey
ezavesky@research.att.com

Feng Qian
Indiana University
Bloomington, Indiana
fengqian@indiana.edu

ABSTRACT

As Augmented Reality (AR) ties closely to the physical world, its users looking at overlapped scenes are likely to be in the vicinity of each other, which naturally enables the collaboration and interaction among them. In this paper, we propose CARS (Collaborative Augmented Reality for Socialization), a framework that leverages the social nature of human beings to improve the user-perceived Quality of Experience (QoE) for AR, especially the end-to-end latency. CARS takes advantage of the unique feature of AR to support intelligent sharing of information between nearby users when it is feasible. It brings various benefits at the user, application and system levels, e.g., reduction of end-to-end latency and reuse of networking and computation resources. We demonstrate the efficacy of CARS through a preliminary evaluation based on a prototype implementation.

CCS CONCEPTS

• **Human-centered computing** → **Ubiquitous and mobile computing design and evaluation methods**; • **Networks** → *Cloud computing*; • **Information systems** → *Image search*;

KEYWORDS

Augmented reality, collaborative augmented reality, cloud offloading, device to device communication

ACM Reference Format:
Wenxiao Zhang, Bo Han, Pan Hui, Vijay Gopalakrishnan, Eric Zavesky, and Feng Qian. 2018. CARS: Collaborative Augmented Reality for Socialization. In *HotMobile '18: 19th International Workshop on Mobile Computing Systems & Applications, February 12–13, 2018, Tempe , AZ, USA.* ACM, New York, NY, USA, 6 pages. https://doi.org/10.1145/3177102.3177107

1 INTRODUCTION

Augmented Reality (AR) enhances the physical world by creating virtual annotations to augment one's perception of reality. AR systems can *recognize* objects inside the camera view of a mobile device and *augment* them with annotations [5, 11]. AR has found applications in various areas, such as training [13], healthcare [20], and communication [22]. However, most AR applications operate independently in a standalone way. Thus, the cooperation and interaction among mobile users running the same application are largely neglected.

With the recent advances of communication technologies (*e.g.*, 5G and 802.11ac/ad) and AR devices (*e.g.*, Microsoft HoloLens [19]), AR applications will become prevalent and be widely adopted by consumers and businesses. For example, Apple has released the ARKit [3] in iOS 11 which allows developers to create AR experiences using iPad and iPhone. The increasing popularity of AR offers tremendous opportunities for collaborations among its users. The key reason is that, by its design AR ties tightly with the real world, a unique feature that other applications such as virtual reality do not have. As a result, its users viewing overlapped scenes are in the close proximity and can communicate locally to share their common interests.

In this paper, we advocate to *leverage the social nature of human beings* for enabling the coordination and collaboration of sharing the results of computation intensive AR tasks, high quality AR annotations, and real-time annotation modifications by users. To this end, we propose CARS which, to the best of our knowledge, is the first collaborative AR framework for cloud-based AR. CARS supports instantaneous socialization (*e.g.*, real-time user interactions) and those experiences spread over time via local caches.

CARS brings various benefits at different levels. At the *user* level, it satisfies the general need of human beings for collaborations and interactions and creates an immersive user experience for AR. At the *application* level, CARS allows the exchange of invaluable information, for example, regarding the surrounding environment during a fire hazard for first responders with a single-minded focus. At the *system* level, it improves the efficiency of AR by reducing end-to-end latency, reusing computation resources in the cloud, saving mobile data usage, *etc.*

We illustrate the high level idea and benefits of CARS using an example in Figure 1. Suppose Alice and Bob are visiting a gallery and are appreciating two side-by-side paintings, Vincent and Mona

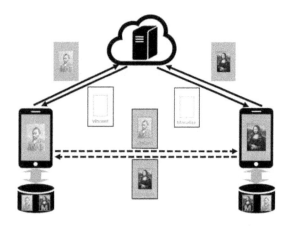

Figure 1: An illustrative example of CARS. **Users can collaboratively perform object recognition: they can exchange results that each has received from the cloud.**

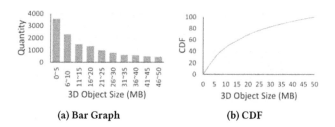

(a) Bar Graph   (b) CDF

Figure 2: Size distribution of typical 3D objects for annotation (Source: Unity Asset Store).

Lisa, separately. They get the results of an AR application (*i.e.,* recognition result and annotation content) from the cloud. Now they change their positions, Alice moving to Mona Lisa and Bob to Vincent. Instead of running cloud-based recognition again which may waste mobile data usage and computation resources in the cloud, they can *collaboratively exchange the results* from previous runs via Device-to-Device (D2D) communications. We will discuss other mechanisms beyond D2D in § 5.

CARS is not limited to indoor environments and *does not require localization*. It is also helpful for outdoor scenarios, such as city sightseeing. Note that localization alone is not enough for AR. Even if we know which painting a user is looking at via localization, it cannot tell us the position of that painting within a camera view for augmentation.

Although the above idea sounds straightforward, there are several practical issues in order to realize CARS. The key challenge is that CARS should maintain, or better improve, the user-perceived QoE (especially the end-to-end latency), when processing locally the shared information from others. Another hurdle is the support of interactions among users, which requires the synchronization of annotations and their changes made by users. To address these challenges, we carefully design the architecture and key components of CARS to make them *lightweight yet efficient and suitable* for mobile devices (§ 3). Our design makes it feasible to collaborate among users by *performing object recognition locally* based on the results from the cloud. We build a prototype of CARS which demonstrates it can reduce object-recognition latency by up to 40%, compared to cloud-based AR (§ 4).

2 BACKGROUND

In this section, we introduce how mobile AR works, by summarizing its pipeline, which was shown in Figure 1 of our previous work [30], and cloud-offloading feature of AR.

2.1 Pipeline of Mobile AR

A typical pipeline of mobile AR systems starts with *Object Detection* that identifies the Regions of Interest (ROIs) for target objects in

a camera frame. For each ROI, *Feature Extraction* is the next step which extracts its feature points. The third step is *Object Recognition* that determines the original image for the target ROI stored in a database of to-be-recognized objects.

We utilize the classic image retrieval technology for object recognition. To compress raw feature points, we first build an offline probabilistic model (*e.g.,* Gaussian Mixture Model, GMM [25]) based on the feature points of all images in the database. Using this model, we encode the feature descriptors of an image into a compact representation (*e.g.,* Fisher Vector, FV [23]). We then store all compact feature representations of the images using a hash function (*e.g.,* Locality Sensitive Hashing, LSH [7]) for faster retrieval. Upon receiving an object recognition request, we process the request frame using the same procedure as described above, to get its compact feature representation. We then check its nearest neighbors in the hash table for the best matching result.

Template Matching validates object recognition result and calculates the pose of the target. *Object Tracking* takes the pose as its input with the goal of avoiding object recognition for every frame. Finally, *Annotation Rendering* renders the virtual content determined by the recognition result to augment the target object. Annotation content is usually a 3D object for achieving a better user experience. We retrieve the size of around 12,000 3D objects from the Asset Store of Unity [28] and plot the distribution and its CDF in Figure 2. The size of a 3D object ranges from a few hundreds of kilobytes to tens of megabytes. The large size of these 3D annotations is one of the motivations to enable collaborative sharing of them among users.

2.2 Cloud-Based Mobile AR

The performance of the current generation of mobile devices is still restricted by their computation power and battery life. AR systems can potentially offload some tasks to the cloud, in order to reduce the computation overhead on mobile devices. There are two common offloading scenarios. AR systems can offload tasks starting from object detection by sending camera frames to the cloud [11], or they can run object detection and feature extraction locally on a mobile device and upload the extracted feature points to the cloud for object recognition [12].

CARS inherits the benefits from cloud offloading of AR. First, image retrieval algorithms are usually computation intensive. Offloading them to the cloud can significantly reduce the end-to-end latency [5]. Second, the size of digital annotations may be large, as shown in Figure 2. It is challenging to store them for a dataset with a reasonable size (*e.g.,* 1,000 images) locally on mobile devices.

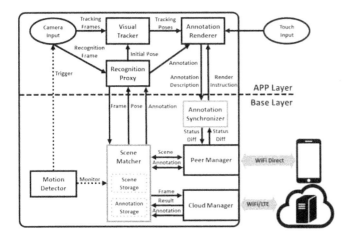

Figure 3: System architecture of CARS framework (dotted lines are for control messages). Its two key components are Scene Matcher and Annotation Synchronizer.

3 CARS SYSTEM DESIGN

In this section, we present an overview of CARS and describe its two key building blocks: the APP and Base layers.

3.1 CARS Overview

Using the pipeline in § 2.1 directly in CARS is not beneficial, as our previous work [30] has demonstrated that it takes several seconds for image retrieval on mobile devices, much longer than cloud-based AR. We show the system architecture of CARS in Figure 3. The major difference between the APP layer and the traditional AR applications (as elaborated in § 2.1) is that it does not handle object recognition itself, which is offloaded to the Base layer. The Base layer hides the details of object recognition and annotation download from the APP layer through a *simplified and lightweight* object-recognition engine.

The main benefit of decoupling the APP and Base layers is that they can evolve independently of each other. For example, we can make the Base layer lightweight and feasible for collaboratively exchanging annotations based on performing locally object recognition. It also makes the integration of traditional AR applications into CARS easy. They can send recognition requests to Recognition Proxy without caring about the operations happening underneath.

3.2 The APP Layer

The APP layer retrieves camera frames for object recognition and tracks recognized objects. It has three components: Recognition Proxy, Visual Tracker and Annotation Renderer.

Recognition Proxy is the bridge between the APP and Base layers for object recognition. Its input is a camera frame and the response contains the pose of the target object in that frame. It offloads the recognition to the cloud for improved latency performance and for supporting a large database of images. If the same object has been processed by the cloud for other nearby users and the result is available in the local cache, the Base layer returns it directly to Recognition Proxy without involving the cloud, as we will explain in § 3.3.

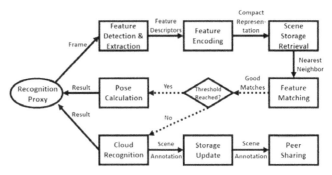

Figure 4: Workflow of Scene Matcher (We use dotted lines for control messages).

Visual Tracker tracks the pose of a recognized target when camera view changes. It is initialized by Recognition Proxy. After that Visual Tracker takes continuous camera frames as input and calculates the object pose frame-by-frame. Object pose contains three dimensions of translation and three dimensions of rotation (*i.e.*, the so-called Six Degrees of Freedom, 6DoF). We utilize feature points to calculate the object pose in each frame, and optical flow tracking [9] to track the feature points in the frame sequence.

Annotation Renderer augments the recognized objects using the virtual content which will be either downloaded directly from the cloud or fetched from others. It calculates a 6DoF pose of an annotation for rendering. We use a 3D graphics engine to render the annotation and to align it precisely with the physical target object. Annotation Renderer also reacts to users' touch input and instructions from Annotation Synchronizer of the Base layer for changes made by others, and modifies annotations accordingly.

3.3 The Base Layer

The Base layer handles object recognition and annotation download and synchronization for the APP layer. It has five components: Motion Detector, Scene Matcher, Annotation Synchronizer, Peer Manager and Cloud Manager.

Motion Detector indicates that a user intends to recognize the object inside the current camera frame. It triggers object recognition by avoiding specific user commands such as screen touch or voice input, which provides a seamless user experience. Object recognition will be initiated when a mobile device is in a relatively steady and vertical status, which filters out blurry images and camera frames with irrelevant objects (*e.g.*, when the camera is facing the ceiling). In order to ensure the accuracy of object recognition, Motion Detector continues monitoring the user's hand movement. It ignores the result if there is a significant movement during the recognition which may cause a mismatch between the request frame and the recognition result.

Scene Matcher is the core of the Base layer. We show its workflow in Figure 4. Upon receiving a recognition request from the APP layer, Scene Matcher first tries to find a local match by computing the feature descriptors and their compact representation of the request frame. It then calculates the distance between this compact feature representation and those in Scene Storage. Using the pair of feature-point sets from the request frame and the local

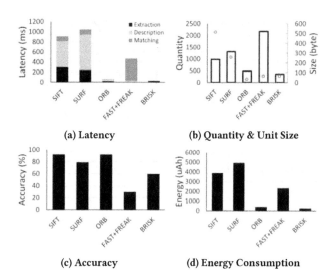

(a) Latency   (b) Quantity & Unit Size

(c) Accuracy   (d) Energy Consumption

Figure 5: Performance comparison of various algorithms using `OpenCV4Android` library on a Xiaomi MI5 phone.

match, Scene Matcher determines the homography between them to find their geometric transformation and adjusts the corresponding recognition result from the local match accordingly.

Scene Matcher offloads object recognition to the cloud when it cannot find a local match, following the procedure described in § 2. When the recognition result is returned from the cloud, besides used by the APP layer, Scene Matcher also inserts it with the request frame into Scene Storage. Similarly, the request frames and results from other devices are cached in Scene Storage. To speed up the local search, Scene Matcher also extracts the feature points from the request frame, generates the compact feature representation, and stores them into Scene Storage. As a result, each scene is represented as a {*frame image, recognition result, feature points, compact feature representation*} tuple.

A key design challenge of Scene Matcher is the selection of a *lightweight yet efficient and suitable* object recognition algorithm for mobile devices. SIFT [18] and SURF [4] have been used extensively in cloud-based AR (*e.g.,* Overlay [11] uses SURF and VisualPrint [12] uses SIFT). Instead of using them blindly for CARS, we evaluate the performance of 5 representative algorithms, SIFT, SURF, ORB [26], FAST+FREAK [1] and BRISK [16]. We use the following metrics, latency, feature quantity (*i.e.,* the number of generated feature descriptors), the size of a single feature descriptor, recognition accuracy and mobile device energy consumption.

We plot the experimental results with a dataset of 100 images (*i.e.,* movie posters) in Figure 5. The results for latency and feature quantity are averaged over the 100 images. We use only 10 images to measure energy consumption, as the results for them already show similar patterns as those of latency in Figure 5a (as expected). Among these algorithms, ORB achieves the best tradeoff between these metrics, higher than 90% accuracy with low latency and energy consumption and small memory space for storage, which is consistent with the result in Rublee *et al.* [26]. Thus, CARS uses ORB in Scene Matcher. A limitation of ORB is that it is less robust to image-scale changes [26], compared to other schemes such as

SIFT and SURF. Thus, we need to resize the camera frame to a scale similar with the original image.

An important design decision we have made is the utilization of a *probabilistic model* to significantly speed up object recognition on mobile devices. Object recognition is relatively slow when comparing raw feature descriptors directly, as the numbers of feature descriptors may be fairly different for various images. There are several probabilistic models available, such as Gaussian Mixture Model [25] and Bernoulli Mixture Model (BMM) [14]. CARS uses BMM as GMM does not fit with binary descriptors such as ORB. Moreover, FV with BMM built upon ORB features is about two orders of magnitude faster than FV with GMM on SIFT features [2].

Scene Matcher contains Annotation Storage to cache annotations along with the scenes. When Scene Matcher finds a local match, Annotation Storage provides the corresponding content without requesting it from the cloud, which reduces the end-to-end latency and mobile data usage.

Annotation Synchronizer enables instantaneous interactions among users via synchronizing the annotation status so that one can see in real-time the modifications made by others. It shares with others the description of annotations (*e.g.,* a 3D object's pose, texture, lightness, *etc.*) generated by Annotation Renderer. Since the objects in the camera view are recognized by Scene Matcher, Peer Manager can learn from it their identities and communicate with others to see if they are looking at the same objects.

Recognition and tracking of common real-world objects guarantee that the coordinate systems of annotations for different users are synchronized (*i.e.,* the coordinate system of the physical world is the reference here). Modifications from a user change only the coordinates of annotations within his/her virtual world, which are shared by Annotation Synchronizer with others. We presently support moving, scaling, and rotating actions from users, and this design is capable of extending to much more complex operations. Annotation Synchronizer can resolve the conflicts among users by utilizing the strategies proposed by Gautier *et al.* [6].

Peer Manager utilizes WiFi Direct or Bluetooth Low Energy for peer discovery and D2D communications. It periodically scans for nearby devices running the same AR application. It maintains a list of peering devices with whom it can collaborate with. A challenge here is how to determine what recognition results and annotations to share and store in the local cache with a small size, which has been investigated extensively in the literature. For example, Psephos [10] is a fully distributed caching policy for content sharing in mobile opportunistic networks. To control the size of the cache, CARS can also optimize the sharing and fetching policy via preference-aware schemes such as PrefCast [17], as we will discuss in § 5. We leave the integration of existing approaches into CARS as our future work.

Although D2D communication is helpful in this paradigm to share locally AR results, its performance depends on the network conditions between mobile devices. As collaborating users have overlapped scenes of common ROIs in their camera views, they should be close to each other which usually leads to a higher bandwidth of WiFi Direct than that when communicating with the cloud. However, if future technologies (*e.g.,* LTE-Advanced and 5G) can offer higher throughput than WiFi Direct, we can also leverage the edge cloud, for CARS (as to be discussed in § 5). In order to

Step	Latency (ms)
ORB Feature Extraction	40.40 ± 2.31
Fisher Encoding with BMM	78.58 ± 6.37
Scene Retrieval	1.750 ± 0.55
ORB Feature Matching	9.738 ± 1.64
Pose Calculation	30.45 ± 4.73

Table 1: Breakdown of latency for different AR tasks on mobile devices. The value after ± is the standard deviation (for 20 experimental runs).

improve the reliability of D2D communication, especially when many users are using CARS in a crowded environment, we can limit the collaboration between only users with good wireless channel quality (*e.g.*, with signal strength higher than a threshold).

Cloud Manager communicates with the cloud via WiFi or LTE for submitting the recognition request and receiving the result and annotation, as described in § 2. Each request contains a compressed file of the camera frame. The result has the identity and 6DoF pose of the target object.

4 PRELIMINARY EVALUATION

In this section, we present the experimental results based on our proof-of-concept implementation of CARS.

4.1 Implementation

We build a prototype of CARS using the OpenCV4Android [21] library on Xiaomi MI5 smartphones (2.15 GHz Snapdragon 820 processor). We use ORB [26] for feature extraction and Fisher Vector [23] with BMM [14] to encode feature descriptors. The phone downloads the BMM model for the entire database from the cloud. Note that the size of BMM model does not depend on the number of images in the database and is only 131.58 KB for our setup. Motion Detector uses gyroscope and accelerometer on the phone to analyze hand motion of users. Annotation Renderer employs a XML file for describing the status of annotations.

We simplify the setup and configuration of the object-recognition pipeline to make it feasible on mobile devices, as our previous work [30] demonstrated when using the same pipeline it takes much longer time than cloud-based object recognition. First, we reduce the number of ORB feature points from ~500 (in cloud-based AR) to 200. This reduction has almost no impact on the recognition accuracy, given the small size of the local cache (with only 100 images). Second, due to the small search space in the local cache, we do not need to use the Local Sensitive Hashing (LSH) of FV. Third, we skip object detection and thus our mobile image retrieval supports the recognition of only one object.

4.2 Experimental Results

Our preliminary performance evaluation focuses on the end-to-end latency, as we believe it should be the first-class citizen for AR. The latency is the processing time from generating the recognition request to displaying the annotation. It has two parts, object recognition and annotation download.

We set up a VM (8 vCPUs @ 2.5GHz and 32GB memory) in a public cloud. The mobile device communicates with the cloud via

WiFi, with a Round Trip Time (RTT) of ~36 ms. With the WiFi interface connected to both an access point (in Station mode) and a peer device (in WiFi Direct mode), the bandwidth is ~13 Mbps between the phone and the cloud, and ~32 Mbps between the phones. When the phone connects to the cloud via cellular networks, the bandwidth of WiFi Direct increases to ~60 Mbps, as it does not need to share the airtime with the Station mode. The RTT of WiFi Direct between the phones is only ~3.5 ms. Using the pipeline described in § 2.1, the latency for cloud-based recognition is ~266 ms. Downloading a 5 MB (the most common size shown in Figure 2a) annotation from the server takes ~3084 ms.

The local object recognition has five steps, and we list their completion time in Table 1. The recognition latency depends on the nearest neighbor search in Scene Matcher. We define the recognition accuracy as the ratio between the number of successful recognition requests over the total number of requests. CARS can achieve ~90% accuracy when searching up to 5 nearest neighbors (*i.e.*, repeating feature matching at most 5 times). Thus, the local recognition latency is at most ~200 ms. When considering only the nearest neighbor (*i.e.*, executing feature matching only once), the recognition latency is ~161 ms with close to 60% accuracy.

Downloading the same 5 MB annotation via WiFi Direct takes only ~1266 ms, much faster than downloading from the cloud. If the phone communicates with the cloud via cellular networks, this download time would be even shorter (due to the higher throughput). Note that since annotations are usually shared before recognition happens, users may not perceive this download latency. In a nutshell, the reduction of end-to-end latency mainly benefits from the fact that CARS can *perform lightweight object recognition on mobile devices by leveraging the results of cloud-based AR*.

5 DISCUSSION AND FUTURE WORK

In this section, we discuss several unsolved issues and directions of future work.

Preemptive Caching. Other than D2D communication, CARS can also benefit from cloud-initiated push to enable collaborative AR. For example, if CARS knows there are three more paintings on the left side of Mona Lisa and Bob is moving toward that direction, it can request, *in advance*, the cloud to push existing recognition results from others for these paintings if available. In this case, the collaboration does not happen directly over D2D, but utilizes the cloud as a *remote cache* for sharing. Note that this approach requires localization/mobility prediction and may consume extra mobile data, especially for outdoor scenarios. AR applications can utilize the edge cloud, *e.g.*, Cloudlets [27], to further improve the QoE of the preemptive caching.

Sharing Policy. Regarding the sharing policy of CARS, users can express their personal interests via preferences (*i.e.*, utility for an object) [17], which reduces the chance of exchanging objects that a user may not be curious about. To further minimize the communication overhead on D2D, CARS users will not forward recognition results and annotations from others and should avoid always-on-sharing for reducing energy consumption. Moreover, we can assign a time-to-live (as a geographical bound) for the scene a user plans to share with others, which decreases the probability that the scene will not be consumed by them.

Evaluation and Deployment. The performance evaluation in this paper is preliminary. For example, we use only two smartphones in the experiments, measure mainly the latency reduction, and the target objects are all movie posters. As shown in CoMon [15], opportunistic cooperation among nearby users can reduce energy consumption of mobile sensing. As our future work, we plan to conduct large-scale real-world experiments by deploying CARS in places such as museums and galleries, and evaluate its performance thoroughly (*e.g.*, by measuring energy consumption on mobile devices).

6 RELATED WORK

We divide existing work into two categories: cloud-based augmented reality and mobile image recognition.

Cloud-Based AR can be either non-continuous or continuous. For the former, users cannot move their mobile devices before getting the results from the cloud. For example, it takes around 500 ms for Overlay [11] to finish object recognition and rendering, during which a user needs to pause the camera at the interested object. VisualPrint [12] optimizes the uplink bandwidth requirements by uploading fingerprints extracted from the feature points of a camera frame to the cloud for recognition. In contrast to Overlay and VisualPrint, Glimpse [5] is a continuous face and road-sign recognition system. It uses an active cache of camera frames to hide the cloud-offloading latency by tracking objects in real time.

Image Recognition is a key component of augmented reality. CrowdSearch [29] combines image search and real-time human validation via crowdsourcing systems, such as the Amazon Mechanical Turk. ThirdEye [24] tracks the browsing behaviors of customers in retail stores by identifying the item a user is gazing at through an online image search service. Gabriel [8] assists users with their cognitive abilities using Google Glass, which leverages mobile edge computing for reducing the end-to-end latency of image recognition. Different from the above work, CARS explores the collaborative nature of mobile users for cloud-based AR systems to improve the quality of user experience.

7 CONCLUSION

In this paper, we propose CARS, a collaborative AR framework for socialization. CARS leverages the unique feature of AR that its users who share common scenes are usually close to each other. By enabling the social nature of human beings, CARS supports the interaction and coordination among users of cloud-based AR applications. Given that the size of local cache is usually small, we simplify the pipeline of object recognition to make it feasible on mobile devices. We build a proof-of-concept for CARS on smartphones and demonstrate it can reduce the object-recognition latency by up to 40%, compared to purely cloud-based AR.

ACKNOWLEDGEMENT

We thank the anonymous reviewers for their insightful comments. The research of Pan Hui was supported in part by the General Research Fund from the Research Grants Council of Hong Kong under Grant 26211515 and Grant 16214817. The research of Feng Qian was supported in part by a Google Faculty Award.

REFERENCES

[1] Alexandre Alahi, Raphael Ortiz, and Pierre Vandergheynst. 2012. Freak: Fast Retina Keypoint. In *Proceedings of CVPR*.
[2] Giuseppe Amato, Fabrizio Falchi, and Lucia Vadicamo. 2016. Aggregating binary local descriptors for image retrieval. *Multimedia Tools and Applications* (2016), 1–31.
[3] Apple Inc. 2017. Introducing ARKit: Augmented Reality for iOS. https://developer.apple.com/arkit/. (2017). [accessed on 20-October-2017].
[4] Herbert Bay, Tinne Tuytelaars, and Luc Van Gool. 2006. SURF: Speeded Up Robust Features. *Proceedings of ECCV* (2006).
[5] Tiffany Yu-Han Chen, Lenin Ravindranath, Shuo Deng, Paramvir Bahl, and Hari Balakrishnan. 2015. Glimpse: Continuous, Real-Time Object Recognition on Mobile Devices. In *Proceedings of SenSys*.
[6] Laurent Gautier, Christophe Diot, and Jim Kurose. 1999. End-to-end transmission control mechanisms for multiparty interactive applications on the Internet. In *Proceedings of INFOCOM*.
[7] Aristides Gionis, Piotr Indyk, Rajeev Motwani, and others. 1999. Similarity Search in High Dimensions via Hashing. In *VLDB*, Vol. 99. 518–529.
[8] Kiryong Ha, Zhuo Chen, Wenlu Hu, Wolfgang Richter, Padmanabhan Pillai, and Mahadev Satyanarayanan. 2014. Towards Wearable Cognitive Assistance. In *Proceedings of MobiSys*.
[9] Berthold KP Horn and Brian G Schunck. 1981. Determining Optical Flow. *Artificial intelligence* 17, 1-3 (1981), 185–203.
[10] Stratis Ioannidis, Laurent Massoulié, and Augustin Chaintreau. 2010. Distributed Caching over Heterogeneous Mobile Networks . In *Proceedings of SIGMETRICS*.
[11] Puneet Jain, Justin Manweiler, and Romit Roy Choudhury. 2015. Overlay: Practical Mobile Augmented Reality. In *Proceedings of MobiSys*.
[12] Puneet Jain, Justin Manweiler, and Romit Roy Choudhury. 2016. Low Bandwidth Offload for Mobile AR. In *Proceedings of CoNEXT*.
[13] Eric Johnson. 2015. Boeing Says Augmented Reality Can Make Workers Better, Faster. http://www.recode.net/2015/6/8/11563374/boeing-says-augmented-reality-can-make-workers-better-faster. (2015). [accessed on 20-October-2017].
[14] Alfons Juan and Enrique Vidal. 2004. Bernoulli mixture models for binary images. In *Proceedings of ICPR*.
[15] Youngki Lee, Younghyun Ju, Chulhong Min, Seungwoo Kang, Inseok Hwang, and Junehwa Song. 2011. CoMon: Cooperative Ambience Monitoring Platform with Continuity and Benefit Awareness. In *Proceedings of MobiSys*.
[16] Stefan Leutenegger, Margarita Chli, and Roland Y Siegwart. 2011. BRISK: Binary robust invariant scalable keypoints. In *Proceedings of ICCV*.
[17] Kate Ching-Ju Lin, Chun-Wei Chen, and Cheng-Fu Chou. 2012. Preference-aware content dissemination in opportunistic mobile social networks. In *Proceedings of INFOCOM*.
[18] David G Lowe. 2004. Distinctive image features from scale-invariant keypoints. *Journal of Computer Vision* 60, 2 (2004), 91–110.
[19] Microsoft. 2017. HoloLens. https://www.microsoft.com/microsoft-hololens/. (2017). [accessed on 20-October-2017].
[20] Ben Nelson. 2017. VR/AR Challenge finalist WayPoint RX take the guess work out of filling prescriptions. https://developer.att.com/blog/vr-ar-challenge-waypoint-rx. (2017). [accessed on 20-October-2017].
[21] OpenCV. 2017. OpenCV4Android. http://opencv.org/platforms/android/. (2017). [accessed on 20-October-2017].
[22] Sergio Orts-Escolano, Christoph Rhemann, and others. 2016. Holoportation: Virtual 3D Teleportation in Real-time. In *Proceedings of the 29th Annual Symposium on User Interface Software and Technology (UIST)*.
[23] Florent Perronnin, Yan Liu, Jorge Sánchez, and Hervé Poirier. 2010. Large-scale image retrieval with compressed Fisher vectors. In *Proceedings of CVPR*.
[24] Swati Rallapalli, Aishwarya Ganesan, Krishna Chintalapudi, Venkat N Padmanabhan, and Lili Qiu. 2014. Enabling Physical Analytics in Retail Stores Using Smart Glasses. In *Proceedings of MobiCom*.
[25] Douglas A Reynolds, Thomas F Quatieri, and Robert B Dunn. 2000. Speaker Verification Using Adapted Gaussian Mixture Models. *Digital Signal Processing* 10, 1-3 (2000), 19–41.
[26] Ethan Rublee, Vincent Rabaud, Kurt Konolige, and Gary Bradski. 2011. ORB: An efficient alternative to SIFT or SURF. In *Proceedings ICCV*.
[27] Mahadev Satyanarayanan, Paramvir Bahl, RamÃşn Caceres, and Nigel Davies. 2009. The Case for VM-Based Cloudlets in Mobile Computing. *IEEE Pervasive Computing* 8, 4 (2009), 14–23.
[28] Unity. 2017. Asset Store. https://www.assetstore.unity3d.com/. (2017). [accessed on 20-October-2017].
[29] Tingxin Yan, Vikas Kumar, and Deepak Ganesan. 2010. CrowdSearch: Exploiting Crowds for Accurate Real-Time Image Search on Mobile Phones. In *Proceedings of MobiSys*.
[30] Wenxiao Zhang, Bo Han, and Pan Hui. 2017. On the Networking Challenges of Mobile Augmented Reality . In *Proceedings of VR/AR Network*.

Unsupervised Workflow Extraction from First-Person Video of Mechanical Assembly

Truong-An Pham
Aalto University
Espoo, Finland
truong.pham@aalto.fi

Yu Xiao
Aalto University
Espoo, Finland
yu.xiao@aalto.fi

ABSTRACT

Recently, Augmented Reality (AR) applications have proved to help improve the efficiency in accomplishing assembly tasks. However, due to the lack of approaches to automatic workflow extraction, the existing AR-based assembly assistance applications require manual authoring, which hampers scalability. Moreover, most of these applications only support information visualization and video documentation. To tackle the challenge of scalability and to enable more intelligent functionalities, such as real-time quality control, we propose in this paper a novel solution for unsupervised workflow extraction from first-person video of mechanical assembly, without any pre-labeled training data or pre-trained classifiers. Our proposed system automatically discovers a sequence of operations from the input video, and describes the extracted workflow process with semantics. Preliminary evaluation demonstrates the feasibility of our solution and highlights the technical challenges.

CCS CONCEPTS

• **Computing methodologies** → *Computer vision tasks*;

KEYWORDS

Video analytics; Workflow extraction

ACM Reference Format:
Truong-An Pham and Yu Xiao. 2018. Unsupervised Workflow Extraction from First-Person Video of Mechanical Assembly. In *HotMobile '18: 19th International Workshop on Mobile Computing Systems & Applications, February 12–13, 2018, Tempe , AZ, USA*. ACM, New York, NY, USA, 6 pages. https://doi.org/10.1145/3177102.3177112

1 INTRODUCTION

Augmented Reality (AR) allows computer-generated virtual content to be overlaid on the view of real world. Receiving instructions in AR mode, compared to reading paper-based manuals, has proved to significantly shorten the completion time of the same maintenance tasks [10]. Additionally, AR-based guidance could be more helpful for assembly than disassembly during maintenance [2]. However, the adoption of AR-based assembly assistance has been hampered, due to the lack of approaches to automatic authoring.

Authoring is the process of creating visual overlays and associating them with certain objects or process steps. For AR-based

assembly assistance applications, authoring includes defining contexts (e.g. completion status of a process step) and the AR content in different context (e.g. instruction for each step). Manual authoring is time consuming, though there are several software tools available for creating and editing the step-to-step instructions [10, 23]. To implement automatic authoring, it is essential to enable automatic workflow extraction, the capability of recognizing the order of the working steps and the context (e.g. objects, hand-object interactions) of each step. This capability is also needed for developing more intelligent functionalities, such as real-time quality control and workflow optimization, than information visualization and video documentation [25].

In this paper, we propose an unsupervised workflow extraction system which automatically discovers the working steps and the operations in each step from first-person video of mechanical assembly. Concerning the lack and scarcity of labeled data, we combine object detection and tracking to implement unsupervised object recognition, which does not require any pre-labeled data or pre-trained classifiers. Based on the recognized objects and human-object interaction, our system infers the working steps included in a workflow, and describes the operations in each step with semantics.

We have evaluated the feasibility of our system with 40 10-minute first-person videos captured by Microsoft Hololens during the implementation of two assembly tasks. Firstly, we measure how accurately our system can recognize working steps and the operations in each step. Our preliminary results show that our system can extract 81% of working steps and 76% of the operations. Secondly, we test whether the accuracy of object recognition would increase with the amount of input through the self-learning process. Compared with the first result without any pre-trained classifier, the accuracy of unsupervised object recognition increases by 7.24% after processing 16 10-minute videos.

Concerning the remained challenges, we plan to develop a robust hand gesture recognition solution that can detect various hand gestures from visual and motion sensor data. In addition, we will work on semantic workflow modeling to enable workflow optimization and situation-aware authoring for mechanical assembly.

2 RELATED WORKS

This section reviews the previous works related to workflow discovery and wearable cognitive assistance for mechanical assembly. Here workflow discovery refers to the process of discovering the working steps involved in a workflow.

2.1 Workflow Discovery

Previous works on workflow discovery [18–20] have managed to segment a video in the way that each segment represents one working step in the workflow. However, they did not provide detailed information about the objects or operations involved in each step. In other words, these works only considered the cycles of working

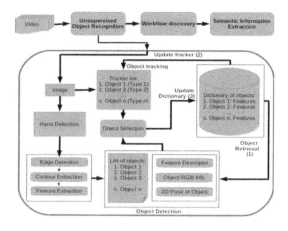

Figure 1: The process of unsupervised object recognition.

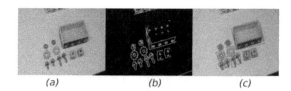

Figure 2: Edge- and contour-based detection of object-like regions. (a) Original image. (b) edges. (c) contours.

steps [19], or the detection of working steps based on the dissimilarity between image frames [18, 20]. In addition, previous works assumed that RGB cameras were always placed in certain locations to capture the ongoing activities. When the camera poses change, or when the cameras are relocated, the system is highly unlikely to recognize the same activities, because the image distance metric used for measuring similarity is not robust for transformations like rotation and scaling. In this paper, we present a novel solution that extracts semantic information about each working step from first-person video. The semantic information can later be applied for error detection, progress control and workflow optimization.

2.2 Wearable Cognitive Assistance

A few wearable cognitive assistance systems [9, 12] have been developed, with the goal of providing context-aware instructions during assembly process. However, they rely on pre-defined workflow scripts [9], or pre-defined object positions in a pre-setup working environment [12]. In other words, these works require a lot of efforts for manually defining the working steps and the operations in each step, preparing labeled training data, and training the classifiers for object recognition. Concerning the large variance in assembly process in the era of mass customization, these previous works are not scalable, due to massive labor cost. Our system provides scalability by applying unsupervised machine learning which learns by itself to detect objects from unlabeled video.

3 SYSTEM DESIGN

Our system is implemented as a pipeline that contains three main process modules, namely, unsupervised object recognition, workflow discovery, and semantic information extraction. In this section, we will describe the design of these process modules.

3.1 Unsupervised Object Recognition

Our system implements unsupervised object recognition which automatically detects and tracks objects appearing in the video. This differs from supervised object recognition [16, 21] which requires manual collection of labeled training data. As illustrated in Figure 1, given a first-person video of an assembly process, our system executes the following steps on each image frame.

(1) Execute human hand detection and remove the hand regions from each image frame. This step is implemented using open

egohands [4–7]. After this step, objects such as tools and assembly components will be separated from human hands.

(2) Extract edges and contours from the image, as shown in Figure 2. The output of this step includes object-like regions, bounded by contours.

(3) Filter out the bounded regions which have low probability of containing any object. The filtering follows two criteria: a) the contour in question covers more than two thirds of the frame, or is smaller than a certain threshold (e.g. a 10x10 pixel area), or b) the contour covers a small amount (e.g. less than 10) of SIFT (Scale-Invariant Feature Transform) features. SIFT is robust against some affine transformation types like scaling, reflection, rotation. According to Perspective-Three-Point principle [13], at least 4 SIFT feature points are needed for estimating a camera pose. With that camera pose, we can later evaluate whether bounded region in question is transformed from any reference. According to our tests, at least 10 SIFT features are expected, in order to provide robust object detection with acceptable accuracy.

(4) If the object dictionary is empty, add all the objects detected in Step (3) to the dictionary. Otherwise, skip this step. Here the object dictionary stores the features and the bounding box of each type of object. For each type of object, there can be more than one entries.

(5) For each object-like region, conduct feature-based object detection using SIFT [17] and RANSAC [11]. The purpose of this step is to recognize the objects already included in the object dictionary, and to eliminate the false positive output of Step (3). In the first scenario, the system will use the bounding boxes stored in the object dictionary as references to refine the bounding boxes of the recognized object in the image based on feature matching and 2D projective transformation. We call the refined bounding box (e.g. the green bounding box in Figure 3) in the image as *detected bounding box*. The reference bounding box in the object dictionary will be used for calculating the distance information in Eq. (1).

(6) In parallel with Step (5), track the detected objects using MIL object tracker [24] which is robust to occlusion and is stable with abrupt changes in video. The bounding box of the tracked object (e.g. the blue bounding box in Figure 3) is called *tracked bounding box*. This method may work even when the feature matching in the process of object detection fails.

(7) Given the two bounding boxes obtained from Step (5) and (6), respectively, the system decides which one to use based on Eq. (1). As input for the calculation in Eq. (1), each bounding box is divided into 4x4 subregions.

$$\alpha D_d(x, y) + (1 - \alpha)D_t(x, y) < \theta (\alpha \in [0, 1], \theta \in [0, 1]), \quad (1)$$

where $D_d(x, y)$ is the normalized distance between a subregion centered at (x, y) in the detected bounding box and the corresponding subregion in the reference bounding box mentioned

Figure 3: Feature-based object detection with bounding box in green and object tracking with bounding box in blue

in Step (5). Similarly, $D_t(x, y)$ refers to the normalized distance for the tracked bounding box obtained from Step (6). θ is a threshold used for controlling the acceptable dissimilarity or distance between subregions.

(8) Add to the object dictionary the bounding box chosen in Step (7) and the newly detected SIFT features. The more features to be accumulated into the object dictionary, the higher probability to have for correctly recognizing objects.

(9) Repeat from Step (1) until the end of the video.

After executing all these 9 steps on an image, the output includes an updated object dictionary and a new entry to be added to the operation log. The entry includes the positions of the detected hands, the types of the recognized objects from the image, and/or the changes in the positions of any tracked objects.

3.2 Workflow Discovery and Semantic Information Extraction

We propose to separate working steps by idle state, and then recognize the operations involved in each step. Here idle state refers to the status where no hand-object interaction is happening. In this work, we define 4 basic operations. Besides idle state, the other three are plugging, searching, and pose changing. Plugging refers to the action of attaching any objects to the assembled product through hand-object interaction. Searching is about changing the camera view to look for objects for example, while pose changing refers to the operation of changing the pose of the assembled product. Each working step contains a series of operations, and causes change in the product pose or in the state of the assembly process. Given the output of unsupervised object recognition, the process of workflow discovery is implemented as follows.

Firstly, by tracking the movement of hands and the relative positions of the hands to the objects, the system can memorize the objects associated with each hand-object interaction. As illustrated in Figure 4, the system infers hand-object interaction and the product pose change caused by the interaction. The detailed inference rules are listed below.

$$A \wedge B \Rightarrow C_1 \text{ Plugging} \qquad (2)$$

$$\neg A \wedge B \Rightarrow C_2 \text{ Changing pose} \qquad (3)$$

$$\neg A \wedge \neg B \Rightarrow C_3 \text{ Idle state} \qquad (4)$$

$$D \Rightarrow C_4 \text{ Searching} \qquad (5)$$

Here A is defined as a boolean value that indicates whether the assembly state has changed. B represents hand-object interaction, which can be detected based on the similarity in trajectories of the hand and the object. D represents the scenario where the assembled product disappears from the camera view while for example the user is searching tools from a toolbox. C indicates the type of the inferred operation. All the recognized operations are recorded also in the operation log.

Secondly, regarding the change in assembly state, the system needs to check whether the appearance of the product changes, because the change in the appearance may indicate the completion of a working step. In practice, the appearance of the product may also change when the product pose changes, as shown in Figure 5. Therefore, to reduce the error in the detection of the assembly state change, we conduct the following two steps.

(1) Extract RGB-Local Binary Pattern (RGB-LBP)[3] features of the assembled product. These features are used for describing the appearance of the assembled product.

(2) Match the output of the previous step with the product poses recorded in the operation log, using the RGB-LBP features. If no match is found, the change in the appearance is caused by pose change. Otherwise, check whether the number of objects included in the assembled product has changed. If yes, it is considered as an assembly state change.

After recognizing the operations in each working step, the next task is to describe the step with semantic information. We describe each working step with a set of the two-element tuple *([operation type], [object name list])* following the order of the operations.

4 PRELIMINARY EVALUATION

4.1 Experimental setup

To emulate the assembly tasks in industrial environment, we conducted two assembly tasks using a Hape kid's wooden tool box set [1]. As the original instruction provided by the manufacturer (see Figure 6) ignores a lot of details, we redefine it to include detailed description of each working step. As listed in Table 1, the first assembly task then consists of 25 steps, while the second one contains 16 steps.

Regarding data collection, one user wearing a Microsoft Hololens was asked to repeat the assembly tasks for 20 times following the step-by-step instruction listed in Table 1. We collected in total 40 first-person videos from the RGB camera embedded in the Microsoft Hololens. Each video lasts approximately 10 minutes.[1] These videos have been used for evaluating the accuracy of each process module in our system. Note that we have manually checked all the videos and make sure that the user had strictly followed the instruction. This means the instruction we gave to the user can be considered as the ground truth for evaluating the accuracy of the system.

Intersection over Union (IoU), as defined in [26], has been commonly used for evaluating the accuracy of object detectors. IoU measures the overlap between the groundtruth bounding box and the detected bounding box. When the value of IoU is set to 0.5, the result is considered as a true positive if the detected bounding box overlaps with at least 50% of the groundtruth bounding box. Thus, the higher the value of IoU is, the more strict the evaluation criteria is. In our experiment, we compare the precision and recall of unsupervised object recognition between the scenarios where the value of IoU is set to 0.5, 0.7, and 0.9, respectively. We also compare the results with different settings of the parameters α and θ defined in Eq. (1).

We use Recall (or detection rate) to measure the accuracy of workflow discovery and semantic information extraction. For example, the recall of workflow discovery shows how many working steps have been detected correctly in each assembly task. As described in Section 3.2, the workflow can be described with semantic information. The description of a working step is correct, when the

---
[1]The videos can be downloaded from https://goo.gl/Z24Xe3

| (a) Hand detection | (b) Interaction | (c) Changing pose | (d) Changing view | (e) Interaction | (f) Interaction |

Figure 4: Illustration of 3 basic operations. (a)-(c) changing product pose. (c)-(d) searching (c)-(f) plugging

Step	Assembly Task 1	Assembly Task 2
1	Put the red gear to one side of the container	Put a 3-hole bar to one side of the container
2	Attach the red gear to one side of the container by screw	Put a triangle to a 3-hole bar
3	Put the green gear to one side of the container	Use screw for attaching 1 and 2 to the container
4	Attach the green gear to the side of the container by screw	Use screw for attaching 1 and 2 to the container
5	Put the cube under the container	Use screw for attaching 1 and 2 to the container
6	Attach the cube to the bottom of the container by screw	Attach an axle to the 3-hole bar in 1 with another 3-hole bar to the other side of the container
7	Put the cube under the container	Put a triangle to a new 3-hole bar in 4
8	Attach the cube to the bottom of the container by screw	Use screw for attaching the combination in 5 to the container
9	Put 2-hole bar to a side of attached cube in 5	Use screw for attaching the combination in 5 to the container
10	Put 3-hole bar to the 2-hole bar in 9	Use screw for attaching the combination in 5 to the container
11	Attach two bars and attached cube together by screw	Put a wheel on a side of the container
12	Put 2-hole bar to a side of attached cube in 7	Use screw for attaching combination in 11 to the container
13	Put 3-hole bar to the 2-hole bar in 12	Put a cube on the same side of the container
14	Attach two bars and attached cube together by screw	Use screw for attaching that cube to the container
15	Attach a circle, a wheel into 3-hole bar in 10 by screw	Put two gears on the cube in 13
16	Attach a circle, a wheel into 3-hole bar in 10 by screw	Use screw for attaching that cube to the container
17	Attach a circle, a wheel into 3-hole bar in 13 by screw	
18	Attach a circle, a wheel into 3-hole bar in 13 by screw	
19	Attach a 3-hole bar to a side of the container by screw	
20	Attach an axle to 3-hole bar in 19 with another 3-hole bar in other side	
21	Attach another 3-hole bar in 20 to a side of the container by screw	
22	Attach a triangle to a rectangle bar by screw	
23	Attach the combination in 22 to 3 hole bar in 19 by screw	
24	Attach a triangle to a rectangle bar by screw	
25	Attach the combination in 23 to the 3-hole bar in 21 by screw	

Table 1: Pre-defined step-to-step instructions

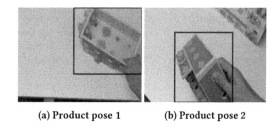

| (a) Product pose 1 | (b) Product pose 2 |

Figure 5: Change in product pose in a working step

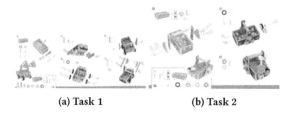

| (a) Task 1 | (b) Task 2 |

Figure 6: Instruction of two assembly tasks provided by Hape [1].

order of the step, the types of the objects, and the types of the operations involved match the groundtruth. Regarding the groundtruth of semantic information extraction, we observe from the 20 videos of the first assembly task 25 "idle", 25 "searching", 25 "plugging", and 6 "changing pose" operations. In the videos of the second assembly tasks, there are 16 "idle", 16 "searching", 16 "plugging", and 4 "changing pose" operations.

4.2 Unsupervised object recognition

The precision and recall of unsupervised object recognition with different parameter settings are presented in Figure 7. When α is set to 0.6, the system achieves the highest precision and recall at the same time. We also measure Area under the Curve (AUC) for each curve in Figure 7. The results listed in Table 2 confirm the observation that our system reduces both false positive and false negative.

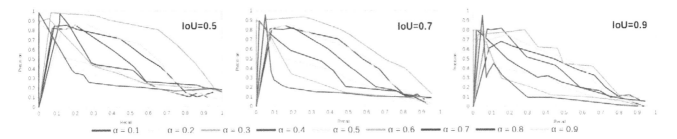

Figure 7: Precision and Recall evaluation on unsupervised object recognition

Area Under the Curve(AUC)									
Criteria / α	0.1	0.2	0.3	0.4	0.5	0.6	0.7	0.8	0.9
IoU 0.5	0.3	0.32	0.4	0.4	0.51	**0.73**	0.5	0.42	0.33
IoU 0.7	0.16	0.15	0.24	0.34	0.49	**0.64**	0.45	0.41	0.31
IoU 0.9	0.14	0.11	0.19	0.29	0.4	**0.47**	0.34	0.35	0.24

Table 2: AUC with different settings of IoU and α

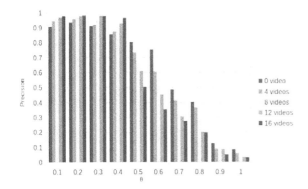

Figure 8: Precision of unsupervised object recognition at 5 different phases with different settings of θ

With unsupervised object recognition, the accuracy of object recognition is supposed to increase with the amount of input. To prove that, we divide the learning process into 5 phases, and compare the precision of object recognition at different phase. The number of video already fed into the system at the beginning of each phase is 0, 4, 8, 12, and 16, respectively. We set the value of α to 0.6, and tune the value of θ. According to Table 2, the value of IoU does not affect the impact analysis of the parameter α. Therefore, we set IoU to 0.7 for case study. As shown in Figure 8, when θ is smaller or equal to 0.4, the accuracy of unsupervised object recognition increases gradually when the number of processed videos increases from 0 to 16. On average, the accuracy increases by 2.28% after each phase. When θ is bigger than 0.4, the accuracy starts to drop significantly. This is because a bigger value of θ allows more wrongly detected features to be added to the object dictionary.

4.3 Workflow Discovery

The overall detection rate of working steps in the 40 videos is 80.73%. When several objects are involved in one working step, the operation becomes more complex. For example, in Table 1, Step 20, 22, and 24 in the first assembly task, and Step 6 in the second

assembly task are relatively complex than the others. According to Figure 9, the accuracy of these complex working steps ranges between 0.5 and 0.65. It is a bit lower compared with the results of other working steps, which range from 0.7 and 1.0. The low recognition accuracy is mainly caused by the limitation of video-based hand gesture recognition. In a simple working step, one operation can be completed without a break. However, in a complex working step that involves multiple objects and operations, the intervals between operations may be identified as the idle state between working steps. Therefore, one complex working step may in practice be recognized as a set of simple working steps.

4.4 Semantic Information Extraction

Overall, 76.05% of operations involved in the 40 video have been correctly recognized. As illustrated in Figure 10, our system can better recognize "plugging" and "searching" than "idle" and "changing pose". "Plugging" involves long-term contact between hands and the assembly products, while "searching" can be recognized by abrupt changes in the scene. In case of "idle", the error comes from the limitation of color-based hand detection. For example, errors occur when the hand detection algorithm by accident classifies non-hand object regions as hand regions when the illumination changes. In case of "changing pose", the new pose may have not appeared in previous image frames, which results in the lack of the features to be matched.

5 REMARKING CHALLENGES AND FUTURE WORK

Although preliminary results on extracting workflow are quite positive, more work is needed for improving the accuracy of object recognition and hand gesture recognition methods. In addition, we plan to work on semantic workflow modeling and to build model-based automatic authoring tools for AR-based assembly assistance applications.

1) Video-based hand gesture recognition supports few types of gestures, and does not perform well due to occlusions and variations in gestures of different users. Besides visual information, we plan to leverage also motion sensors with high sampling frequency (e.g. 4KHz) for recognizing different types of hand gestures and improving the accuracy of hand gesture recognition [15].

2) Hand-crafted features such as SIFT are not robust against variant illumination conditions of working environments. To overcome this challenge, we plan to test other feature descriptors, and to explore the feasibility of combining our approach with deep object recognition techniques such as Faster-CNN [22].

3) With our proposed semantic information extraction, we aim to propose a novel semantic workflow modeling mechanism for

(a) Assembly Task 1

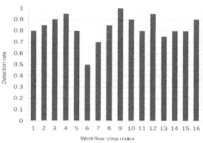

(b) Assembly Task 2

Figure 9: Recall of workflow discovery.

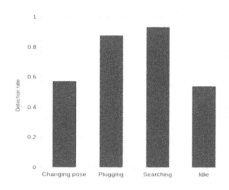

Figure 10: Recall of operations recognition

automatic authoring in the future work. Meanwhile, we would like to explore a novel way to support diversity [14] and correctness diagnose [8] in semantic workflow models, and to develop solutions for workflow optimization in order to optimize the efficiency in assembly process.

4) We plan to implement tools for automatic authoring and example applications like wearable assembly assistance for real-time error detection. With extracted semantic information, the applications will be able to provide contextualized instructions for users.

6 CONCLUSIONS

In this paper we propose an unsupervised workflow extraction system that automatically discovers the working steps and the operations involved in each step, without any pre-labeled data. The system is implemented based on unsupervised object recognition, workflow discovery, and semantic information extraction. Our preliminary evaluation with two assembly tasks show that our system extracts accurate workflow description from first-person video. The limitation of video-based hand gesture recognition will be tackled in the future work. We believe our system can help increase the scalability of AR-based assembly assistance systems by enabling automatic authoring, and can provide semantic information for quality control, progress management, and workflow optimization in assembly process.

REFERENCES

[1] Hape International AG. 2017 (accessed Oct 1, 2017). *Hape kid toys company*. https://www.hape.com
[2] Susanna Aromaa et al. 2016. Use of Wearable and Augmented Reality Technologies in Industrial Maintenance Work. In *Proceedings of the 20th International Academic Mindtrek Conference (AcademicMindtrek '16)*. ACM, New York, NY, USA, 235–242.
[3] Sugata Banerji et al. 2012. LBP and Color Descriptors for Image Classification. (2012).
[4] Alejandro Betancourt et al. 2014. A sequential classifier for hand detection in the framework of egocentric vision. In *Proceedings of the IEEE CVPR Workshops*. 586–591.
[5] Alejandro Betancourt et al. 2015. A dynamic approach and a new dataset for hand-detection in first person vision. In *CAIP 2015*. Springer, 274–287.
[6] Alejandro Betancourt et al. 2015. Filtering SVM frame-by-frame binary classification in a detection framework. In *Proceedings of the IEEE ICIP 2015*. IEEE, 2552–2556.
[7] Alejandro Betancourt et al. 2015. Towards a unified framework for hand-based methods in first person vision. In *Proceedings of 2015 IEEE International Conference on Multimedia & Expo Workshops (ICMEW)*. IEEE, 1–6.
[8] Diana Borrego et al. 2013. Diagnosing correctness of semantic workflow models. *Data & Knowledge Engineering* 87 (2013), 167–184.
[9] Zhuo Chen et al. 2015. Early implementation experience with wearable cognitive assistance applications. In *Proceedings of the 2015 workshop on Wearable Systems and Applications*. ACM, 33–38.
[10] John Ahmet Erkoyuncu et al. 2017. Improving efficiency of industrial maintenance with context aware adaptive authoring in augmented reality. *CIRP Annals* 66, 1 (2017), 465 – 468.
[11] Martin A Fischler and Robert C Bolles. 1981. Random sample consensus: a paradigm for model fitting with applications to image analysis and automated cartography. *Commun. ACM* 24, 6 (1981), 381–395.
[12] Markus Funk and Albrecht Schmidt. 2015. Cognitive assistance in the workplace. *IEEE Pervasive Computing* 14, 3 (2015), 53–55.
[13] Xiao-Shan Gao et al. 2003. Complete solution classification for the perspective-three-point problem. *IEEE TPAMI* 25, 8 (2003), 930–943.
[14] Gregor Grambow et al. 2010. Semantic workflow adaption in support of workflow diversity. (2010).
[15] Gierad Laput et al. 2016. Viband: High-fidelity bio-acoustic sensing using commodity smartwatch accelerometers. In *Proceedings of UIST 2016*. ACM, 321–333.
[16] Tsung-Yi Lin et al. 2014. Microsoft coco: Common objects in context. In *ECCV*. Springer, 740–755.
[17] David G Lowe. 1999. Object recognition from local scale-invariant features. In *Computer vision, 1999. The proceedings of the seventh IEEE international conference on*, Vol. 2. Ieee, 1150–1157.
[18] Katharina Mura et al. 2013. IBES: a tool for creating instructions based on event segmentation. *Frontiers in psychology* 4 (2013).
[19] Fabian Nater et al. 2011. Unsupervised workflow discovery in industrial environments. In *ICCV Workshop 2011*. IEEE, 1912–1919.
[20] Nils Petersen and Didier Stricker. 2012. Learning task structure from video examples for workflow tracking and authoring. In *ISMAR 2012*. IEEE, 237–246.
[21] Joseph Redmon and Ali Farhadi. 2016. YOLO9000: Better, Faster, Stronger. *arXiv preprint arXiv:1612.08242* (2016).
[22] Shaoqing Ren, Kaiming He, Ross Girshick, and Jian Sun. 2015. Faster R-CNN: Towards real-time object detection with region proposal networks. In *Advances in neural information processing systems*. 91–99.
[23] Andrea Sanna et al. 2015. A Flexible AR-based Training System for Industrial Maintenance. In *Proceedings of the Second International Conference on Augmented and Virtual Reality - Volume 9254*. Springer-Verlag New York, Inc., New York, NY, USA, 314–331.
[24] Vijay K Sharma and Kamala K Mahapatra. 2017. MIL based visual object tracking with kernel and scale adaptation. *Signal Processing: Image Communication* 53 (2017), 51–64.
[25] X Wang et al. 2016. A comprehensive survey of augmented reality assembly research. *Advances in Manufacturing* 4, 1 (2016), 1–22.
[26] C Lawrence Zitnick and Piotr Dollár. 2014. Edge boxes: Locating object proposals from edges. In *ECCV*. Springer, 391–405.

VVRRM: Vehicular Vibration-based Heart RR-Interval Monitoring System

Amelie Bonde
Carnegie Mellon University
Electrical and Computer Engineering
Moffett Field, California
amelie@cmu.edu

Shijia Pan
Carnegie Mellon University
Electrical and Computer Engineering
Moffett Field, California
shijiapan@cmu.edu

Zhenhua Jia
Rutgers University
Wireless Information Network
Laboratory
North Brunswick, New Jersey
zhenhua@winlab.rutgers.edu

Yanyong Zhang
Rutgers University
Wireless Information Network
Laboratory
North Brunswick, New Jersey
yyzhang@winlab.rutgers.edu

Hae Young Noh
Carnegie Mellon University
Civil and Environmental Engineering
Pittsburgh, Pennsylvania
noh@cmu.edu

Pei Zhang
Carnegie Mellon University
Electrical and Computer Engineering
Moffett Field, California
peizhang@cmu.edu

ABSTRACT

Continuous heart rate variability (HRV) monitoring in cars can allow ambient health monitoring and help track driver stress and fatigue. Current approaches that involve wearable or externally mounted sensors are accurate but inconvenient for the user. In particular, prior approaches often fail when noise from human motion or car noise are present.

In this paper, we present *VVRRM*, an ambient heartbeat monitoring system in an automobile which uses a set of accelerometers in a car seat to monitor a subject's heart RR-intervals. The system removes high energy motion noise and periodic noise using a combination of peak detection with extracted wavelet coefficients. Furthermore, it tracks human heart locations through sensor selection to maximize the heart signal energy. We tested the system with both a manufactured heartbeat signal and experiments with human subjects. Overall our mean absolute error for RR-interval estimation was 54 ms across all human subjects, and 3 ms with our manufactured heartbeat signal.

CCS CONCEPTS

• **Human-centered computing** → **Ubiquitous and mobile computing systems and tools**;

KEYWORDS

vibration; heart rate variability (HRV); vehicular sensing; human condition monitoring

ACM Reference Format:
Amelie Bonde, Shijia Pan, Zhenhua Jia, Yanyong Zhang, Hae Young Noh, and Pei Zhang. 2018. VVRRM: Vehicular Vibration-based Heart RR-Interval Monitoring System. In *Proceedings of 19th International Workshop on Mobile Computing Systems & Applications (HotMobile '18)*. ACM, New York, NY, USA, 6 pages. https://doi.org/10.1145/3177102.3177110

1 INTRODUCTION

Continuous heart rate and heart rate variability (HRV) monitoring in cars can allow for ambient health monitoring in an environment people inhabit regularly. Short-term heart rate variability monitoring in terms of RR-intervals (the distance between successive heartbeats) is particularly useful. It has been used to help track stress and fatigue, which are important driver safety issues [4, 13, 16].

Prior work takes a number of approaches including photoplethysmography, electrocardiography (ECG) and cameras, sometimes in combination, to retrieve heart rate from people [8, 9, 14, 18]. These methods can be useful for heart-rate monitoring in static environments but are inconvenient to the user or are inaccurate for RR-interval measurements. In particular, these approaches fail for high-noise in-car environments subject to periodic noise such as car engine vibration and impulsive noise from subject movement.

We present *VVRRM*, a non-intrusive, heart RR-interval measurement system for the in-car environment. *VVRRM* first collects accelerometer data from our sensing module embedded in car seats. We then remove high-energy non-periodic motion segments resulting from body motion and periodic noise resulting from the engine and other noise. We choose between multiple sensors to account for variations in body size and position. Finally, we perform peak detection to obtain the RR-interval using the distance between the peaks.

We chose to study an idling car instead of a driving scenario because we wanted to focus on engine and human motion noise before tackling the noise caused by the car's movement on the road. We felt the noise of the moving car would overwhelm the other types of noise and should be studied separately.

Our paper provides three contributions:

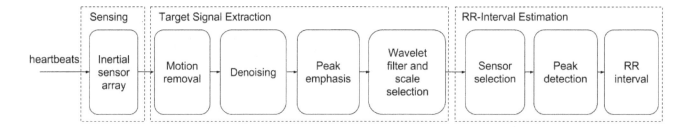

Figure 1: System Overview

(1) We introduce *VVRRM*, a real-time system that uses ambient car seat vibration to monitor the RR-intervals of a subject in a (currently stationary) car.

(2) We characterize the motion noise caused by human movement and the motion noise caused by an idling car and present an adaptive sensing algorithm to detect the heartbeat signal in the midst of high levels of noise.

(3) We present a comprehensive evaluation of our system using both characterization data with heartbeat recordings and human subject experiments.

The rest of this paper is organized as follows: We discuss related work in Section 2, and also discuss background information related to heart rate and heart rate variability. Section 3 describes our overall system, and we describe our evaluation and go over results in Section 4. Finally, in Section 5 we conclude our work.

2 BACKGROUND AND RELATED WORK

Definition of Heart RR-Interval: At every beat, the heart is polarized and depolarized to trigger its contraction, an electrical activity which can be measured by an ECG. The depolarization of the main mass of the ventricle causes the largest peak in an ECG, called the R wave. The RR-interval is defined as the distance between the peaks of two R waves and describes the duration of one complete cardiac cycle. The peaks of the waves *VVRRM* measures correspond to the heart's movement, and the distance between the two peaks is the same as the RR-interval.

Heart RR-interval as an Indicator of Stress: As stress level increases, the heart rhythm is affected and becomes unstable [3]. This instability is reflected in RR-interval measurements [11]. Thus RR-intervals provide a key indicator of stress. Prior work in the medical domain has defined that the error of this indicator needs to be lower than 100ms [6].

Monitoring Methods: Various ways of monitoring heart rate have been explored in the noisy vehicle environment. One common approach relies on the use of electrocardiogram (ECG) sensors [5, 9, 17]. These approaches, in general, require mounting that allows direct skin contact between the driver and the sensors to avoid unacceptable noise levels. While their performance is promising, this mounting requirement prevents these approaches from becoming mainstream.

Wearable devices can be inconvenient for the user, so we prefer an approach that is integrated with the car. A variety of approaches have been tried including the use of capacitive sensors in the seat, high-resolution cameras to capture skin tone fluctuations, and thermal imaging. While these approaches work well in a static environment in the lab, in the vehicle they are subject to non-ideal situations (e.g. light conditions, vibrations, etc.), these approaches fail to provide accurate measurements of individual heartbeat intervals [2, 14, 18], which is not useful for stress and fatigue inference. Placing sensors in a steering wheel is also subject to real-world problems, as drivers place their hands in different positions and often wear gloves in cold weather[8].

In non-vehicle environments, vibration-based approaches have been utilized in beds [7]. These approaches utilize the mechanical motion of the heart to detect and sense heartbeat without intrusive sensors. These approaches hold promise for non-skin-contact sensing. Unlike vibration-based approaches, capacitive sensors that are not worn next to the body can be sensitive to environmental noise, including noise that does not involve motion (e.g., humidity, the distance of body parts from the sensor), while accelerometers only measure motion from the parts of the body they are in contact with. (e.g., if a person moves a part of the body not in contact with the accelerometer, such as their arms, the sensor values do not change significantly due to motion). This means that when using accelerometers, the noise sources would be greatly reduced. Using accelerometers has some limitations: along with motion noise and placement concerns, which we address, they may be sensitive to clothing thickness.

3 SYSTEM DESCRIPTION

VVRRM accurately detects the vibration of heartbeats through the body's forces on the car seat in an automobile to measure RR-intervals. This poses many challenges which our system addresses with a multifold approach. Our main challenges are the sometimes low signal to noise ratio (heartbeat forces on the seats are small), human motion noise (movement noise can overwhelm the signal), engine noise (periodic engine noise increases the noise floor), and sensor placement (the best location to capture the heart motion varies between persons and over time. We can intuitively understand this because people are different heights and they sit in different ways). Figure 1 shows the system overview. The sensing module acquires the signal using a grid of accelerometers to capture the heart motion that can occur at **different locations**. The target signal extraction module removes high motion parts induced by **human motion**. Then it performs denoising on the remaining signal to remove **periodic noise** (e.g. engine noise). Next, it smooths the signal to **enhance peaks**, followed by a wavelet filter to further enhance the impulse signal in the heart rate frequency range.

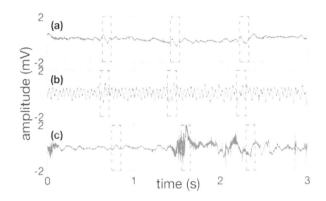

Figure 2: Raw data for a human subject with (a): engine off, (b): engine on, and (c) with subject laughing. Red boxes mark the heartbeat location. With no engine noise, the heartbeat signal in (a) is fairly clear. In (b), it is harder to see because of engine noise, while in (c), it is obscured by noise from laughter.

Finally, the RR-interval estimation module addresses the sensor placement challenge with a sensor selection algorithm, and outputs the final RR-interval estimation.

3.1 Sensing

VVRRM uses a set of inertial sensors to pick up movement caused by the subject's beating heart as the subject sits in the seat. The heartbeat causes their chest and stomach to vibrate. Because we detect the vibration of heartbeats from the vibration of the seat, the location of the sensor relative to the body greatly impacts the signal magnitude. Intuitively, the closer the sensor is to the heart, the stronger the signal. This raises two challenges: 1) People are different heights, so when they sit in the car their hearts are in different locations. And 2) people sometimes shift position and do not always sit leaning back. To address the first challenge, we use a network of sensors that lie against the backrest of the car seat and can pick up signals from a larger area. To address the second challenge, we use a sensor in the seat belt to pick up the stomach vibration caused by the heartbeat. We choose a sparse sensor array instead of many sensors for a lower-cost and low-computational-power design. We use piezoelectric accelerometers, which are excellent for vibration monitoring due to their wide frequency response, linear frequency response curve, and high sensitivity. We describe the sensor selection algorithm in Section 3.3.1.

Accelerometers are very sensitive to vibration and changes in motion: this allows us to see the very small signal caused by the motion of the beating heart. Figure 2(a) shows raw data from a human subject sitting in a car. We can see clear heartbeat-induced vibrations as small peaks marked by the dashed red boxes. That same sensitivity also makes accelerometers very sensitive to vibration and motion noise. Figure 2(b) shows a human subject sitting in an idling car. The **engine noise** makes the heartbeat signal less clear. Figure 2(c) shows a human subject laughing. The **human motion noise** of laughter completely overwhelms the heartbeat signal. We describe how *VVRRM* handles these types of noise in the following sections.

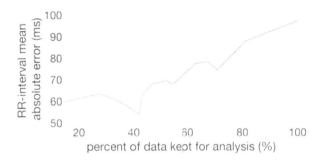

Figure 3: As we lower our noise threshold and keep less data, our error lowers and then increases.

3.2 Target Signal Extraction

The target signal extraction module handles both human motion and engine noise. It first extracts windows of data where there is less human motion noise. It then applies denoising and a wavelet filter to remove engine noise.

3.2.1 Windowing for Human Motion Noise Extraction. Our first step is recognizing and discarding portions of the signal that are excessively noisy due to person movement. We found that most large spikes of noise in the data were due to person movement, either talking, coughing, laughing, gesturing, or shifting positions. To identify this type of signal, we use a sliding window on the vibration signal and extract the maximum value of the window. If this value is above a threshold, we skip one second of data (i.e., label it as motion noise) and try again with a new window, moving forward by one second each time until we have a window that doesn't exceed our threshold. We skip one second at a time because we observe experimentally that noise in the data tends to last from between half a second to several seconds and takes about half a second to subside. We set our threshold by fitting a probability distribution to the first minute of data for each person using kernel density estimation and then using the inverse cumulative distribution function (ICDF) to compute a threshold to detect high motion noise. The threshold is determined empirically, considering the tradeoff between data preservation and accuracy (i.e., high threshold leads to more data but lower accuracy, while low threshold increases accuracy but wastes lots of data).

We note that as we lower our noise threshold, there are sometimes small peaks that buck the general trend. This is because our thresholding method occasionally cuts out some data that gives good results, causing a small rise in our error. We observe that at about 41% of data from the optimal sensor kept across all subjects, the error starts to rise. Setting the threshold to the ICDF function for 89% minimizes this error.

3.2.2 Denoising for Engine Noise Reduction. We then do denoising to further reduce the noise in the signal. We place one sensor near the bottom of the backrest, away from the heart, to characterize noise. We observed that the level of noise recorded by each sensor is different, so it works best to partially subtract one sensor's signal from the other. We multiply the noise sensor signal by a fraction (we obtained 20% heuristically) and subtract it from the rest of the sensors.

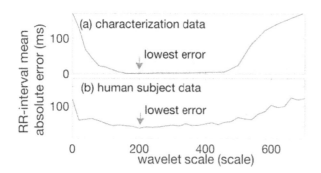

Figure 4: The mean absolute RR-interval error with different wavelet scales, (a), with characterization data, and (b) with human subject data. Using a scale of 200 minimized our error.

3.2.3   Peak Emphasis to Enhance Heartbeat Signal. In order to enhance the weak peaks of the heartbeat signal, we do root-mean-square averaging, which preserves the peaks in the data and smooths the high-frequency noise.

3.2.4   The Continuous Wavelet Transform for Heartbeat Isolation. To further reduce the noise, we isolate the periodic nature of the heartbeat using a continuous wavelet transform (*CWT*)[1]. The *CWT* compares the signal to compressed and stretched versions of a wavelet, the *CWT*'s analyzing function. The Mexican hat wavelet has been widely used for characterizing impulse signals, which fits our target signal profiling. It is described by

$$\psi(t) = \frac{2}{\sqrt{3}\pi^{\frac{1}{4}}}(1-t^2)e^{\frac{-t^2}{2}} \qquad (1)$$

The stretching and compressing of the wavelet performed by the *CWT* is known as "scaling": the *CWT* is a function of scale (*a*) and position (*b*):

$$C(a,b;f(t),\psi(t)) = \int_{-\infty}^{\infty} f(t)\frac{1}{a}\psi(\frac{t-b}{a})dt \qquad (2)$$

$f(t)$ is the signal, t is time, and $\psi(t)$ is the wavelet function.

By varying the values of the scale parameter, a, and the position parameter, b, we obtain the cwt coefficients $C(a, b)$. We chose the scale that best represents our data and varied the position coefficients to obtain a one-dimensional filtered signal. Figure 4 shows the result of the wavelet transform using scales between 1 and 700. *VVRRM* chose the scale that gives the lowest error, in this case, scale 200. Scale 200 corresponds to a frequency of 2.5 Hz, which, at 150 beats per minute, is higher than any heart rate we expect to see. This makes sense because the heartbeat is made up of several components, described in the background section. Choosing too low a frequency would lose information from these different components, while too high a frequency wouldn't filter out engine noise.

3.3   RR-Interval Estimation

Once the signal is enhanced and filtered, we calculate RR-interval with the sensor with the highest signal amplitude.

3.3.1   Sensor Selection. To adapt to a wide range of heart positions with sparse sensors, we displace the sensors with minimum overlapping sensing range and choose the sensor closest to the heart. In each window, we calculate the mean of the wavelet coefficients for each sensor, and select the one with highest mean, indicating highest Signal-to-Noise Ratio. This algorithm depends on our having removed noisy parts in the signal and reduced the noise in the remaining signal, as high amounts of noise could also cause a higher mean, and cause the incorrect selection of a sensor as "optimal".

3.3.2   Peak Detection for Peaks of Heartbeat Motion. For the first step in our peak detection algorithm, we do root-mean-square averaging of the wavelet coefficients, which smooths the data, limiting small false peaks and emphasizing larger peaks. We find local maxima by calculating the derivative of our signal in two points in time and comparing them to see if the difference lies above a given threshold [10]. Then we pick points near the local maxima and apply Least Squares Curve Fitting over them to refine the peak location [10].

3.3.3   RR-Interval Estimation. We occasionally detect extra peaks or drifted peaks from noise in the signal, which we remove to get accurate RR-intervals. Since heartbeats occur at periodic intervals, we discard the lowest magnitude peak of any pair of peaks that are closer than 220 beats per minute, which we take as our maximum heart rate (well above the normal resting heart rate of 60-100 beats per minute). This will not affect HRV monitoring in healthy subjects, because while heart rate does oscillate over time, it is not so irregular that it would have beats this close together and maintain a normal heart rate. Then we find the distance in time between the first two peaks in our sliding window and consider that our RR-interval. Now that we have our RR-interval, we take our next window of data starting at a location just past the 1st peak, ensuring that we don't miss any heartbeats as we move the window forward.

4   EXPERIMENTATION AND CHARACTERIZATION

We evaluated our system with two sets of experiments: controlled heartbeat characterization input, and uncontrolled human subject input.

4.1   Experimental Setup

We use the W354C03_010G10 piezoelectric accelerometer, sampled at 2 kHz [12]. We chose to put the sensors on the passenger seat because passengers move more freely and would give us more varied motion noise. We plan to test the system with steering and other driving motions in a future driving scenario. We put sensors at different heights on the backrest to accommodate different heights of drivers and passengers. The sensor layout is shown in Figure 5. For the characterization experiments, we have three sensors at different heights on the backrest (sensors 1, 2, and 3), while for the human subject experiments we put two sensors on the backrest at different heights and one sensor on the seat belt across the lap (sensors 1, 2, and 5). This is so that if the person leans forward, we can still pick up the motion of the heartbeat through their stomach. Sensor 4, the noise sensor, helps us characterize and remove the

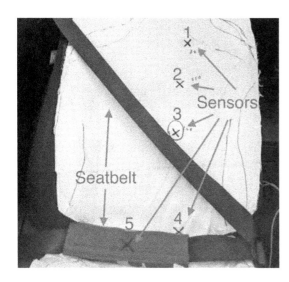

Figure 5: Hardware setup. Sensor 3 was only in characterization experiments, while sensor 5 was only for human subject experiments. Sensor 4 measured noise.

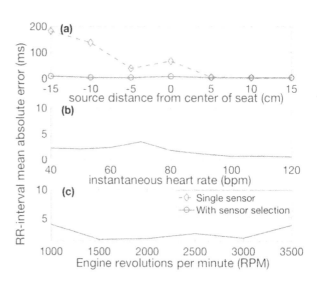

Figure 6: In (a), we compare the sensor selection algorithm with using a single sensor, and see that using sensor selection lowers the average error compared to using a single sensor. In (b), we see that our algorithm is not significantly affected by heart rate. In (c), we see that different engine speeds do not greatly affect error.

noise in the system. For the characterization experiments, we use a small set of speakers as the input that lean against the seat and play the sound of a heart beating. This allows us to control the height and rate of the heart. For the human subject experiments, we have human subjects sit in the seat, wearing a Zephyr Bioharness belt (capacitive ECG) as the ground truth [15].

4.2 Heartbeat Characterization

In our characterization experiments, we tested different heights and rates of the heart, and different car engine speeds. In order to control heartbeat characteristics in a realistic setting, in our heartbeat characterization experiments, we manufactured a heartbeat signal by putting a set of speakers against the backrest of the car seat, and playing the sound of heartbeats at different rates and with the speakers in different positions against the seat.

To test the effect of heights, we put the simulated heart at 7 different heights against the backrest of the car seat and played heartbeat sounds at 60 BPM. The results are shown in Figure 6(a). Using a single sensor, as the simulated heart got further from the sensor the error increased, but with our sensor selection algorithm, the sensor closest to the heartbeat was consistently chosen and that error was minimized.

4.2.1 Different rates. Figure 6(b) shows the accuracy for different heart rates. In this experiment, we kept the simulated heart in the same place and changed the rate of the heartbeat signal. We found that while there was a small difference in error, with lower heart rates having a slightly larger error, our system performed well across the range. This tells us that our algorithm is not affected by heart rate.

4.2.2 Engine noise evaluation. Figure 6(c) shows the result with the engine revving at different speeds with the car in neutral. We see that different engine speeds did not greatly affect our error. This

shows the continuous wavelet filter effectively removed engine noise.

Overall the mean absolute error for our characterization experiments was 3 ms, and we accurately categorized 100% of our data to within 100 ms of the ground truth (The error of RR-intervals should be lower than 100ms [6]).

4.3 Human Subject Experiments

For our human subject experiments, we asked 4 subjects, 3 men and 1 woman, to sit in an idling car. The participants were between the ages of 25 and 42. We collected 4 minutes of data from each of them for a total of 16 minutes. We noted the time when talking, laughing, coughing, gesturing or shifting positions happened, and found that laughing and coughing caused the most obvious noise in the data. Figure 7 shows the results of the human subject experiments. From this figure, we can see that the system is able to effectively recognize and ignore these noisy parts of the data by fitting a distribution to the data and introducing a threshold, as described in Section 3. When we look at the data by subject, we can see that there is some variation in the data. This can partly be explained by the way the subjects behaved. The extent to which the different subjects talked, laughed, coughed and shifted positions is reflected in the error rate and percent of data under the noise threshold for each subject.

Subject 1 watched funny videos while sitting in the car, and his frequent laughter caused significant noise in the data. However, data with laughing noise was effectively ignored by our algorithm, which greatly reduced both the amount of his data that we used and the error associated with it.

Subject 2 talked frequently and fidgeted. The thresholding algorithm also discarded a lot of her data, but it didn't reduce the

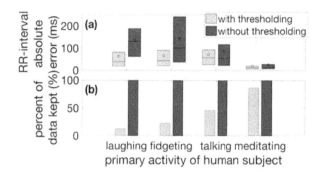

Figure 7: Graph (a) shows the 25% and 75% confidence intervals of the RR-interval absolute error for each human subject. The circles mark the mean error and the horizontal lines mark the median error. (b) shows how much data for each human subject was kept before and after the thresholding algorithm. One can see that there is variation per person in the amount of data under the noise threshold and the error.

error by as much. This could be because some of her periodic fidgeting was confused with heart motion. Subjects 1, 3 and 4 were all between 177 and 180 cm, while subject 2 was 167 cm, significantly shorter than the other subjects. Additionally, the sensor selected for Subject 2 was the one across the lap, while for the other subjects it was a sensor in the backrest. This suggests that either Subject 2 spent a lot of time leaning forward, or the sensors in the backrest were in a bad location to pick up heart rate for shorter subjects. In the future, more subjects with varying heights will help us determine this.

Subject 3 also talked during most of the data collection, with occasional coughing or laughing. This behavior occurred less than subject 1, so less of his data was discarded.

Subject 4 preferred to sit quietly and meditate, so his data had much less motion noise and the lowest error. Subject 4's results suggest that keeping as much data as possible to acquire RR-intervals is a crucial component of obtaining accurate HRV measurements.

Overall the mean absolute error for RR-intervals was 54 ms across all subjects. 84% of our data under threshold was accurately categorized to within the 100 ms error defined in medical literature [6].

5 CONCLUSION

In this paper, we introduced *VVRRM*, a real-time system that uses ambient car seat vibration to monitor the individual heartbeats of a subject in a car. *VVRRM* characterizes and removes the motion noise caused by an idling car and the movement of people, and presents an adaptive sensing algorithm to detect the heartbeat signal in the midst of high levels of noise. Our evaluation shows that we can accurately estimate RR-intervals with the high levels of noise present in an automobile, with on average 54 ms mean absolute error for human subjects and 3 ms mean absolute error for characterization experiments, significantly lower than the 100 ms requirement for RR intervals. Work is still needed to expand

characterization and further noise removal in multiple highway driving scenarios and with more human subjects.

ACKNOWLEDGEMENTS

This research was supported in part by the National Science Foundation (under grants CNS-1149611, CMMI-1653550, CNS-1404118, and CNS-1423020), the National Science Foundation Graduate Research Fellowship Program (under Grant No. DGE 1745016), Intel and Google. The views and conclusions contained here are those of the authors and should not be interpreted as necessarily representing the official policies or endorsements, either express or implied, of Carnegie Mellon University, the National Science Foundation, or the U.S. Government or any of its agencies.

REFERENCES

[1] MJ Burke and M Nasor. 2012. ECG analysis using the Mexican-Hat wavelet. In *Int. Conf. Multirate Systems & Wavelet Analysis*. 1–6.
[2] Sergey Y Chekmenev, Aly A Farag, William M Miller, Edward A Essock, and Aruni Bhatnagar. 2009. Multiresolution approach for noncontact measurements of arterial pulse using thermal imaging. In *Augmented vision perception in infrared*. Springer, 87–112.
[3] Hagit Cohen, Moshe Kotler, Mike A Matar, Zeev Kaplan, Uri Loewenthal, Hanoch Miodownik, and Yair Cassuto. 1998. Analysis of heart rate variability in posttraumatic stress disorder patients in response to a trauma-related reminder. *Biological psychiatry* 44, 10 (1998), 1054–1059.
[4] Niels Egelund. 1982. Spectral analysis of heart rate variability as an indicator of driver fatigue. *Ergonomics* 25, 7 (1982), 663–672.
[5] Jennifer A Healey and Rosalind W Picard. 2005. Detecting stress during real-world driving tasks using physiological sensors. *IEEE Transactions on intelligent transportation systems* 6, 2 (2005), 156–166.
[6] Keri J Heilman, Mika Handelman, Gregory Lewis, and Stephen W Porges. 2008. Accuracy of the StressEraser® in the detection of cardiac rhythms. *Applied psychophysiology and biofeedback* 33, 2 (2008), 83–89.
[7] Zhenhua Jia, Musaab Alaziz, Xiang Chi, Richard E Howard, Yanyong Zhang, Pei Zhang, Wade Trappe, Anand Sivasubramaniam, and Ning An. 2016. HB-phone: a bed-mounted geophone-based heartbeat monitoring system. In *Information Processing in Sensor Networks (IPSN), 2016 15th ACM/IEEE International Conference on*.
[8] Boon-Giin Lee and Wan-Young Chung. 2012. A smartphone-based driver safety monitoring system using data fusion. *Sensors* 12, 12 (2012), 17536–17552.
[9] Nermine Munla, Mohamad Khalil, Ahmad Shahin, and Azzam Mourad. 2015. Driver stress level detection using HRV analysis. In *Advances in Biomedical Engineering (ICABME), 2015 International Conference on*. IEEE, 61–64.
[10] Thomas C. O'Haver. 2008. Peak finding and measurement. (2008). https://terpconnect.umd.edu/~toh/spectrum/PeakFindingandMeasurement.htm
[11] Massimo Pagani, Raffaello Furlan, Paolo Pizzinelli, Wilma Crivellaro, Sergio Cerutti, and Alberto Malliani. 1989. Spectral analysis of RR and arterial pressure variabilities to assess sympatho-vagal interaction during mental stress in humans. *Journal of hypertension. Supplement: official journal of the International Society of Hypertension* 7, 6 (1989), S14–5.
[12] PCB Piezotronics. [n. d.]. W354C03_010G10 datasheet. ([n. d.]). http://www.pcb.com/Products.aspx?m=W354C03_010G10.
[13] Melvin L Selzer and Amiram Vinokur. 1974. Life events, subjective stress, and traffic accidents. *American Journal of Psychiatry* 131, 8 (1974), 903–906.
[14] Ye Sun and Xiong Bill Yu. 2014. An innovative nonintrusive driver assistance system for vital signal monitoring. *IEEE journal of biomedical and health informatics* 18, 6 (2014), 1932–1939.
[15] Zephyr Performance Systems. [n. d.]. Zephyr BioModule Device. ([n. d.]). https://www.zephyranywhere.com/benefits/physiological-biomechanical.
[16] Adrian H Taylor and Lisa Dorn. 2006. Stress, fatigue, health, and risk of road traffic accidents among professional drivers: the contribution of physical inactivity. *Annu. Rev. Public Health* 27 (2006), 371–391.
[17] José Vicente, Pablo Laguna, Ariadna Bartra, and Raquel Bailón. 2016. Drowsiness detection using heart rate variability. *Medical & Biological Engineering & Computing* 54, 6 (01 Jun 2016), 927–937. https://doi.org/10.1007/s11517-015-1448-7
[18] Qi Zhang, Guo-qing Xu, Ming Wang, Yimin Zhou, and Wei Feng. [n. d.]. Webcam based non-contact real-time monitoring for the physiological parameters of drivers. In *Cyber Technology in Automation, Control, and Intelligent Systems (CYBER), 2014 IEEE 4th Annual International Conference on*.

iCare: Automatic and User-friendly Child Identification on Smartphones

Xiaopeng Li
University of South Carolina
xl4@cec.sc.edu

Sharaf Malebary
University of South Carolina
malebary@cec.sc.edu

Xianshan Qu
University of South Carolina
xqu@cec.sc.edu

Xiaoyu Ji
Zhejiang University & AZTF[1]
xji@zju.edu.cn

Yushi Cheng
Zhejiang University
yushicheng@zju.edu.cn

Wenyuan Xu
Zhejiang University & AZTF[1]
xuwenyuan@zju.edu.cn

ABSTRACT

With the proliferation of smartphones, children often use the same smartphones of their parents to play games or surf Internet, and can potentially access kid-unfriendly content from the Internet jungle. It is critical to employ parent patrol mechanisms such that children are limited to child-friendly contents only. A successful parent patrol strategy has to be user-friendly and privacy-aware. The apps that require explicit actions from parents may not be effective when parents forget to enable them, and the ones that use built-in cameras to detect children may impose privacy violations. In this paper, we propose iCare, which can identify child users automatically and seamlessly as users operate smartphones. In particular, iCare investigates the intrinsic differences of screen-touch patterns between child and adult users. We discover that users' touch behaviors depend on a user's age. Thus, iCare records the touch behaviors and extracts hand-geometry and finger dexterity features that capture the age information. We conducted experiments on 31 people including 17 elementary school kids (3 to 11 years old) and 14 adults (22 to 60). Results show that iCare can achieve 84% accuracy for child identification using only a single swipe on the screen, and the accuracy becomes 97% with 8 consecutive swipes.

ACM Reference Format:
Xiaopeng Li, Sharaf Malebary, Xianshan Qu, Xiaoyu Ji, Yushi Cheng, and Wenyuan Xu. 2018. iCare: Automatic and User-friendly Child Identification on Smartphones. In *HotMobile '18: 19th International Workshop on Mobile Computing Systems & Applications, February 12–13, 2018, Tempe , AZ, USA.* ACM, New York, NY, USA, 6 pages. https://doi.org/10.1145/3177102.3177119

1 INTRODUCTION

Mobile devices (e.g., smartphones) provide us numerous services, ranging from web surfing, information sharing, to entertainment. Not surprisingly, it is common that children in their early age start to use mobile devices. Often, we observe kids with smartphones

[1] Alibaba-Zhejiang University Joint Research Institute of Frontier Technologies.

playing games, watching videos, and taking pictures. According to recent studies [4, 15], almost 90% of modern children had a moderate ability to use a tablet and child users can be even as young as 2-year-old, and most 3 and 4-year-old children are capable of using smart devices before even starting to read without any help.

Because Internet hosts a variety of content, if not guided properly, children can be exposed to violent or adult-only materials that may lead to serious negative consequences [9, 14]. For example, children are more likely to be attracted by games and become addicted due to limited self-control ability, resulting in both physical and mental illness. It is reported that children nowadays with anxiety have become more common than before [11], not to mention the impact of adult-only contents from the Internet. Parent patrol mechanisms is in great need. In addition, since parents and children often share the same mobile devices, children may be able to cause privacy or monetary damage to their parents, e.g., leak private photos or account information unintentionally, or purchase goods without parents' consent. In summary, both parent patrol and parent asset protection mechanisms are necessary to protect both children and parents when they share the same devices.

Existing mechanisms for child-oriented access control on mobile devices are not user-friendly. Traditionally, parents take the full responsibility for monitoring and guiding their children to use smartphones. However, it is challenging to ensure continuous and effective monitoring. Alternatively, parent patrol apps installed on smartphones can help parents restrict the content their children can access, but those apps may not be effective when parents forget to active them before giving their phones to their children. Some approach exploits collecting sensitive data to enable accesses. For instance, an image taken from a camera [7] or a 3D depth camera [1], or an audio clip recorded by a microphone can be used to determine the legitimacy of users [6, 8].

In this paper, we ask "*Can we identify child users in an automatic and friendly way?*", which means that the identification requires no explicit user involvement and can automatically differentiate child and adult users transparently. To this end, we examine the underlying difference between child and adult users in terms of their gesture behaviors when operating smart devices. Specifically, we investigate the touch operations during device interaction, and find age-related differences between adults and children. Motivated by this observation, we propose and design iCare to identify child users based on their touch behaviors in an **automatic** and **implicit** manner. We extracted and exploited two key features, i.e.,

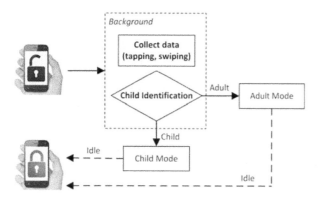

Figure 1: Illustration of an application of iCare.

hand *geometry* and finger *dexterity* that are represented in 35 sub-features, to capture the distinct characteristics of children. We further explored three machine learning algorithms for classification. A dataset on 31 people including 17 children (3 to 11 years old) and 14 adults (22 to 60 years old) is collected and tested to verify the effectiveness of iCare. Evaluation results indicate that iCare can achieve an accuracy as high as 84% and 97% with single and multiple consecutive swipes, respectively.

We envision that iCare can be used as follows. As shown in Figure 1, once a smartphone's screen is unlocked, iCare starts to monitor the touch data in the background and further identifies the age group of the user. If the user is a child, the smartphone will enter child mode and automatically block the child user from inappropriate content. Each time unlocking the smartphone will automatically trigger iCare once and change the smartphone mode accordingly. To the best of our knowledge, this is the first work on detecting child users based on the touch patterns. The main contributions are summarized as follows:

- We propose iCare, which is an effective approach to automatically detect child users on smartphones without compromising user experience and violating privacy.
- We explore the possibility of using continuous touches on the smartphone to detect child users. We explore hand *geometry* and finger *dexterity* features to assist on detection accuracy.
- We evaluate the classifiers using the dataset collected from 17 child users aged from 3 to 11 years old and 14 adults. Our dataset is collected during users' normal operations without any constraints.

2 RELATED WORK

Touch-based User Authentication. Frank *et al.* investigate the applicability of using touchscreen inputs to continuously authenticate users [2]. They extract 30 behavioral features from raw touchscreen logs and justify that simple touch movements are sufficient to authenticate a user. Li *et al.* describe a continuous user authentication mechanism for smartphones by checking user's finger movement patterns [5]. Zheng *et al.* extract four features (acceleration, pressure, size, and time) from smartphone sensors, and implement a verification mechanism to validate whether an authenticating user has the true ownership of a smartphone [16]. In HMOG [10], authors introduce a new set of biometric behavioral features (hand

movement, orientation, and grasp) for continuous authentication on smartphones. These features can unobtrusively capture subtle micro-movements generated when users tap a screen. These studies mainly focus on finding distinctive characteristics for a specific user to recognize the user, while our work aims at exploring common distinctive characteristics among a group of users at similar ages. Identifying group characteristics can be challenging because characteristics may have large variance for a group of users and result in overlap between two groups of users.

Child Identification. Basaran *et al.* introduce a classification system (ChildSafe) which exploits human skeletal features collected by 3D depth cameras to identifying children [1]. Pental *et al.* study the possibility of inferring users' age and gender based on keystrokes from keyboard and mouse [9]. Two closely related papers [3, 13] to ours are based on a publicly available dataset containing 2912 touch records on touchscreen devices. Vatavu *et al.* utilize touch coordinates to divide users into age groups [13]. Hernandez-Ortega *et al.* propose a method based on the Sigma-Lognormal theory to capture users' neuromotor skills which can distinguish children from adults [3]. These two studies have significant differences with ours in the problem setting. First, unlike prior work [3, 13] that collects particular gestures such as dragging two targets simultaneously with two fingers, our work allows users to perform normal operations as they like on screens. Second, in prior work [3, 13] the starting and ending points of each gesture are predefined for the user to authenticate, while we aim at an automatic and implicit way. In addition, these two studies doesn't consider children older than 6 years, who may have less difference to adults.

3 OVERVIEW

In this section, we discuss the goals and provide a bird's-eye view on the idea of detecting children's use of smartphones.

Goals. Our goal is to explore the possibility of detecting child users of smartphones in real time without compromising user experience and violating the privacy. In particular, we want to answer the following questions:

- Is it feasible to distinguish child users from adult users based on natural screen touches? What touch gestures can be used to accomplish the goal, and which performs better?
- Would there be any difference for classifying adults and children in different age groups (e.g., 3 to 5 and 6 to 11)? Will they achieve the same level of accuracy?
- Will the classification accuracy improve with an increasing number of samples? How many consecutive strokes of screen touch are needed to detect a child user confidently?

Basic Idea. Human engineering and kinesiology have shown that we can potentially find common characteristics among similar age groups of people [12]. The main assumption of this study is that children interact with smartphones in a distinctive way from adults. We want to extract the characteristics of child users from their normal touch operations on smartphones. Our idea is based on the following two observations.

First, hand *geometry* is different between children and adults in terms of the size: children have smaller hands as well as shorter fingertips than adults in general. Consequently, children tend to

(a) Enter numeric passwords   (b) Merge attachable same numbers

Figure 2: Two scenarios for data collection.

touch in a narrower range of the screen and swipe for a shorter trajectory length.

Second, the *dexterity* associated with children's interactions with smartphones is poor compared to adults'. According to our observation, children perform each touch stroke on smartphones slower and less flexible than adults do. This is the same case when they try to switch between two touch actions, i.e., from tap to swipe. This can be attributed to the fact that children's bodies and fingers have yet been matured and fully developed, and thus it impacts their reactions when implementing a task using fingers.

Therefore, we take the aforementioned attributes (i.e., *hand-geometry* and *dexterity*) into consideration when extracting features from touch data.

4 EXPERIMENT

4.1 Data Collection

Experimental Setup. Our study obtained Institutional Review Board approval at the University of South Carolina (IRB number 73819). In the experiment we used the same smartphone (Google Nexus 5X manufactured by LG, running Android v.7.1.1) across all the subjects to eliminate biases caused by different phones, and turned off its rotation function to eliminate biases associated with various holding ways. We designed a two-phase App based on two common activities with smartphones: unlocking phones and playing games. Tap gestures are collected in the first phase. As shown in Figure 2(a), a pin number appears on the top side of the screen and users are asked to input it. Our app generates two four-digit and two six-digit pin numbers and each pin appears twice randomly. Each user unlocks the phone for eight times if they succeed every time. We set the maximum number of unlocking attempts to be ten. As an incentive, we reward the user a star for each time they enter the correct number.

The swipe gestures are collected in the second phase. We modified a popular puzzle game named 2048 [1] as shown in Figure 2(b).

[1] https://github.com/uberspot/2048-android

Table 1: Participants and collected data.

Group	Age	# of users	# of swipes	# of taps
G-Children	3~5	7	1055	727
	6~11	10	2387	630
G-Adults	20~29	8	2144	466
	30+	6	1514	296

Table 2: A sample of swipe data.

Time	Action	X	Y	Pressure	Size	Finger ID
276416631	0	712	1257	0.775	0.339	0
276416644	1	710	1262	0.763	0.321	0
⋮	⋮	⋮	⋮	⋮	⋮	
276416702	1	668	1414	0.638	0.286	0
276416710	2	-	-	-	-	-

Table 3: A sample of tap data.

Time	Action	X	Y	Pressure	Size	Finger ID
276381043	0	131	112	0.925	0.429	0
276381108	2	-	-	-	-	-

Users swipe vertically or horizontally to combine two attachable blocks with the same number (e.g., swipe up or down to merge the two vertical "2"s in the left most column in Figure 2(b)). Then, a single one containing the sum will replace them automatically and a new number (2/4) appears randomly in one of blank blocks after each valid swipe. The game is over when all the spaces are filled with numbers and no move is available to merge two same blocks. Users are allowed to swipe at any direction to play the game. Surprisingly, a fair amount of children stated that they have played this particular game or a similar one before. Most of children between 3-5 years were able to reach 64 or larger, while the ones between 6-11 years reached at least 128, and the highest block reached was 512 by a 5th grader (10 years old).

Without loss of generality, all participants were required to keep sitting to play and holding the phone in their hands. All child participants reported that they have previously used touch-screen phones. Before the start of the experiment, we briefly explained to users how to play with the app and let them play it for a while until they felt familiar with it.

Data. We recruited two groups of users in our experiment: *G-Children* with 17 children aged 3 to 11 years old and *G-Adults* with 14 adults aged 20 to 59 years old. Table 1 summarizes the demographics of the participants. All of the participants finished the two phase tasks. In the phase of unlocking phones, we collected 1357 taps among the *G-Children* group and 762 taps among the *G-Adults* group. Note that although the number of children aged 3 to 5 years old is not the greatest, we collected the most taps compared to older children and adults. That's because children in this age group were more likely to enter pins incorrectly and they had more attempts. In the second phase, we collected 3442 and 3658 swipes

Table 4: Extracted features from touch data.

No.	Category	Feature description
1	hand geometry	relative start position of x (Tap)
2	hand geometry	relative stop position of x
3	hand geometry	relative start position of y (Tap)
4	hand geometry	relative stop position of y
5	hand geometry	direct end-to-end distance
6	hand geometry	trajectory distance
7	hand geometry	direction of end-to-end line
8	hand geometry	touch size at down (Tap)
9	hand geometry	touch size at mid-stroke
10	hand geometry	average touch size
11	hand geometry	std of touch size
12	hand geometry	pressure at down (Tap)
13	hand geometry	pressure at mid-stroke
14	hand geometry	average pressure
15	hand geometry	std of pressure
16	hand geometry	x displacement of two consecutive downs (Tap)
17	hand geometry	y displacement of two consecutive downs (Tap)
18	hand geometry	x displacement of down and last up
19	hand geometry	y displacement of down and last up
20	dexterity	average velocity
21	dexterity	maximum pairwise velocity
22	dexterity	relative time of feature 21
23	dexterity	std of pairwise velocity
24	dexterity	maximum pairwise acceleration
25	dexterity	relative time of feature 24
26	dexterity	std of pairwise acceleration
27	dexterity	median velocity of first 3 points
28	dexterity	median velocity of last 3 points
29	dexterity	velocity at mid-stroke
30	dexterity	median acceleration of first 3 points
31	dexterity	median acceleration of last 3 points
32	dexterity	acceleration at mid-stroke
33	dexterity	mean resultant length
34	dexterity	stroke duration (Tap)
35	dexterity	inter stroke time (Tap)

from the group of *G-Children* and *G-Adults* respectively. In general, the *G-Adults* group did better in the 2048 game and more swipes were collected among this group.

Table 2 gives a sample of swipe data and Table 3 is a sample of tap data. A tap generally consists of two actions: touch down ("0") and up ("2"), while a swipe has one more action: touch move ("1"). A swipe consists of a sequence of touch points. It starts from touching the screen and ends with finger lifting. At each point, we record the time occurred, its X-Y coordinates, the pressure and size of the touch area, and the finger ID. The event time is in milliseconds and based on the smartphone's non-sleep uptime since boot. Both the pressure and size values are normalized to a range between 0 and 1, where 0 means no pressure and no size at all.

4.2 Data Processing

We extract features from the collected touch data from two aspects: hand *geometry* and *dexterity*. Table 4 shows the feature descriptions for swipe and tap gestures. In total, we extracted 35 features in swipe and 8 features in tap.

Hand Geometry. The variances of hand geometry will result in differences in terms of the touch range, the touch distance, the touch pressure and size. In particular, the features numbered from 1 to 19 in Table 4 are extracted based on hand geometry.

Dexterity. Considering finger dexterity, we extracted 16 features numbered from 20 to 35. The finger dexterity mainly impacts the velocity, acceleration and task duration.

4.3 Classifiers and Metrics

Classifier Choices. To classify children and adults based on the above features, we implement three machine learning classifiers

namely support-vector machine (SVM), Random Forests (RF) and k-nearest-neighbors (kNN). SVM is a popular and powerful tool for binary classification, which can output an optimal hyperplane that maximizes the margin between two classes. Most importantly, it is able to solve non-linearly separable problem by mapping data into a higher-dimensional space using the kernel trick. Here, we use radial basis function (RBF) as our non-linear kernel. kNN is a nonparametric method which has no underlying assumption of data and each sample is assigned to one class based on a majority vote of its neighbors. kNN doesn't do any generalization based on the training data, but it's simple and fast while with highly competitive results. RF is another efficient algorithm which is able to classify large amounts of data with accuracy. It is an ensemble method which constructs a number of decision trees during training time and outputs the class label with the most votes from all models. It also gives estimates of the importance of each feature in classification.

Metrics. To evaluate the performance of the binary classifiers, we choose the commonly used performance metrics: the area under the ROC (AUC) curve and equal error rate (EER). An ROC curve represents Receiver Operating Characteristic curve and is created by plotting true accept rate (TAR) against false accept rate (FAR), as the threshold varies. TAR is the probability of correctly identifying a child, while FAR is the probability that the classifier incorrectly accepts a child. AUC is a value between 0 and 1 and a larger value is usually better. EER is the rate when both accept and reject errors are equal, and the lower this value, the better the classifier.

4.4 Results

Classifier Impact. In this section, we evaluate the performance of the three classification methods in identifying child users. Firstly, we label our dataset based on which group a stroke sample is from. All the stroke samples from *G-Adults* are labeled as class 0 and the strokes from *G-Children* are labeled as class 1. We use stratified 5-fold cross-validation to avoid overfitting and report the average result of 5 validations as the final result. For the swipe dataset, we train the SVM classifier by selecting the complexity parameter $c = 1.4$ and the gamma parameter $\gamma = 0.15$, and setting the number of trees in RF to be 200 and the parameter k in kNN classifier to be 7. For the tap dataset, the choice of $c = 1.4$ and $\gamma = 0.7$, the tree number is 100, and $k = 9$. All the parameters are determined and optimized by the grid search.

Figure 3 shows the ROC curves of the three classifiers based on the swipe dataset and tap dataset respectively. The results of SVM, RF and kNN are colored in red, blue and green respectively. For both datasets, SVM and RF classifiers outperform kNN. And the difference is more obvious for the swipe dataset. Note that all the classifiers can achieve better performance on the swipe dataset than that on the tap dataset. As a swipe usually contains more data points, more features can be extracted for classification. Overall, SVM and RF can reach a roughly 16% EER and a 0.9 AUC on swipe dataset. The result is promising for identifying children through only a swipe. Even using a single tap, the RF algorithm can still achieve a 18.8% EER and a 0.88 AUC. Finally, we choose RF as our classification algorithm for the following experiments.

Influence of Different Age Groups. To understand the influence of children from different age groups on the classification

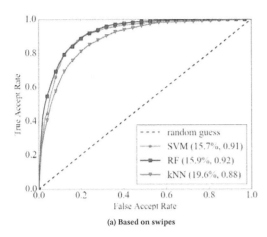 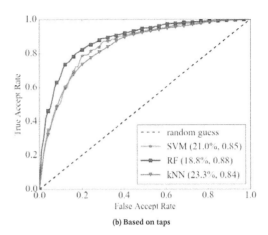

(a) Based on swipes   (b) Based on taps

Figure 3: ROC curves of three classifiers. Legends are in form "label (EER, AUC)", where label indicates one of the three classifiers, EER is the equal error rate, and AUC is the area under ROC.

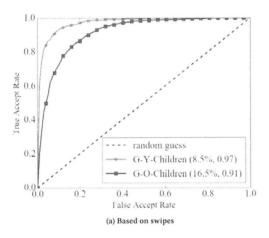 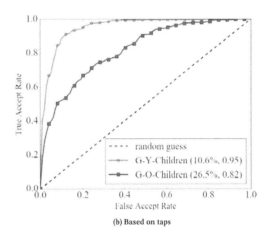

(a) Based on swipes   (b) Based on taps

Figure 4: ROC curves for two age groups of children. Legends are in form "label (EER, AUC)", where label indicates one of the two child groups.

results, we perform an analysis on two child groups: children aged 3 to 5 years old (*G-Y-Children*) and children aged 6 to 11 years old (*G-O-Children*). Firstly, we separate the touch data from children into two sets corresponding to the two age groups. We consider all the adult data as negative samples and train a separate RF classifier for each age group of children based on stratified 5-fold cross-validation. After the grid search of parameters, we select the tree number to be 200 for swiping and 100 for tapping. Figure 4 shows the comparisons of ROC curves with the two age groups. For both swiping and tapping, we have a much better performance in classifying the *G-Y-Children* group. This is reasonable as younger children tend to be more different from adults in terms of *hand geometry* and *dexterity*.

Multiple Swipes. In this section, we explore the impact of combining different numbers of consecutive swipes for classification on the performance. So far, we only use the swipe dataset that is relatively large to conduct multiple stroke evaluation. First, we separate

the dataset into training and testing sets. We prepare the testing dataset by randomly choosing 10% consecutive samples from participants at each age. Overall, the testing dataset consists of 660 samples which are evenly distributed among children and adults. We train a RF model using the remaining samples and choose tree number to be 200. Instead of classifying all swipes individually and reaching a final decision by the majority vote, we combine multiple consecutive outputs at an earlier stage by their probabilities, and take the average of them as our final predicted probability. Figure 5 shows the ROC curves by varying the number of swipes taken for a classification decision. The classification error can be greatly decreased when increasing the number of swipes. And the EER converges locally to 3.0% as we increase the number of swipes to eight. Although the limited size of the dataset doesn't allow us to increase the number of swipes further, the results have clearly demonstrated that using multiple swipes is able to improve the accuracy.

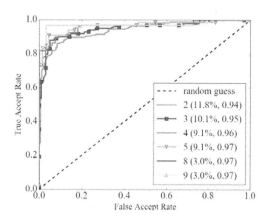

Figure 5: ROC curves with different numbers of swipes. Legends are in form "label (EER, AUC)", where label indicates the number of consecutive swipes used.

5 LIMITATIONS AND FUTURE WORK

Several issues remain to be explored.

Task-dependent Biases. Although there are no constraints on how the users perform the touch gestures, the context of the applications (i.e., the tasks) in the experiments may limit the diversity of the gesture geometry. Thus, task-dependent diversity may affect the accuracy of iCare. It is worth studying how gestures and corresponding features vary with different tasks and therefore affect the classifiers.

Diversities of Child Users. Considering the different developing rates of their bodies among girls and boys, it is worth checking the touch patterns across genders. Additionally, as children's dexterity develops significantly every year, training the classifier for finer age groups possibly increases the overall accuracy. We also observed that children older than 3 years can unlock a smartphone with PINs even they cannot read numbers. It is interesting to analyze how poor numeracy will affect touch patterns.

Limited Gestures. There are many other gestures (e.g., scroll, fling) that haven't been explored in our study. In reality, users may have to change among different types of gestures back and forth to complete a task on smartphones. Fusing all types of gestures together can result in a faster classification decision and possibly improve the accuracy.

Improving Accuracy. Given eight consecutive swipes and the accuracy, our method can be a good supplement for existing parent patrol apps. However, before real world deployment, the accuracy shall be improved. We can improve the accuracy by solving the above three limitations. In addition, there are other built-in sensors on smartphones (e.g, gyroscope and accelerometer) that can be exploited to derive users' characteristics for refining classification results.

6 CONCLUSION

Existing methods for parent patrol are far from satisfactory. In this paper, we introduced an implicit approach to detect that a child is operating a smartphone without users' special attention. Specifically, we extracted the features of hand geometry and finger

dexterity from swipe and tap gestures, and explored three machine learning algorithms to classify children. Our pilot study with 17 children and 14 adults shows that the trained SVM and RF models can achieve an equal error rate of 16% with a single swipe. A higher accuracy can be achieved with children aged 3 to 5 years old. We also find that the performance can be greatly improved using eight consecutive swipes.

ACKNOWLEDGMENT

We would like to thank the anonymous reviewers for their insightful comments. This work is supported by NSFC under Grant No. 61472358, 61702451, and the Fundamental Research Funds for the Central Universities 2017QNA4017.

REFERENCES

[1] Can Basaran, Hee Jung Yoon, Ho Kyung Ra, Sang Hyuk Son, Taejoon Park, and JeongGil Ko. 2014. Classifying Children with 3D Depth Cameras for Enabling Children's Safety Applications. In *Proceedings of the 2014 ACM International Joint Conference on Pervasive and Ubiquitous Computing (UbiComp '14)*. 343–347.
[2] Mario Frank, Ralf Biedert, Eugene Ma, Ivan Martinovic, and Dawn Song. 2013. Touchalytics: On the Applicability of Touchscreen Input As a Behavioral Biometric for Continuous Authentication. *IEEE Transactions on Information Forensics and Security* 8, 1 (Jan. 2013), 136–148.
[3] Javier Hernandez-Ortega, Aythami Morales, Julian Fierrez, and Alejandro Acien. 2017. Predicting Age Groups from Touch Patterns based on Neuromotor Models. In *8th International Conference on Pattern Recognition Systems (ICPRS-17)*. 1–6.
[4] Hilda K Kabali, Matilde M Irigoyen, Rosemary Nunez-Davis, Jennifer G Budacki, Sweta H Mohanty, Kristin P Leister, and Robert L Bonner. 2015. Exposure and use of mobile media devices by young children. *Pediatrics* 136, 6 (2015), 1044–1050.
[5] Lingjun Li, Xinxin Zhao, and Guoliang Xue. 2013. Unobservable Re-authentication for Smartphones. In *Proceedings of the 20th Annual Network Distributed System Security Symposium*.
[6] Hugo Meinedo and Isabel Trancoso. 2010. Age and gender classification using fusion of acoustic and prosodic features. In *INTERSPEECH 2010, 11th Annual Conference of the International Speech Communication Association, Makuhari, Chiba, Japan, September 26-30, 2010*. 2818–2821.
[7] Microsoft. [n. d.]. How do I look? ([n. d.]). https://how old.nct/
[8] Seyed Mostafa Mirhassani, Alireza Zourmand, and Hua-Nong Ting. [n. d.]. Age Estimation Based on Children's Voice: A Fuzzy-Based Decision Fusion Strategy. *The Scientific World Journal* 2014 ([n. d.]).
[9] Avar Pentel. 2017. Predicting Age and Gender by Keystroke Dynamics and Mouse Patterns. In *Adjunct Publication of the 25th Conference on User Modeling, Adaptation and Personalization (UMAP '17)*. ACM, New York, NY, USA, 381–385.
[10] Zdeňka Sitová, Jaroslav Šeděnka, Qing Yang, Ge Peng, Gang Zhou, Paolo Gasti, and Kiran S Balagani. 2016. HMOG: New behavioral biometric features for continuous authentication of smartphone users. *IEEE Transactions on Information Forensics and Security* 11, 5 (2016), 877–892.
[11] Michael Ungar. 2016. Why Are Kids So Anxious These Days? (2016). https://www.psychologytoday.com/blog/nurturing-resilience/201609/why-are-kids-so-anxious-these-days
[12] WILLEM VAN MECHELEN, JOS W. R. TWISK, G. BERTHEKE POST, JAN SNEL, and HAN C. G. KEMPER. 2000. Physical activity of young people: the Amsterdam Longitudinal Growth and Health Study. *MSSE* 32, 9 (2000), 1610–1616.
[13] Radu-Daniel Vatavu, Lisa Anthony, and Quincy Brown. 2015. *Child or Adult? Inferring Smartphone Users' Age Group from Touch Measurements Alone*. Springer International Publishing, Cham, 1–9.
[14] Radu-Daniel Vatavu, Gabriel Cramariuc, and Doina Maria Schipor. 2015. Touch interaction for children aged 3 to 6 years: Experimental findings and relationship to motor skills. *International Journal of Human-Computer Studies* 74 (2015), 54–76.
[15] Elyse Wanshel. [n. d.]. 10 Reasons Why You Shouldnât Give A Child A Smartphone Or Tablet. ([n. d.]). https://www.littlethings.com/reasons-not-to-give-children-technology
[16] N. Zheng, K. Bai, H. Huang, and H. Wang. 2014. You Are How You Touch: User Verification on Smartphones via Tapping Behaviors. In *2014 IEEE 22nd International Conference on Network Protocols*. 221–232.

HappyFeet: Recognizing and Assessing Dance on the Floor

Abu Zaher Md Faridee*, Sreenivasan Ramasamy Ramamurthy[†], H M Sajjad Hossain, Nirmalya Roy

Department of Information Systems, University of Maryland Baltimore County

{faridee1,rsreeni1,hmsajja1,nroy}@umbc.edu

ABSTRACT

The widespread availability of Internet-of-Thing (IoT) devices, wearable sensors and smart watches have been promoting innovative activity recognition applications in our everyday lives. Recognizing dance steps with fine granularity using wearables is one of those exciting applications. In a typical dance classroom scenario where the instructors are frequently outnumbered by the students, accelerometer sensors can be utilized to automatically compare the performance of the dancers and provide informative feedback to all the stakeholders, for example the instructors and the learners. However, owing to the complexity of the movement kinematics of human body, building a sufficiently accurate and reliable system can be a daunting task. Utilization of multiple sensors can help improve the reliability, however most wearable sensors do not boast sufficient resolution for such tasks and often suffer from various data sampling, device heterogeneity and instability issues. To address these challenges, we introduce *HappyFeet*, a convolutional neural network based deep, self-evolving feature learning model that accurately recognizes the micro steps of various dance activities. We show that our model consistently outperforms feature engineering based shallow learning approaches by a margin ≈7% accuracy on data collected from dance routines (Indian classical) performed by a professional dancer. We also posit a *Body Sensor Network* model and discuss the underpinning challenges and possible solutions associated with multiple sensors' signal variations.

ACM Reference Format:
Abu Zaher Md Faridee, Sreenivasan Ramasamy Ramamurthy, H M Sajjad Hossain, Nirmalya Roy. 2018. HappyFeet: Recognizing and Assessing Dance on the Floor. In *HotMobile'18: 19th International Workshop on Mobile Computing Systems & Applications, February 12–13, 2018, Tempe , AZ, USA*. ACM, New York, NY, USA, 6 pages. https://doi.org/10.1145/3177102.3177116

1 INTRODUCTION

With the proliferation of wearable sensors over the last few years, a plethora of exciting new applications is evolving every day. The inbuilt accelerometer, gyroscope, ambient light sensor, altimeter, GPS and heart rate sensors of these wearable devices are being exploited in various application domains ranging from health care,

---

*Equally Contributing authors
[†]Equally Contributing authors

HotMobile'18, February 12–13, 2018, Tempe , AZ, USA
© 2018 Association for Computing Machinery.
ACM ISBN 978-1-4503-5630-5/18/02...$15.00
https://doi.org/10.1145/3177102.3177116

sports, fitness, entertainment etc. While video camera based sensors have also been used widely in various application domains, majority of them suffer from user privacy concerns and overlapped field of view in presence of multiple users such as in case of our proposed dance activity recognition scenario.

Dance activity involves subtle movements of limbs and other body parts in a sequenced fashion. In a professional dance-learning environment, in general there are more students than instructors, which makes it harder for the instructor to dance, teach, and assess the performance of the students simultaneously and divert attention equally to each of the students. Therefore, In this work, we propose to develop "Dance Activity Recognition" (DAR) system which can provide feedback on the steps performed by the students to an instructor. The proposed system helps the instructor to readily identify the mistakes and postulate corrections in mind while the DAR system needs to deal with very fine-grained labeling followed by accurate classification of various dance steps. Recognizing the dance activity is fundamentally different from recognizing and learning the traditional *Activities of Daily Living (ADLs)*. Dancing requires grace and finesse, and involves repetitive movements of the fingers, hands, forearm, elbow, arm, legs, toes, waist, heads etc., in a rhythmic fashion. It also reflects the delicacy and rhythm of different postures along with the cognitive ability and physical fitness of an individual. One step alone may consist of multiple micro steps which span across the various movements of legs, hands, fingers, shoulder, elbow etc. Capturing these movements with a minimal number of accelerometer sensors, recognizing and delimiting these micro steps, and defining a repetitive pattern out of it to recognize the entire dance episode are non-trivial activity recognition problems. This makes a *Dance Activity Recognition (DAR)* system unique in its own context than the traditional *Human Activity Recognition (HAR)* problem.

The fine-grained modifications of the movements needed to enhance the overall performance of a dancer are not always apparent, and therefore assessed appropriately by an instructor. In this context, an autonomous *Dance Activity Recognition (DAR)* system can play an integral role by providing meaningful qualitative feedback to help improve the learning capabilities of the participants. The design of such a system can also help postulate how an individual participant is grasping the dance activity progressively in a group setting compared to a one-to-one learning environment. In order to capture the full extent of movements of the limbs during the dance activities which can vary drastically from subtle to pronounced, a full-fledged Body Sensor Network may be required. However, deploying sensors with different modalities which is prevalent in commercially available devices, introduces heterogeneity, synchronization and sampling instability problems. Considering the complexity of properly capturing the micro steps of dance moves, and

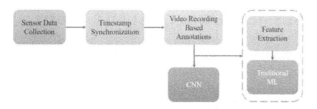

Figure 1: Overall framework of dance activity recognition system

the challenges introduced by employing multiple devices, we make the following contributions in this paper.

- We design an accelerometer-based multi-channel data collection prototype that helps capture the subtle movements of a dancer accurately.
- We propose a multi-channel deep convolutional neural network model that learns the dance moves by automatically and hierarchically learning the features that represent the raw data.
- We investigate empirically the coexistence of multiple heterogeneous devices and the inherent sensor biases, sampling rate heterogeneity, and sampling rate instability.

2 RELATED WORK

It has recently been shown that accelerometer can be used to quantify the performance during simple ballet dance activity [23]. The physical activities of children and adolescents in 7 different dance styles using accelerometer have been investigated and noted that the children were more active than the adolescents [2]. In addition, authors have also hypothesized that there is a requirement for a better teaching method to increase the physical activity. In contrast to a single accelerometer sensor, a sensor network was used as a viable input system for control in a video game involving dance activity called *Dance, Dance, Evolution*; a popular game in Asia [4]. A recurrent and convolutional neural network based models has been used to design and revamp the dynamisms of the game by generating new dance steps [6]. A motion capture and composition system for dance motion was developed by exploiting multiple RGB and depth sensors [12]. Another interesting study in an attempt to preserve the ancient Chinese folk dance, the authors transcribed the motion data into lab annotation which was captured by OptiTrack system [24]. A model that performs classification of Korean pop (K-pop) dances based on human skeletal motion data captured using Kinect sensor in a motion-capture studio environment has been studied [11]. The authors proposed an efficient Rectified Linear Unit (ReLU)-based neural network model without implementing weight learning which is efficient than conventional neural network. [7] proposed a novel technique that helps decompose the dance motions using the Hilbert-Huang transform and compare Waltz and Salsa dance movements with the dance of a Japanese pop group "Perfume". A Kinect-based Thai dance evaluation system was demonstrated in [17] which rates the user's performance and provides helpful and real-time feedback to the user. Recognizing Greek folk dances and their variations using Kinetc II sensor has been proposed in [18]. A mobile based dance education system has been proposed in [8] using wearables. A dance performance evaluation system was developed to decode the performed dance gestures as captured using high-precision motion capture system which

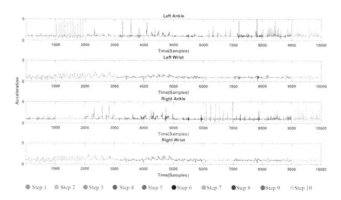

Figure 2: Accelerometer Signals of different activities captured from four *Actigraph* sensors

showed a likelihood value of the recognized gesture in terms of a score [14]. Skeletal pose based dance step recognition system has been proposed in [19] [10]. An image based classical Indian dance norms classification model was demonstrated in [20]. [5] proposed a dance training system using foot mounted inertial sensor which leverages the orientation and position of the foot to evaluate the trainee's movements. [26] depicts that an expert shows a consistent and repeatable pattern of dance activities, an intermediate participant shows a consistent action but is different to that of an expert and the novice shows a pattern which appears disjoint and noisy. Most of the dance recognition related literatures employed video based motion capture system, which requires delicate equipments and fixed installation in a confined setting. In this paper, we propose a Convolutional Neural Network (CNN) based dance activity recognition model using ubiquitous wearable devices focusing on detecting the micro steps of the dancers and mitigating the sensor bias, sampling rate heterogeneity, sampling rate instability, and synchronization problems.

3 OVERALL DESIGN AND SYSTEM SETUP

Figure 1 depicts the overall framework of *HappyFeet*, our proposed dance activity recognition system. Since dance involves different movements of limbs to perform distinct steps, it warrants more than one sensor to capture the user's actions with required accuracy. We used four *Actigraphs*, an *Empatica E4* and two *Microsoft Bands* (the details of the placement are described in subsection 3.2). The use of heterogeneous sensors pose challenges associated with multiple sensors data stream synchronization, sensor biases, and sampling rate instability [22], which are discussed in detail in section 4.1. In order to precisely annotate the ground truth, we employed a video recording based labeler called ELAN [15]. Thereafter we fed this annotated data to a hierarchical self-evolving feature-based deep convolutional neural network model to recognize the dance activities. We also posit a feature-based shallow machine learning model as a baseline to compare against the deep learning model. Next, we describe our *HappyFeet* setup and discuss the dance micro steps, sensor data collection process, data stream time synchronization, ground truth annotation and construction of shallow and deep learning models.

Table 1: Description of Activities

Class Label	Description
Step 1	Wave both hands from left to right
Step 2	Stepping right leg forward
Step 3	Clockwise Rotational Movement
Step 4	Walking forward with extended arms
Step 5	Anti-clockwise Rotational Movement
Step 6	Stepping left leg forward
Step 7	Step-by-step slow rotational movement (Clockwise)
Step 8	Step-by-step slow rotational movement (Anti-Clockwise)
Step 9	Step-by-step rapid rotational movement (Clockwise)
Step 10	Step-by-step rapid rotational movement (Anti-Clockwise)

3.1 Defining Dance Steps

In our experiment, we chose to study a classical Indian dance style: *Lasya* which is a subcategory of Manipuri [25] dance form; the dance is noted for its gentle, smooth and subtle limb movements. We collected data from one professional dancer and four learners. We designed a specific dance script for *Lasya* which a beginner would learn during the first few dance sessions. The steps of the dance script are described in Table 1 and depicted in Figure 2. The dance activities described in Table 1 are similar to normal daily activities in many ways, however, these activities involve a large number of minute finer movements. For instance, the first activity which is "Wave both hands from left to right" involves different *mudras* (hand postures) at different positions. Unlike ADLs or other activities, dance activities involves a combination of very short movements which forms the micro level activities. A sequence of such smaller combination of activities helps form a dance routine. In this study, we have recorded 10 such micro level activities. These fine-grained steps have no specific names in the dance literature but the sequence of these steps do have names. This study deals with the micro level dance steps and the sequence of the micro level steps is outside the scope of this study.

3.2 Data Collection

The participants were asked to wear the actigraph (model *wGT3X-BT*) [1] on all the limbs. In addition, to capture the heterogeneity across different devices, the participants were also asked to wear a *Microsoft Band* on the waist and the left hand, and a *Empatica E4* device on the right hand. The *ActiGraph wGT3X-BT* device has much higher sensitivity compared to the Microsoft band. When kept at at rest (Zero g test) [22] Actigraph and Empatica E4 showed constant 1g acceleration, indicating that Actigraph and Empatica have less *Sensor Biases*[22]. However, the Microsoft Band did not pass the Zero g offset test, the resultant acceleration signal was contaminated with noise; hence a low pass filter was used to nullify the sensor bias. Before each data collection session, we also synchronized the clocks of all of the sensors. We collected data for 20 trials out of which the first 10 trials were conducted as such that the participants danced only the specific micro steps repetitively. The remaining 10 trials were recorded as a sequence of all micro steps.

3.3 Synchronization and Annotations

The *ActiGraph wGT3X-BT* has a tri-axis accelerometer sensor, that gives us acceleration data for x, y and z axis at the desired sampling frequency (in this case 100 Hz) along with the UNIX time-stamp of each of the readings. The *Lasya* dance form in our experiment contains ten separate micro steps. The granularity of the steps can be varied if desired, for finer granular step identification the annotation, training and inference would warrant extensively more data collection over more dance sessions. In our case, the dance routine lasted for roughly one minute and each of the dance steps taking up between six to fourteen seconds (they are not of equal lengths). We recorded each dance session using a video camera and annotated each micro step of the dance session by synchronizing the video with the accelerometer data stream. We synchronized the signals from each sensor, the video and the timestamps associated with them using *ELAN* software [15]. At the start of each dance routine, the participants were asked to jump thrice as high as possible. These three jumps showed a peak in the resultant acceleration signal. The annotator used the peaks to synchronize the sensor data stream and the video feed, all at the same time. We deduced the starting and ending frame for each of the micro level dance moves and labeled them accordingly. Annotation is done with respect to the video feed not the accelerometer data as ELAN is originally a linguistic annotation tool. When doing the alignment, we also noted the video and accelerometer synchronization offset. With this information, we were able to derive the standardized time stamps across devices and crop the data that is of interest using the equation $T_{acc.} = T_{video} - O_{video} + O_{acc}$ (T_{acc} denotes the accelerometer time, T_{video} is the video time, O_{video} is synchronization offset of the video and O_{acc} is the synchronization offset of the accelerometer). Because of the initial clock synchronization, all sensor samples are also properly aligned with each other in the end.

3.4 Model Building

We design a deep learning model for recognizing the dance steps and compare its performance against several shallow learning approaches after the extraction, synchronization and annotation of the data, we carefully split the data between train and test set while also ensuring that both the sets have similar label distribution. This early separation of training and test samples ensures absolute zero overlapping between the samples. First, we applied filtering to nullify the effect of noise. We applied both *Kalman* filter and *Median* filter and noted that the frequency response of the filtered signals were similar. Therefore, we chose Median filter instead of *Kalman* filter as it has lower computational complexity. After filtering the noise, we divided the accelerometer data into 50 sample window with a sliding window approach (90% overlap) which helps prevent the model from being dependent on initial positioning of the windows. For shallow learning models, we extracted a total of 46 time and frequency domain features [3]. We calculated *Pearson's correlation coefficient* between the features and used a threshold t to remove the highly correlated features. We optimized the hyper-parameters of the classifiers with 5-fold cross validated (with stratified sampling) *Randomized Search* and performed the final evaluation on the held-out test data using the accuracy, recall and the F1-scores.

The CNN architecture employs three *convolution* layers which is the main building block for the self-evolving feature learning. These layers are followed by the two fully connected layers that take care of the actual classification by working on the features

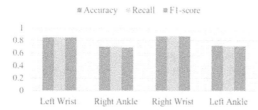

Figure 3: Accuracy, Recall and F1-score for each sensor in identifying all activities using Random Forest

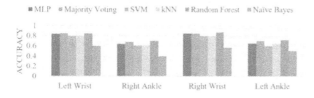

Figure 4: Comparison of Accuracy for each sensor in identifying all activities using all shallow learning algorithms

learned by the previous layers. Each of these layers actually consists of the following fundamental components:

- The convolution layer [13] consists of the following operations in sequence - convolution, batch normalization [9], rectilinear activation function and average pooling.
- The first fully connected layer also has a rectilinear activation function.
- We introduce a dropout [21] layer between the two fully connected layers which helps to make the network robust against over-fitting issue.
- We employ *soft-max* layer to get the final class label from the fully connected layers.

Average Pooling at the end of each *convolution layer* automatically helps smooth out the data as it picks the average value and provides a low pass filtered version of the signal along with dimensionality reduction that nullifies the need to use filtering beforehand. For the CNN based approach we use the same sliding window technique mentioned before. After this preprocessing step, each sample consists of a 50x3 data points as we consider 3 axes in the accelerometer data.

4 EXPERIMENT SETUP AND EVALUATIONS

The experiments were conducted on a Windows platform consisting of Intel i7 6700HQ Quad Core Hyper-threaded CPU, 16GB DDR4 RAM and Nvidia Quadro M1000M workstation class GPU with 2GB of DDR3 RAM. For the signal processing, filtering and shallow learning tasks we used MATLAB R2017a [16] and python (scikit-learn). For the deep learning task, we performed the processing with GPU optimized version of Tensor-flow which cut down training time by 3.5 times compared to running the same code on CPU. The size of the training and testing raw samples for the experiments were of 51148x150 and 25192x150 respectively (66% vs 34% ratio). For this particular experiment, we annotated the dataset with 10 output labels. Table 1 describes the nature of these labels and Figure 2 shows the time series (time vs absolute magnitude) plot of labels. Due to the variable lengths between dance steps, we ended up with a little bit imbalanced distribution of the class labels (Table 2). This

Table 2: Class distribution

Class Label	Percentage	Class Label	Percentage
Step 1	7.96%	Step 6	5.16%
Step 2	3.55%	Step 7	12.19%
Step 3	11.79%	Step 8	13.02%
Step 4	12.74%	Step 9	12.65%
Step 5	9.11%	Step 10	11.77%

kind of class imbalance can make it very difficult to achieve high accuracy with supervised learners. This shows a great point that real world data is often riddled with less than desirable characteristics compared to synthetic datasets.

4.1 Device Heterogeneity

Deploying multiple sensors simultaneously poses some challenging *heterogeneity* issues such as sensor bias, non-uniform sampling rate, sampling rate instability etc. *Sensor bias* is a type of heterogeneity that is caused due to the differences in the precision, resolution, and range values of the devices [22]. *Sampling Rate Heterogeneity* occurs when two different devices starts recording the data at two different sampling rates. For instance, Device X records at 100 Hz and Device Y records at 75 Hz. This heterogeneity is undesirable as the proposed learning framework required equal number of data points from all the devices. A more challenging heterogeneity is *Sampling Rate Instability (SRI)* which is the irregularity between successive timestamps of consequent data points. To control and test the effect of heterogeneity, we maintained redundancy when collecting data with heterogeneous sensors. As described earlier, *Actigraph* was worn on all the limbs, Empatica E4 and Microsoft Band were worn on both of the hands. However, the *Actigraph* collected data at 100 Hz, the *Empatica E4* at 32 Hz and the Microsoft band at 128 Hz. We noticed that the Microsoft band data was suffering from SRI as it was missing certain data points. At the end we categorized these BSN heterogeneity issues into three groups:

(1) All the devices collect data at a constant sampling rate.
(2) Device X collects data at a constant sampling rate and Device Y collects data at a different constant sampling rate.
(3) Devices collect data at a constant rate, however one of the devices collects data at a varying sampling rate.

In this paper, we only focus on building the dance activity recognition system on the first case (multiple sensors collecting data at the same constant rate) and discuss the possible solutions of the other issues in Section 5.

4.2 Results

In this section, we discuss the preliminary results by analyzing the data from the four *Actigraph* sensors (placed on each of the limbs) for the professional dancer. First, we compare the accuracy between the baseline (shallow learning techniques) and CNN model using individual sensors and then we compare the performance of both using multiple sensors referred as BSN. We extracted 46 features from the time windows and used a Pearson's correlation co-efficient threshold of 0.75 to select only 24 of the features. We then train *Naive Bayes*, *K-nearest neighbor* (k=5), *Linear SVM*, *Multilayer Perceptron* and *Random Forest* as the baseline to compare against our CNN model. The classification accuracy is reported in Figure 4. *Random Forest* (with 2000 tress) performed the best (shown in Figure 3) among the shallow learning classifiers so we

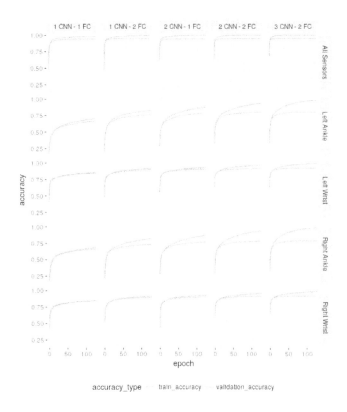

Figure 5: Accuracy comparison across sensors and CNN architectures

refer to it as our baseline henceforth; we then compare the baseline's performance with that of the deep learning model. We run our deep learning model on each of the sensor data separately and noted that the CNN model is consistently performing better than the baseline (*Random Forest*) which is shown in Table 3.

These results encouraged us to move to the next logical step, combining multiple sensors streams to develop CNN based *Body Sensor Network* and investigate whether it improved the discriminative power of the model. For example, Step 7 described in Table 1 is an activity involving step-by-step slow rotational movement in clock wise direction where both the legs should capture similar patterns for the activity. In Figure 2 we see that the patterns of Step 7 for right ankle is more distinctive and repetitive in nature when compared to that of left ankle. For left ankle the baseline classifier accuracy was 69% whereas for the right ankle it was 84% (figure not included due to space constraint). We hypothesized that combining data from multiple sensors would help mitigate the scarcity of discriminative data for certain classes. Our deep learning architecture was fluid in terms of employing multiple sensors requiring no complicated and computationally expensive modification of the current network structure. We have 3 channels per sensor data stream on which the CNN performs 3D convolution operations. With the added homogeneous sensors, the CNN would then be performing *nx3*-dimensional convolution operations (n being the total number of sensors). We already had the sensor data aligned (section 3.3) so this was a fairly straightforward process and without any special change in the current CNN structure we were able

to get 93.81% hold-out test accuracy. This is not surprising; as we have stated previously, the intuition behind using CNN for dance activity recognition was to generate self developing features that are able to capture the truer representation of the data compared to the hand-crafted heuristics. In contrast to 3 channel single sensor data stream, the 12 channel 4 sensors (two Actigraphs, one Empatica, one Microsoft band) data stream gives CNN more patterns to holistically analyze and yield better accuracy. We experimented with different CNN architectures for both the individual sensors and BSN model to find the optimal hyper-parameters and the network structure. The details of the hyper-parameters are described in Table 4. In Figure 5, we compare the training and validation set accuracy for the combined BSN and each of the sensors (placed row-wise) and five network structures of increasing complexity (more convolutional and fully connected layers, placed column-wise). Table 5 shows the accuracy on held-out test dataset for each model. It can be noted that for each of the individual sensors, adding more layers improves the accuracy; adding the 2nd CNN layer over base 2 layer network seems to provide the higher boost ($\approx$ 8%) compared to just adding 2nd fully connected layer. Adding another CNN and fully connected layer each provide $\approx$1% more accuracy gain. Surprisingly, the BSN model achieved high accuracy with even the simplest network model (1 CNN layer and 1 Fully Connected layer), the difference between this model and the most complex model was just $\approx$0.67%, hinting that a simpler CNN architectures become as effective as complex models when larger supplementary sensor data streams are available.

5 LIMITATIONS AND FUTURE DIRECTIONS

This paper only discusses the preliminary findings of our BSN architecture, a lot of areas still remain unexplored and we would like to keep investigating and improve the model. Although we did capture the dance activity data from four *Actigraph* sensors, two *Microsoft Bands* and one *Empatica E4* sensor, in this paper we limited the BSN model to use just the *Actigraphs*. As mentioned in Section 3.2, we faced issues related with failed zero-g test, mismatched sampling rates, missing data points (either due to sensor fault or sampling rate instability) etc. The next challenge is to deal with the heterogeneity issues both experimentally and analytically (Section 4.1). We plan to investigate the effectiveness of recent deep learning architectures such as *Restricted Boltzmann Machine* and *Generative adversarial networks (GANs)* in reconstruction of these erroneous data samples. As stated previously, we collected redundant data with multiple sensors on the same limb; with large quantities of such unlabeled data from a high precision sensors, we can train an RBM to learn the intrinsic probability distribution of the dance activities and use that to reconstruct the missing data points. During this preliminary study, we limited ourselves to detecting 10 beginner level dance steps, but we would like to detect more advanced dance steps in future that consists of more complex micro-level gestures with a more advanced data collection and annotation setup. We also had to restrict ourselves to using the data collected on the dance steps performed by the professional dancer as the data collected from the students had extreme and unpredictable variances (due to their unfamiliarity with the dance routines). This complicated the process of building a consistent dance activity recognition model. In order to provide feedback to the instructor about the dance routines

Table 3: Comparison between CNN and Random Forest for each sensor

Sensor Position	CNN			Random Forest		
	Accuracy	Precision	Recall	Accuracy	Precision	Recall
Left Ankle	79.45%	79.66%	79.36%	71.87%	72.08%	71.87%
Left Wrist	91.90%	92.44%	91.32%	84.34%	84.26%	84.34%
Right Ankle	76.75%	76.91%	76.66%	69.40%	69.88%	69.40%
Right Wrist	91.84%	91.79%	91.30%	87.95%	88.13%	97.96%

Table 4: Hyper-parameters of CNN model

Hyper-parameters	Values
No. of maximum convolution layers	3
No. of filters in convolution layers	32, 48, 64
Convolution filter dimensions	21x1, 15x1, 7x1
No. of maximum fully connected layers	2
No. of neurons in fully connected layers	64, 10
Batch size	64
Dropout rate	1.0
Max number of epochs	128

Table 5: Final Test Accuracy across sensors and CNN architectures

Sensor Position	1 CNN 1 FC	1 CNN 2 FC	2 CNN 1 FC	2 CNN 2 FC	3 CNN 2 FC
All Sensors	93.53%	93.44%	94.20%	93.56%	93.81%
Left Ankle	65.67%	73.42%	77.13%	78.65%	79.45%
Left Wrist	85.23%	88.29%	90.50%	90.96%	91.90%
Right Ankle	64.17%	72.05%	74.94%	75.15%	76.75%
Right Wrist	83.77%	88.21%	89.29%	90.69%	91.84%

performed by the students and track their progress, we will need to extend the model; it will also be interesting to investigate the qualitative improvements of the model and whether the adoption of the model improve the overall teaching and learning experience of both the students and the instructors. We also want to investigate whether the model can be adopted to a mobile/cloud based settings and the possibility of providing real time feedback to the users. Finally, the efficacy of a multi-modal combination of the BSN based approach with vision based approaches could also be investigated.

6 CONCLUSION

In this paper, we have presented the initial stages of a deep convolutional neural network based dance activity recognition model that can automatically learn the morphologically distinct features from multi-channel sensor data and then use those features to correctly identify the dance steps. We achieved ≈7% better accuracy than existing popular hand-crafted feature engineered machine learning approaches. The fact that the CNN architecture, apart from a few hyper-parameter tuning steps does not require time consuming feature engineering, without which the traditional models perform poorly. This supports our initiative of using deep learning architectures for daily activity recognition tasks. We also described the problem of heterogeneity and sampling rate instability for different sensor modalities in body sensor network and discussed how to overcome this adversity. We demonstrated a video recording based ground truth data annotation synchronizer for accurate labeling of large amount of dance activity data. Finally, we demonstrated the flexibility of the CNN approach, and showed that our Dance Activity Recognition system, *HappyFeet* can be easily extended reliably to heterogeneous body sensor network.

REFERENCES

[1] ActiGraph. 2017. (2017). http://www.actigraphcorp.com/
[2] Kelli L Cain, Kavita A Gavand, and Terry L Conway et al. 2015. Physical activity in youth dance classes. *Pediatrics* (2015), peds–2014.
[3] Diane J Cook and Narayanan C Krishnan. 2015. *Activity learning: discovering, recognizing, and predicting human behavior from sensor data.*
[4] Nick Crampton and Kaitlyn Fox et al. 2007. Dance, dance evolution: Accelerometer sensor networks as input to video games. In *Haptic, Audio and Visual Environments and Games, 2007. HAVE 2007. IEEE International Workshop on*. IEEE, 107–112.
[5] Quoc Khanh Dang, Duy Duong Pham, and Young Soo Suh. 2015. Dance training system using foot mounted sensors. In *SICE*. 732–737.
[6] Chris Donahue, Zachary C. Lipton, and Julian McAuley. 2017. Dance Convolution. In *ICML*. 1039–1048.
[7] Ran Dong, DongSheng Cai, and Nobuyoshi Asai. 2017. Nonlinear dance motion analysis and motion editing using Hilbert-Huang transform. In *CGI*. 35:1–35:6.
[8] Augusto Dias Pereira dos Santos. 2017. Smart Technology for Supporting Dance Education. In *UMAP*. 335–338.
[9] Sergey Ioffe and Christian Szegedy. 2015. Batch normalization: Accelerating deep network training by reducing internal covariate shift. In *International Conference on Machine Learning*. 448–456.
[10] Sotiris Karavarsamis and Dimitrios Ververidis et al. 2016. Classifying Salsa dance steps from skeletal poses. In *CBMI*. 1–6.
[11] Dohyung Kim, Donghyeon Kim, and Keun-Chang Kwak. 2017. Classification of K-Pop Dance Movements Based on Skeleton Information Obtained by a Kinect Sensor. *Sensors* 17, 6 (2017), 1261.
[12] Yejin Kim. 2017. Dance motion capture and composition using multiple RGB and depth sensors. *IJDSN* 13, 2 (2017).
[13] Alex Krizhevsky, Ilya Sutskever, and Geoffrey E Hinton. 2012. Imagenet classification with deep convolutional neural networks. In *Advances in neural information processing systems*. 1097–1105.
[14] Sohaib Laraba and Joëlle Tilmanne. 2016. Dance performance evaluation using hidden Markov models. *Journal of Visualization and Computer Animation* 27, 3-4 (2016), 321–329.
[15] Hedda Lausberg and Han Sloetjes. 2009. Coding gestural behavior with the NEUROGES-ELAN system. *Behavior research methods* 41, 3 (2009), 841–849.
[16] MATLAB. 2017. *version 9.2.0 (R2017a)*. The MathWorks Inc., Natick, Massachusetts.
[17] Ob-orm Muangmoon, Pradorn Sureephong, and Karim Tabia. 2017. Dance Training Tool Using Kinect-Based Skeleton Tracking and Evaluating Dancer's Performance. In *IEA/AIE 2017, Part II*. 27–32.
[18] Eftychios Protopapadakis and Athanasios Voulodimos et al. 2017. A Study on the Use of Kinect Sensor in Traditional Folk Dances Recognition via Posture Analysis. In *PETRA*. 305–310.
[19] Sriparna Saha and Rimita Lahiri et al. 2016. Human skeleton matching for e-learning of dance using a probabilistic neural network. In *IJCNN*. 1754–1761.
[20] Shubhangi and Uma Shanker Tiwary. 2016. Classification of Indian Classical Dance Forms. In *IHCI*. 67–80.
[21] Nitish Srivastava and Geoffrey E Hinton et al. 2014. Dropout: a simple way to prevent neural networks from overfitting. *JMLR* (2014).
[22] Allan Stisen and Henrik Blunck et al. 2015. Smart devices are different: Assessing and mitigatingmobile sensing heterogeneities for activity recognition. In *Proc of the 13th ACM Conference on Embedded Networked Sensor Systems*. 127–140.
[23] Thiel, David V and Quandt, Julian and Carter, Sarah JL and Moyle, Gene. 2014. Accelerometer based performance assessment of basic routines in classical ballet. *Procedia Engineering* 72 (2014), 14–19.
[24] Jiaji Wang, Zhenjiang Miao, and et al. 2017. Using automatic generation of Labanotation to protect folk dance. *J. Electronic Imaging* 26, 1 (2017).
[25] Wikipedia. 2017. Manipuri Dance — Wikipedia, The Free Encyclopedia. (2017). https://en.wikipedia.org/wiki/Manipuri_dance
[26] Miguel Xochicale, Chris Baber, and Mourad Oussalah. 2017. Analysis of the Movement Variability in Dance Activities Using Wearable Sensors. In *Wearable Robotics: Challenges and Trends*. Springer, 149–154.

UniverSense: IoT Device Pairing through Heterogeneous Sensing Signals

Shijia Pan
Carnegie Mellon University
Electrical and Computer Engineering
Moffett Field, California
shijiapan@cmu.edu

Carlos Ruiz
Carnegie Mellon University
Electrical and Computer Engineering
Moffett Field, California
carlosrd@cmu.edu

Jun Han
Carnegie Mellon University
Electrical and Computer Engineering
Moffett Field, California
junhan@cmu.edu

Adeola Bannis
Carnegie Mellon University
Electrical and Computer Engineering
Pittsburgh, Pennsylvania
abannis@andrew.cmu.edu

Patrick Tague
Carnegie Mellon University
Electrical and Computer Engineering
Moffett Field, California
tague@cmu.edu

Hae Young Noh
Carnegie Mellon University
Civil and Environmental Engineering
Pittsburgh, Pennsylvania
noh@cmu.edu

Pei Zhang
Carnegie Mellon University
Electrical and Computer Engineering
Moffett Field, California
peizhang@cmu.edu

ABSTRACT

Easily establishing pairing between Internet-of-Things (IoT) devices is important for fast deployment in many smart home scenarios. Traditional pairing methods, including passkey, QR code, and RFID, often require specific user interfaces, surface's shape/material, or additional tags/readers. The growing number of low-resource IoT devices without an interface may not meet these requirements, which makes their pairing a challenge. On the other hand, these devices often already have sensors embedded for sensing tasks, such as inertial sensors. These sensors can be used for limited user interaction with the devices, but are not suitable for pairing on their own.

In this paper, we present *UniverSense*, an alternative pairing method between low-resource IoT devices with an inertial sensor and a more powerful networked device equipped with a camera. To establish pairing between them, the user moves the low-resource IoT device in front of the camera. Both the camera and the on-device sensors capture the physical motion of the low-resource device. *UniverSense* converts these signals into a common state-space to generate fingerprints for pairing. We conduct real-world experiments to evaluate *UniverSense* and it achieves an F1 score of 99.9% in experiments carried out by five participants.

HotMobile '18, February 12–13, 2018, Tempe , AZ, USA
© 2018 Association for Computing Machinery.
ACM ISBN 978-1-4503-5630-5/18/02...$15.00
https://doi.org/10.1145/3177102.3177108

CCS CONCEPTS

• **Networks** → *Cyber-physical networks*; • **Computer systems organization** → *Embedded and cyber-physical systems*;

KEYWORDS

Internet-of-Things, Heterogeneous sensing, Pairing

ACM Reference Format:
Shijia Pan, Carlos Ruiz, Jun Han, Adeola Bannis, Patrick Tague, Hae Young Noh, and Pei Zhang. 2018. *UniverSense*: IoT Device Pairing through Heterogeneous Sensing Signals. In *Proceedings of 19th International Workshop on Mobile Computing Systems & Applications (HotMobile '18)*. ACM, New York, NY, USA, 6 pages. https://doi.org/10.1145/3177102.3177108

1 INTRODUCTION

The Internet-of-Things (IoT) requires a configured network to perform sensing and actuation tasks. Pairing is a common way to configure the network by authorizing a device with a specific MAC address to transmit on the network. With the rapid growth of IoT devices in the smart home environment, each user will have an average of over 13 devices by 2020, inevitably some will have significantly more [19]. Various pairing methods have been explored to allow easy and fast network setup, including passkeys, QR codes, and RFID tags, and each has their limitations. For example, passkey-based methods require I/O hardware such as a display and a keypad [3]. QR-code based methods require the device to have a flat surface to print or glue the QR code on. In addition, they limit the device to using a static MAC address, which may cause unexpected consequences for user privacy [15]. RFID-based methods require additional hardware to conduct pairing, such as tags and readers [24].

However, more and more IoT devices are designed with no interface [16, 21], which makes it difficult, if not impossible, to conduct the traditional device pairing methods [9]. Research has been

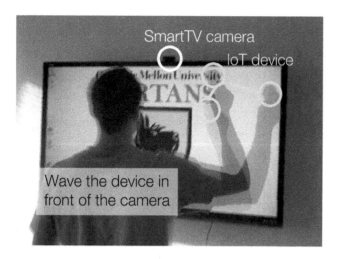

Figure 1: *UniverSense* **pairing concept.**

done on utilizing existing on-device sensors to achieve pairing via detecting co-sensed events. They mainly fall into two categories: interaction-free and interaction-based methods. Interaction-free methods rely the fact that co-presented devices can sense events occurring in the shared physical world [17, 29]. They require no human interaction to establish the pairing between devices in the environment. However, this process usually takes a long time, especially when the frequency of detected events is low, as there is less opportunity to correlate co-sensed events. Interaction-based methods leverage human intention to designate pairing devices [13, 22, 28]. The state-of-the-art approaches require either a designated device [22] or the devices on both ends to be moved together to generate fingerprints [13], which is difficult for pairing between devices of various sizes.

We present *UniverSense*, an alternative pairing solution that enables network setup of IoT devices without an interface, by using their existing sensors. Our solution targets at the pairing between 1) interactive IoT devices (*e.g.*, smart TVs[25]), which already have I/Os, camera, and network connection, and 2) IoT devices with Inertial Measurement Units (IMU) and no interfaces [16, 21]. Figure 1 shows a concept scenario where a user moves an IoT device in front of the smart TV camera to conduct pairing. Both the camera and the IoT device itself sense the motion of the IoT device. It is challenging to extract information comparable enough for pairing from the 2-D image signal and the 3-D inertial signal. *UniverSense* achieves this by converting the co-sensed motion to a common state space and generating fingerprints for pairing. The contributions of this work include:

- We introduce an IoT device pairing mechanism, *UniverSense*, that allows devices with different sensing modalities to pair through motion sensing.
- We present a fingerprint generating and pairing method for heterogeneous sensing signals that extracts shared physics representations of the motion from sensors of different modalities.
- We conducted real-world experiment to evaluate our pairing mechanism.

The rest of the paper is organized as follows. Section 2 introduce our pairing mechanism *UniverSense*. Then, we evaluate *UniverSense* through real-world experiments in Section 3. Next, we discuss the potential expansion of this work in Section 4. Finally, we compare this work with related work in Section 5 and conclude in Section 6.

2 *UNIVERSENSE* SYSTEM OVERVIEW

UniverSense pairs devices based on detecting shared physical motion. Figure 2 shows the pairing process. *UniverSense* first obtains the motion signals (Section 2.1), which are observed by each device involved in the pairing. Then, *UniverSense* converts each motion signal –detected by different sensor modalities– into a common state space (Section 2.2). Next, each device generates a fingerprint based on the converted signal (Section 2.3). Finally, the fingerprints are used to determine whether a successful pairing should be established (Section 2.4).

2.1 Heterogeneous Sensing

The heterogeneity of the pairing devices allows the more 'powerful' IoT devices (*i.e.*, computational power, sensors, interface, network) to complement the low-resource IoT device with no interface, allowing for pairing between them and potentially to the rest of the home network. The 'powerful' devices include 1) interactive devices, such as smart TVs equipped with camera(s) to enable user interaction [25] and 2) ambient sensing devices, such as security cameras [12]. These cameras capture image frames that contain the position/movement of the IoT device. On the other hand, low-resource IoT devices are likely to be equipped with an IMU [16, 21]. An IMU consists of an accelerometer, a gyroscope and a magnetometer, which measure the linear acceleration, the rotation rate of the device, and the magnetic field respectively in body coordinates of the IoT device. We assume that in this paper the low-resource IoT device has IMU internally.

2.2 Conversion to a Common State-Space

The challenge of heterogeneous sensing-based pairing is that the measured signals are in different sensing state-spaces and therefore cannot be directly compared. However, if a user moves the low-resource IoT device in front of the camera, both sensors can obtain common information about the motion (in the form of position, acceleration, etc.) of the low-resource IoT device **in world coordinates** (*i.e.*, with respect to *down* and *North*). Integration or differentiation could transform acceleration and position into a common magnitude. In this regard, the literature is unanimous with respect to avoiding integration of acceleration signals measured on devices that can move freely in space [7, 18]. Integration is unsuitable for two main reasons that cause the error to accumulate faster than linearly over time: the propagation of the error in the orientation estimate (which is used to remove gravity from the raw acceleration) and the drift induced by integration of noisy signals. Therefore, we use differentiation to convert displacement into acceleration, and define the **world coordinates acceleration** as the common state-space of our camera-IMU sensor pair.

2.2.1 Converting IMU signal to device acceleration. To obtain the acceleration of IMU in world coordinates, *UniverSense* estimates the device orientation from a 9-axis IMU signal and projects the raw

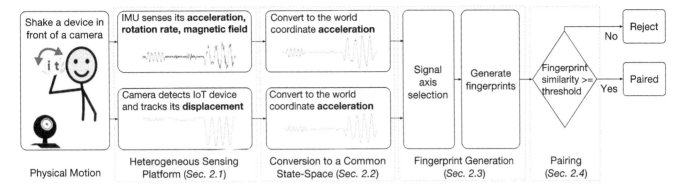

Figure 2: *UniverSense* system overview.

acceleration readings to a global frame of reference. This process basically consists of obtaining a rotation matrix ${}_B^W R$ that converts **B**ody coordinates into **W**orld coordinates. Then, *UniverSense* utilizes ${}_W^B R = i {}_B^W R^{-1}$ to project *gravity* into body coordinates so it can be removed from the raw acceleration signal. Finally, the result is expressed in world coordinates by multiplying by ${}_B^W R$ [18].

2.2.2 Converting camera stream to device acceleration. To extract the acceleration of the low-resource IoT device, *UniverSense* first detects the device from the video stream, then calculates the position of the device, and finally converts the position into acceleration. Object *detection* methods take a still image as the input, and provide a set of pixel coordinates for each target found [1, 8]. Then, object *tracking* processes the detection on consecutive frames and assigns a common ID to each target found in both images. Finally, the position of the IoT device can be tracked over time by converting pixel coordinates to the world frame. This conversion requires knowledge of the camera extrinsics (*i.e.*, the camera's ${}_B^W R$, estimated through *e.g.*, an IMU or a pre-calibration) as well as intrinsics (obtained from the manufacturer) [30]. Once the camera obtains the world coordinate position of the device, *UniverSense* performs a double differentiation on the estimated 3-D position of the IoT device to obtain the corresponding acceleration. In this work we assume the motion is performed perpendicular to the view of the camera at a known distance; in a real implementation, the 3-D position can be mapped into the camera view plane.

2.3 Fingerprint Generation

UniverSense generates binary fingerprints from acceleration signals to reduce the data exchanged. It takes two main steps: signal axis selection and fingerprint generation.

Signal axis selection Due to the noise of the sensor, when the motion of the device is not significant on the investigated axis, the low Signal-to-Noise Ratio (SNR) may cause low pairing success rate. *UniverSense* collects signals of all axises and selects the axis that has the highest signal energy to conduct fingerprint generation on.

Fingerprint generation *UniverSense* projects the acceleration signal into a binary signal by setting a threshold. If the absolute value of the signal is over the threshold, the bit is 1, otherwise, the bit is 0. Since the mean acceleration signal is close to 0, we specifically select an offset away from 0. With a sampling rate of 30

Hz, we estimate a 5-second motion can be used to generate a 128-bit fingerprint, and an 18-second motion can be used to generate a 512-bit fingerprint. Figure 3 shows an example of the fingerprint generated from IMU and camera measurements.

2.4 Pairing

To initiate the pairing, the 'powerful' device broadcasts a pairing request and start to generate fingerprint FP_{cam}. Once the low-resource IoT device receives the request, it starts to generate its fingerprint FP_{IMU}. Once the fingerprint reaches the designated length, the low-resource device sends its MAC address with the generated fingerprint. The 'powerful' device compares the received FP_{IMU} to its FP_{cam} and calculates the fingerprint similarity. If the two fingerprints have similarity over a threshold, *UniverSense* considers them as paired.

3 EVALUATION

We implemented *UniverSense* to evaluate our pairing method in a real-world environment (Section 3.1). We evaluate the motion variable (Section 3.2) and pairing performance (Section 3.3) respectively.

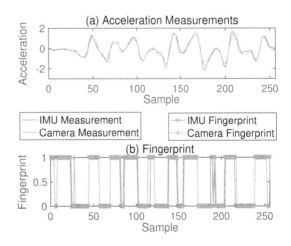

Figure 3: Fingerprint generation example.

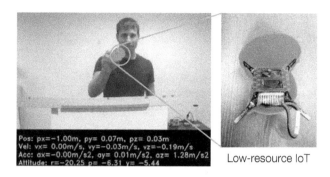

Low-resource IoT

Figure 4: Experiment settings (camera view).

3.1 Implementation

To evaluate *UniverSense*, we conducted real-world experiments with an off-the-shelf RGB camera (ELP 3.0 MegaPixel USB camera) for the 'capable' device, and IMU device from an IoT sensing platform, CrazyFlie 2.0, as the 'low-resource' device [4]. We covered the CrazyFlie with an orange plastic cap and used a color (hue) detector in OpenCV, together with an object tracker [11] to ensure we correctly follow the target. For real use cases, a more robust object detector could easily replace the current simplified version, without requiring any hardware modifications. In order to reduce the effect of sensing noise in the visual position estimation, we obtain good results with a traditional Savitzky-Golay (also known as Least-Squares) smoothing differentiation filter [27]. On the CrazyFlie, we use the popular Madgwick orientation filter [14] to minimize the drift in the orientation estimation. Figure 4 shows our experiment setup from the camera view, where the camera is 1.5m away from the motion area. Fingerprints used in the evaluation are 512 bits.

3.2 Motion Variable Analysis

We evaluate the system feasibility to match motion accelerations measured by camera and IMU under different motion variables: amplitude and velocity. We fix one parameter when evaluating the other. We asked one participant to conduct a designated motion 10 times and demonstrate the similarity of the pairwise fingerprints from camera and IMU.

3.2.1 Motion amplitude. We evaluate four different motion amplitudes, including 10, 20, 40, and 80 cm, with the motion velocity fixed. We control the motion velocity by asking the participant to conduct the motion of designated length within a given duration. We plot the fingerprint similarity against motion amplitude in Figure 5 (a). When the motion amplitude is 20 cm, the system achieves highest fingerprint similarity 0.95. When the motion amplitudes are 40 and 80 cm, the average fingerprint similarity drops below 0.9. The reason is that when the motion is in a large range, the velocity change is relatively small during the motion, and therefore the acceleration signal amplitude is low.

3.2.2 Motion velocity. Since *UniverSense* projects different sensing modalities into acceleration, the motion velocity affects the acceleration signal amplitude. We mainly investigate 5 different motion velocities controlled by metronome beats: 40, 60, 80, 100, 120 beats per minute (BPM) with a motion amplitude of 20 cm. We

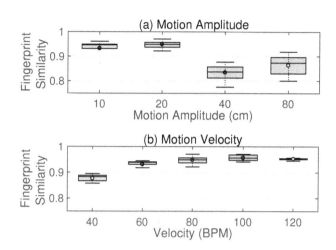

Figure 5: Motion variables' effect on fingerprint similarity. (a) shows the effects of motion amplitude. (b) shows the effect of motion velocity.

demonstrate the fingerprint similarity against motion velocities in Figure 5 (b). We observe an increasing trend of the fingerprint similarity for velocities lower than 80 BPM. However, when the velocity increases above 80 BPM, the increase of the motion velocity has little effect on the fingerprint similarity.

3.3 Pairing Performance

We further evaluate the pairing performance from two aspects: 1) human factors, and 2) the efficiency of fingerprints. We first investigate the human factor by asking multiple people to conduct experiment and evaluate the robustness of *UniverSense* through different users. Then we evaluate the fingerprint efficiency by analyzing the fingerprint similarity of the same motion and across different motions, and the pairing success rate with a selected pairing threshold.

3.3.1 Human factors. Different people may perform pairing motions differently. Therefore, we conduct experiments with multiple users and ask them to move the IoT device within a designated area

Figure 6: Different signal axes' fingerprint similarity.

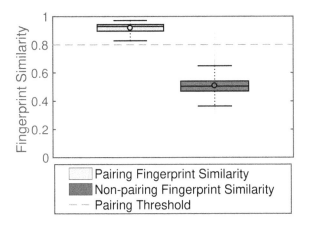

Figure 7: Compare fingerprint similarity of the same motion v.s. of different motions.

(a circle of 45 cm radius) arbitrarily for 20s. We compare multiple users' pairing fingerprint similarity calculated from different signal axises to demonstrate the system robustness, and the results are shown in Figure 6. The average fingerprint similarity across 5 participants using X-axis, Y-axis, and our axis-selection approach are respectively 0.845, 0.915, and 0.917, with standard deviations of 0.146, 0.038, and 0.036. Our approach achieves the highest fingerprint similarity and demonstrates stable matching performance. This is because different people may come up with different pairing motions. If a fingerprint is generated using an axis that lacks significant movement, the SNR will be low, giving a low fingerprint similarity. Our approach uses the axis with the highest SNR among the available signal axises to achieve high fingerprint similarity.

3.3.2 Fingerprint similarity analysis. We further analyze the fingerprint similarity between camera and IMU signals originating from world coordinate acceleration of the same motion, versus those from different motions and show it in Figure 7. The fingerprint similarity of the same motion, even detected by sensors of different modalities, is often over 0.8, which we set as the **pairing threshold**. On the other hand, the fingerprint similarity across different motions are relatively low, with an average of around 0.5. This indicates the feasibility of our system. We consider a successful pairing when the fingerprint similarity between the camera and an IMU device is above the pairing threshold. With a threshold of 0.8, the system achieves a precision of 100%, a recall of 99.8%, and an F1 score of 99.9% in 50 trials.

4   DISCUSSION

The previous section demonstrated the feasibility of our pairing mechanism. Here we discuss some limitations and potential extensions of this work.

4.1   Secure Pairing through *UniverSense*

UniverSense provides efficient device pairing for low-resource IoT devices that do not have a direct interaction I/O. On the other hand, establishing secure network is very important considering the growing number of IoT devices. Compared to current scan-based pairing, *e.g.*, Samsung SmartThings [26], *UniverSense* can be further extended to achieve secure pairing.

Prior work has been done to achieve secure pairing through protocols that utilize similar fingerprints generated from the sensing of shared physical events for IoT devices and vehicles [10, 17]. Therefore, fingerprints generated by *UniverSense* can be used to establish shared keys for secure pairing protocols. The challenges for secure pairing through *UniverSense* include designing a pairing protocol that can effectively defend against attacker models (*e.g.*, eavesdropping, Man-in-the-Middle).

4.2   Movement Tracking and Auto-Pairing

The implementation of this work relies on color markers to recognize the IoT device and a fixed depth to track its motion. Various work has been done on single camera depth estimation and human motion tracking [5, 23]. With these trending new approaches for robust object/human recognition and tracking, we believe that the pairing introduced in this work can be done without requiring users to intentionally move the device nor at a specific distance to the camera.

When the user interacts with the device during the installation, the camera can capture the posture of the person in the form of displacements and the low-resource IoT devices can capture the motion of the person in the form of accelerations. The challenges include selecting the representative point of a person's motion as the motion of the device and linking the physical objects/device to their virtual ID.

5   RELATED WORK

Device pairing has been explored using various sensing approaches. Traditional methods include passkey, QR code, and RFID, all of which face certain sensing limitations. Passkey-based methods require I/O hardware such as a display and a keypad [3]. QR-code based methods require either a flat surface or a screen to show the QR-code [2], but either case requires specific types of surfaces that certain devices may not meet. RFID relies on tags and readers specifically used for pairing [24], adding unnecessary hardware. These traditional methods do not apply to our problem because the type of low-resource IoT devices we focus on in this paper does not have I/O or extra hardware.

Sensing shared physical phenomena through co-presented devices has been applied under different scenarios to tackle these limitations. These methods mainly fall into two different categories: context-based and interaction-based. **Context-based pairing** methods generally utilize everyday events that can be detected by co-presented sensors [17, 31]. These methods often require zero-interaction and establish the secured network automatically. However, due to the randomness of human activities, this process can take a very long time (*e.g.*, days) to identify the shared context.

Interaction-based pairing methods often utilize human intention to designate pairing devices, such as shared motions induced by human activities [13, 28] or pointing to the targets [22]. Involving human interaction leads to reduced pairing times (*e.g.*, seconds). However, the state-of-the-art either requires a specific device, the 'wand' [22] or provides this type of pairing when the same motion is applied to both devices simultaneously [13, 28], thus limiting the variety of devices that can be paired (*e.g.*, shaking a smart TV with an IoT device might be difficult). *UniverSense* provides an alternative flexible pairing through conversion of multi-modal sensing signals, which allows the pairing between IoT devices of heterogeneous systems without additional devices.

Prior work has been done utilizing sensors of different modalities to achieve various sensing tasks. Nguyen et al. combine camera and Wi-Fi signals to localize and identify people in an indoor environment while they carry their smartphones [20]. Chen et al. utilize inertial and depth sensors to accurately link the detected motion on both devices and use this information to estimate the fitness of seniors [6]. Among these multi-modal sensing applications, to the best of our knowledge, we are the first to apply the shared physical-phenomena detected by sensors of different sensing modalities on device pairing.

6 CONCLUSION

In this paper, we present *UniverSense*, a multi-modal sensing based pairing method that pairs 'powerful' devices equipped with a camera to low-resource IoT devices with no interface. The user moves the low-resource IoT device in front of the camera so that the camera can capture the device motion. The low-resource IoT device, on the other hand, measures its own motion through its embedded IMU. These sensed motion signals are then converted into a common state-space to generate pairing fingerprints. We evaluate *UniverSense* through real-world experiments with multiple participants, and it achieves a 99.9% F1 score for the pairing success rate.

ACKNOWLEDGEMENTS

This research was supported in part by the National Science Foundation (under grants CNS-1149611, CMMI-1653550 and CNS-1645759), Intel and Google. The views and conclusions contained here are those of the authors and should not be interpreted as necessarily representing the official policies or endorsements, either express or implied, of CMU, NSF, or the U.S. Government or any of its agencies.

REFERENCES

[1] J. G. Allen, R. Y. Xu, and J. S. Jin. Object tracking using camshift algorithm and multiple quantized feature spaces. In *Proceedings of the Pan-Sydney area workshop on Visual information processing*, pages 3–7. Australian Computer Society, Inc., 2004.

[2] M. Baldauf, M. Salo, S. Suette, and P. Fröhlich. The screen is yours-comparing handheld pairing techniques for public displays. In *International Joint Conference on Ambient Intelligence*. Springer, 2013.

[3] A. Bannis and J. A. Burke. Creating a secure, integrated home network of things with named data networking, 2015.

[4] Bitcraze, AB. Crazyflie 2.0, 2016.

[5] Z. Cao, T. Simon, S.-E. Wei, and Y. Sheikh. Realtime multi-person 2d pose estimation using part affinity fields. In *CVPR*, 2017.

[6] C. Chen, K. Liu, R. Jafari, and N. Kehtarnavaz. Home-based senior fitness test measurement system using collaborative inertial and depth sensors. In *Engineering in Medicine and Biology Society (EMBC), 2014 36th Annual International*

Conference of the IEEE, pages 4135–4138. IEEE, 2014.

[7] J. Farrell and M. Barth. *The global positioning system and inertial navigation*, volume 61. McGraw-Hill New York, NY, USA:, 1999.

[8] R. Girshick, J. Donahue, T. Darrell, and J. Malik. Rich feature hierarchies for accurate object detection and semantic segmentation. In *Proceedings of the IEEE conference on computer vision and pattern recognition*, pages 580–587, 2014.

[9] Gruman, Galen.   *IoT silliness: 'Headless' devices without a UI.*, 2015.   https://www.infoworld.com/article/2867356/internet-of-things/beware-this-iot-fallacy-the-headless-device.html.

[10] J. Han, M. Harishankar, X. Wang, A. J. Chung, and P. Tague. Convoy: Physical context verification for vehicle platoon admission. In *Proceedings of the 18th International Workshop on Mobile Computing Systems and Applications*, pages 73–78. ACM, 2017.

[11] J. F. Henriques, R. Caseiro, P. Martins, and J. Batista. High-speed tracking with kernelized correlation filters. *IEEE Transactions on Pattern Analysis and Machine Intelligence*, 37(3):583–596, 2015.

[12] Joseph Palenchar. *Security Cameras Lead Smart-Home Adoption.* http://www.twice.com/news/statistics/security-cameras-lead-smart-home-adoption/61081.

[13] L. Kriara, M. Alsup, G. Corbellini, M. Trotter, J. D. Griffin, and S. Mangold. Rfid shakables: Pairing radio-frequency identification tags with the help of gesture recognition. In *Proceedings of the ninth ACM conference on Emerging networking experiments and technologies*, pages 327–332. ACM, 2013.

[14] S. Madgwick. An efficient orientation filter for inertial and inertial/magnetic sensor arrays. *Report x-io and University of Bristol (UK)*.

[15] J. Martin, T. Mayberry, C. Donahue, L. Foppe, L. Brown, C. Riggins, E. C. Rye, and D. Brown. A study of mac address randomization in mobile devices and when it fails. *arXiv preprint arXiv:1703.02874*, 2017.

[16] MetaSensor Inc. *Meet Sensor-1, The security system that fits in the palm of your hand.*, 2017. https://www.metasensor.com/.

[17] M. Miettinen, N. Asokan, T. D. Nguyen, A.-R. Sadeghi, and M. Sobhani. Context-based zero-interaction pairing and key evolution for advanced personal devices. In *Proceedings of the 2014 ACM SIGSAC Conference on Computer and Communications Security*, pages 880–891. ACM, 2014.

[18] P. Neto, J. N. Pires, and A. P. Moreira. 3-d position estimation from inertial sensing: minimizing the error from the process of double integration of accelerations. In *Industrial Electronics Society, IECON 2013-39th Annual Conference of the IEEE*, pages 4026–4031. IEEE, 2013.

[19] Networking, Cisco Visual. Cisco global cloud index: forecast and methodology, 2015-2020. white paper, 2017.

[20] L. T. Nguyen, Y. S. Kim, P. Tague, and J. Zhang. Identitylink: user-device linking through visual and rf-signal cues. In *Proceedings of the 2014 ACM International Joint Conference on Pervasive and Ubiquitous Computing*, pages 529–539. ACM, 2014.

[21] Notion Inc. *Home awareness, simplified. Monitor your home with a single sensor, wherever you are.*, 2017. http://getnotion.com/.

[22] T. J. Pierson, X. Liang, R. Peterson, and D. Kotz. Wanda: securely introducing mobile devices. In *The 35th Annual IEEE International Conference on Computer Communications, IEEE INFOCOM 2016*, pages 1–9. IEEE, 2016.

[23] S. Ren, K. He, R. Girshick, and J. Sun. Faster r-cnn: Towards real-time object detection with region proposal networks. In *Advances in neural information processing systems*, pages 91–99, 2015.

[24] J. Riekki, T. Salminen, and I. Alakärppa. Requesting pervasive services by touching rfid tags. *IEEE Pervasive computing*, 5(1):40–46, 2006.

[25] Samsung Inc. *Use gesture control with the latest Smart Interaction.*, 2017. http://www.samsung.com/uk/tv-accessories/tv-camera-stc5000/.

[26] Samsung Inc. *The easiest way to turn your home into a smart home.*, 2018. https://www.samsung.com/us/smart-home/smartthings/.

[27] A. Savitzky and M. J. Golay. Smoothing and differentiation of data by simplified least squares procedures. *Analytical chemistry*, 36(8), 1964.

[28] A. Studer, T. Passaro, and L. Bauer. Don't bump, shake on it: The exploitation of a popular accelerometer-based smart phone exchange and its secure replacement. In *Proceedings of the 27th Annual Computer Security Applications Conference*, pages 333–342. ACM, 2011.

[29] C. T. Zenger, M. Pietersz, J. Zimmer, J.-F. Posielek, T. Lenze, and C. Paar. Authenticated key establishment for low-resource devices exploiting correlated random channels. *Computer Networks*, 109:105–123, 2016.

[30] Z. Zhang. A flexible new technique for camera calibration. *IEEE Transactions on pattern analysis and machine intelligence*, 22(11), 2000.

[31] C. Zhao, S. Yang, X. Yang, and J. A. McCann. Rapid, user-transparent, and trustworthy device pairing for d2d-enabled mobile crowdsourcing. *IEEE Transactions on Mobile Computing*, 16(7):2008–2022, 2017.

Meeting Future Needs in Mobile Computing

Michael Polley
Samsung
Richardson, TX
mike.polley@samsung.com

ABSTRACT

The mobile consumer market continues to demand new features, increased performance and extended battery life. These demands must be balanced with cost and other practical concerns.

To create a successful next-generation product, we should carefully predict the computations required and create a design without excessive performance and cost. To do this, we consider industry trends and the range of compute engines that can be leveraged on mobiles. We contrast computational capabilities of embedded devices with the evolving requirements of new and existing mobile equipment and applications. In addition to considering how to match next-generation devices with the needs, we will also consider what part of the system should be on-device versus in the cloud.

BIOGRAPHY

Mike is Senior Vice President and Head of the Mobile Processor Innovation Lab at Samsung where he leads a team of world-class algorithm and system designers and chipset architects focused on creating advanced technologies for Samsung's Galaxy smartphones as well as next-generation mobile devices.

Prior to Samsung, Mike worked at Texas Instruments for 18 years defining chipset architectures and leading embedded signal processing R&D. He was recognized for his technical accomplishments by election to TI Fellow in 2008.

Mike received his B.S., M.S., and Ph.D. degrees in electrical engineering from MIT. He holds 32 U.S. patents on a broad range of products across communications and multimedia systems.

Remote-Control Caching: Proxy-based URL Rewriting to Decrease Mobile Browsing Bandwidth

Ravi Netravali
MIT CSAIL
ravinet@mit.edu

James Mickens
Harvard University
mickens@g.harvard.edu

ABSTRACT

Mobile browsers suffer from unnecessary cache misses. The same binary object is often named by multiple URLs which correspond to different cache keys. Furthermore, servers frequently mark objects as uncacheable, even though the objects' content is stable over time.

In this paper, we quantify the excess network traffic that mobile devices generate due to inefficient caching logic. We demonstrate that mobile page loads suffer from more redundant transfers than reported by prior studies which focused on desktop page loads. We then propose a new scheme, called Remote-Control Caching (RC2), in which web proxies (owned by mobile carriers or device manufacturers) track the aliasing relationships between the objects that a client has fetched, and the URLs that were used to fetch those objects. Leveraging knowledge of those aliases, a proxy dynamically rewrites the URLs inside of pages, allowing the client's local browser cache to satisfy a larger fraction of requests. Using a concrete implementation of RC2, we show that, for two loads of a page separated by 8 hours, RC2 reduces bandwidth consumption by a median of 52%. As a result, mobile browsers can save a median of 469 KB per warm-cache page load.

CCS CONCEPTS

• **Information systems** → **Web applications**; • **Networks** → **Middle boxes / network appliances**; **Mobile networks**;

KEYWORDS

Web proxies, caching, content aliasing

ACM Reference Format:
Ravi Netravali and James Mickens. 2018. Remote-Control Caching: Proxy-based URL Rewriting to Decrease Mobile Browsing Bandwidth. In *HotMobile '18: 19th International Workshop on Mobile Computing Systems & Applications, February 12–13, 2018, Tempe , AZ, USA*. ACM, New York, NY, USA, 6 pages. https://doi.org/10.1145/3177102.3177118

1 INTRODUCTION

Users desire web pages that load quickly. However, on mobile devices with limited cellular data plans, users also desire pages that

load with *a minimal amount of network traffic*. The average mobile-optimized web page is still 3.1 MB in size [8], which is close to the 3.6 MB size of the average desktop page [7]. HTTP objects are downloaded not just by traditional browsers, but by the many applications that use GUI-stripped browsers [4, 5] to fetch and render user-facing content. HTTP traffic, regardless of its source, consumes data plan bandwidth that is also coveted by video applications and non-HTTP-based programs. So, reducing the transfer bandwidth for mainline web content (i.e., HTML, CSS, JavaScript, and images) is important.

Mainline content is amenable to client-side caching. Objects like CSS files and JavaScript files are often used by multiple pages; furthermore, a given page will often use the same version of an object across multiple page reloads. Unfortunately, traditional caching suffers from low hit rates on mobile devices. The reasons are myriad. For example, web servers often use time-based expiration instead of content-based ETags expiration [1], resulting in browsers making unnecessary fetches of unchanged content. Caching rules are also defined using *exact match* semantics for URLs. Exact-match semantics can result in cache misses even if the necessary bytes already reside in the cache (§2).

In this paper, we provide two contributions. First, we perform an empirical study of how traditional caching logic misses opportunities to avoid redundant downloads. For example, we show that 89% of mobile pages have at least one object which is named via multiple URLs that only differ in the query string (§3.5). We also find that 95% of pages contain objects that do not change across reloads, but are marked as uncacheable by servers. Comparing our results to those of prior studies which focused on content aliasing in desktop web pages [9, 10], we find that redundant transfers are a *worse* problem in the mobile setting, causing at least twice as many cache misses as in the desktop setting.

Our second contribution is the design and evaluation of *Remote-Control Caching (RC2)*. RC2 allows mobile carriers or device manufacturers to improve cache hit rates without changing mobile browsers or mobile operating systems. In the current world, mobile browsers often use web proxies to compress content [1]; in RC2, proxies also *actively rewrite the embedded URLs in HTML and JavaScript*. In particular, an RC2 proxy tracks information about the contents of a phone's browser cache. When a phone requests a page, the RC2 proxy loads that page using a headless browser, determining the external objects (e.g., images and CSS files) whose raw bits are cached on the phone, but stored under different URLs than the ones used by the page to load. The RC2 proxy rewrites those URLs so that the page references the associated objects via URLs that will guarantee cache hits. The result is that phones download much less data per page load. For example, on an LTE network and a Nexus 5 phone, across the 500 most popular sites, RC2 reduces bandwidth costs by 52% for the median page that was reloaded eight hours after its initial load; this reduction translates into raw bandwidth savings of 469 KB.

2 TRADITIONAL CACHING

A browser cache is a key/value store. A key is a full HTTP request, which includes the URL of the object to fetch, and the HTTP request headers in the fetch. A cache value represents the binary contents of an object, e.g., the bits in an image.

When a web server returns an object to a browser, the server uses HTTP response headers to describe the cacheability of the object. For example, the header `Cache-Control: max-age=500` indicates that a browser may cache the object for 500 seconds. `Cache-control: no-store` indicates that the browser should never cache the object.

A server can also indicate that an object is *conditionally cacheable*, meaning that the browser's cached version should only be used if a particular condition is true. When a server returns a conditionally cacheable object, the response includes a `Last-Modified: timestamp` header, and/or an `ETag: opaque-string` header. A `Last-Modified` header indicates the creation time of the object; an `ETag` header provides a unique id for the object. An `ETag` id may be strong validator like a hash value, or a weak validator like a version number. When the browser issues a request for a conditionally cached object, the request includes the appropriate `If-Modified-Since: timestamp` or `If-None-Match: opaque-string` headers. The server parses those headers, determines whether the requested object has changed, and returns either a `200: OK` response with a new version of the object, or a `304: Not modified` response with no object data.

The problem with the traditional caching protocol is that *cache keys are defined by HTTP request state instead of raw object content.* A single binary object can be named by an arbitrary number of HTTP requests; each of those requests is a different cache key, even though each request maps to the same object. Consider the URL `http://a.foo.com/image.jpg?abcd`.

- **Modified domain names:** Popular sites use CDNs to distribute load and push content servers closer to users. The hostnames for CDN servers often differ in just a few positions (e.g., `a.foo.com` versus `b.foo.com`). However, those differences mean that if a browser fetches the same object twice, from two different CDN servers, the two HTTP requests will represent different cache keys, even if the responses contain the same bits.
- **Modified resource names:** A resource name specifies an object to fetch (e.g., `image.jpg`). Web servers often add client-specific strings to resource names, such that clients refer to the same underlying object using different resource names.
- **Modified query strings:** Query strings like `?abcd` are typically used to embed user-provided data, e.g., from a form. Query strings in an HTTP request convey important information to a server. However, servers often return the same bytes in response to requests with different query strings.
- **Improper caching headers:** Even if a request exactly matches an earlier one, a server may have marked the response to the earlier request as uncacheable. If this happened, the second request will suffer a cache miss, and fetch bytes that already exist on the client.

Metric	Median	95th Percentile
# of objects	95	369
# of bytes	1.4 MB	6.1 MB

Figure 1: Summary of our 500 page test corpus.

As we empirically demonstrate in Section 3.5, all four of these scenarios are common. Note that `ETag` headers are not a solution—`ETag` headers enable content-based caching for a particular URL, but the scenarios that we described above involve *multiple, distinct URLs* that refer to the same object.

3 PREVENTING ALIAS-INDUCED MISSES

In this section, we first describe an optimal content-based caching scheme; this optimal scheme defines an upper bound on the bandwidth savings that a concrete scheme can provide. We then describe the design of RC2. RC2 is a web proxy that rewrites embedded URLs in HTML, allowing the proxy to effectively take control of a phone's cache management strategy. By tracking the content in client-stored objects, and rewriting URLs to refer to those objects whenever possible, RC2 unlocks 99.1% of the optimal bandwidth savings.

3.1 Methodology

We used a 500 page test corpus that was collected using Mahimahi, a tool for recording and replaying HTTP traffic [18]. Each test page was the landing page for an Alexa Top 500 site [2]; we used the mobile-optimized version of a page when such a version existed. Figure 1 provides a high-level summary of the pages in the corpus.

All experiments used a Nexus 5 phone that ran Android 5.1.1 and Google Chrome v53. For experiments that involved page load times, we loaded each individual page five times using cold browser and DNS caches, and five times using warm browser and DNS caches; we recorded the median load time for each scenario. We defined "load time" as the elapsed time between the `navigationStart` and `loadEventEnd` JavaScript events.

3.2 Optimal Content-based Caching

We used Mahimahi to record three versions of each page: an initial version, a version that was recorded a few seconds later, and a version that was recorded eight hours later. The first and second versions represented the pages that a browser would see if it loaded a page and then immediately reloaded it. The first and third versions represented what a browser would see if it loaded a page, and then waited eight hours to reload the page.

For each of the three versions, we examined the caching headers for each object in the version, determining which HTTP requests would incur network fetches in the immediate-reload scenario and the delayed-reload scenario. We also examined the *contents* of the objects in the three versions of each page. For each object, we calculated a SHA1 hash. Using those hashes, we determined when an omniscient content-based cache would incur network fetches in the immediate-reload and delayed-reload scenarios. In particular, let $bits(obj_i)$ correspond to the binary content in obj_i, and let $bits(req, t)$ correspond to the bits associated with the HTTP request req when fetched at time t. For a page reload at $t_{reload} > t_{initial\_load}$, we declared a particular request to hit in the cache if $bits(req, t_{reload}) = bits(obj_i)$ for any obj_i that was fetched at $t_{initial\_load}$. This calculation ignored all of the traditional caching logic; for example, even if an object's response headers at $t_{initial\_load}$ marked the object as uncacheable, the object might still provide a content-based cache hit for some request at t_{reload}. This setup evaluates a perfect content-based cache with infinite storage space and a priori knowledge of the mappings between URLs and raw objects.

3.3 RC2 Caching

An RC2 proxy is a remote dependency resolution (RDR) proxy. Before explaining how RC2 rewrites HTML, we first provide a brief overview of RDR proxying.

RDR Fundamentals: When a mobile browser issues an HTTP fetch for a page's top-level HTML, an RDR proxy loads the entire page locally, using a headless browser that runs on the proxy.[1] The proxy loads the page fully, parsing the top-level HTML and fetching all of the external objects that are referenced by that HTML. After returning the fetched HTML, most RDR proxies will proactively push the fetched external objects to the client, allowing the client to load the objects locally when the associated HTTP requests are generated during the local HTML parse. This approach, used by Amazon Silk [3], Opera Mini [19], and PARCEL [23], reduces page load times, but requires a modified client browser to handle the proxy's object-push logic. In contrast, RC2 is designed to work with unmodified mobile browsers. So, after an RC2 proxy returns HTML to the client, the proxy buffers the fetched external objects, draining the buffer as the phone issues HTTP requests for those objects.

RC2: In addition to an object buffer, an RC2 proxy maintains a per-client data structure that persists across individual page loads; this data structure represents the proxy's belief about which objects are stored in the client's browser cache. The data structure is a table which maps the hash value of a client-resident object to 1) the URL that the client used to fetch that object, and 2) the cache expiration date, as indicated by the HTTP response headers for the associated fetch.

A client's proxy-side table is initially empty. At some point, the client issues an HTTP fetch for a page's top-level HTML. The proxy fetches and loads the HTML in a headless browser, triggering additional proxy-side HTTP fetches for the external objects referenced by the top-level HTML. For each HTTP fetch via URL U_i, the proxy calculates the hash value H of the retrieved object. If the client has no table entry for H, the proxy adds the table entry $t[H] = <U_i, exp_{U_i}>$, where exp_{U_i} is the cache expiration date for the object, as indicated by the HTTP response headers. If $t[H]$ is not empty, then there is an aliasing relationship between $<U_i, exp_{U_i}>$ and some preexisting table value $<U_{alreadyCached}, exp_{U_{alreadyCached}}>$. Assuming that $exp_{U_{alreadyCached}}$ is still in the future, the proxy rewrites the HTML's reference to U_i, changing the reference to $U_{alreadyCached}$;

this change prevents an aliasing-based cache miss on the mobile browser. If $exp_{U_{alreadyCached}}$ has already passed, then the proxy updates $t[H]$ with $<U_i, exp_{U_i}>$, and does *not* rewrite the reference to U_i in the HTML.

An RC2 proxy uses DOM shimming [13] to rewrite the URLs for HTML tags that are dynamically created via DOM methods like document.appendChild(). An RC2 proxy also rewrites URLs for JavaScript-initiated XMLHttpRequests that issue during a page load. The proxy detects aliasing relationships for XMLHttpRequests during the proxy-side page load, creating a map between the baseline URLs and the rewritten ones. The proxy includes this map in a small JavaScript library which the proxy injects into the page's HTML. This library also uses DOM shimming [13] to interpose on the mobile browser's creation of XMLHttpRequest objects. When the mobile browser creates XMLHttpRequests, the shimmed objects consult the URL map to determine which objects to fetch.

An RC2 proxy must avoid situations in which URL rewriting causes a mobile browser to load a page with inconsistent content, i.e., a set of objects which would never be seen in an unmodified load of the page. To avoid these problems, an RC2 proxy uses two mechanisms.

- First, an RC2 proxy always marks top-level HTML as uncacheable, ensuring that the proxy controls the objects fetched for every load of a page. This caching strategy deviates little from the status quo, since top-level HTML is often dynamically-generated and therefore unsuitable for caching. We examined the cache headers for all of the HTML objects in our 500 page test corpus, and found that only 6.7% of objects were naturally marked as cacheable.

- An RC2 proxy also does not rewrite U_i to $U_{alreadyCached}$ if $exp_{U_{alreadyCached}}$ is less than 30 seconds in the future. This policy ensures that the associated object in the client cache will not expire half-way through the page load, resulting in a live fetch for that object which might lead to inconsistent page content.

RC2 must also be wary of users who unilaterally delete some or all of the mobile browser's cache entries. If this happens, then the mobile browser may issue an HTTP fetch for an object which the RC2 proxy (incorrectly) believed would be satisfied by the client's cache. When the proxy receives such an unexpected HTTP request, the proxy forces the request to fail by terminating the TCP connection. The termination induces a client-side onerror JavaScript event; the proxy rewrites each page's HTML to include a custom onerror handler that, when fired, forces the entire page to reload via a call to the browser's Location.reload(true) JavaScript method. Note that passing true to the method forces the reload to bypass the browser cache and load the page directly from the origin server (via the proxy). When the proxy detects such a reload, the proxy discards the entirety of the client's table, under the assumption that the proxy's view of the client-side cache is now totally desynchronized and must be rebuilt from scratch.

As a mobile phone is used, it may switch between different cellular towers, or between cellular service and WiFi service. If the RC2 proxy is maintained by phone vendors, then a phone can redirect its web traffic to the proxy regardless of whether the phone's last-mile link is cellular or WiFi; this network-agnostic approach

---

[1] A headless browser is one that has no GUI, but is otherwise equivalent to a regular browser. PhantomJS [6] is the most popular headless browser, and is the one used by our RC2 prototype.

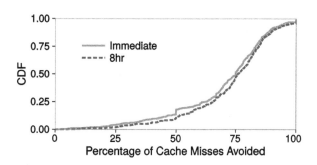

Figure 2: The fraction of cache misses that RC2 avoids, relative to the total number of misses incurred by traditional caching. Results span the 500 page test corpus.

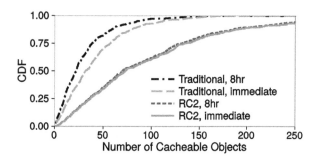

Figure 3: The number of cached objects during an immediate page reload, and an 8-hour-delayed reload.

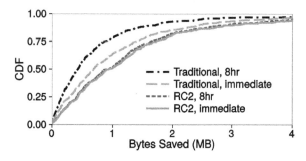

Figure 4: The number of bytes saved during an immediate page reload, and an 8-hour-delayed reload.

is used by Google's compression proxy for Android phones [1]. If the RC2 proxy is instead deployed by a cellular provider, then the proxy will lose visibility into the phone's cache updates when the phone switches to a WiFi network. These updates may cause the phone and the proxy to become desynchronized, forcing the proxy to discard the user's RC2 table when the phone reassociates with the cellular network.

3.4   Bandwidth Savings

We built a prototype RC2 system by modifying the Cumulus RDR proxy [18]. Figure 2 demonstrates the performance of our prototype. For both immediate and delayed page reloads, RC2 eliminates a median of *75% of the cache misses* that would be suffered by a traditional, URL-indexed cache. These savings are roughly *three*

	Raw savings	% savings
Optimal	948 (4420) KB	69.9% (72.5%)
RC2	911 (4284) KB	67.5% (70.3%)
Traditional	682 (3543) KB	50.4% (58.1%)

(a) Immediate reloads.

	Raw savings	% savings
Optimal	909 (4191) KB	67.1% (68.7%)
RC2	901 (4093) KB	66.5% (67.3%)
Traditional	432 (2439) KB	31.9% (40.0%)

(b) Delayed reloads (8 hours).

Figure 5: Bandwidth saved at the median (95th percentile): optimal content-based caching (§3.2), RC2 (§3.3), and traditional caching.

times the savings observed in a 2002 study of content aliasing on the web [10, 14], and roughly *two times* the savings observed in a 2011 study of content aliasing on the web [9]. Both studies focused on traffic involving desktop browsers, so additional research is needed to determine whether our findings generalize to non-mobile pages.

Whereas Figure 2 shows the fractional reduction in cache misses, Figures 3 and 4 provides raw numbers for the cacheable objects found per page reload, and the bandwidth saved per page load due to cache hits. For example, during an immediate reload, traditional caching logic found a median of 32 cacheable objects per page; as a result, the reload needed 50.4% less bandwidth than the initial load. RC2 identified a median of 73 cacheable objects, allowing the reload to use 67.5% less bandwidth than the initial load. The additional cache hits represented a raw bandwidth savings of 229 KB over traditional caching.

In a delayed-reload scenario, both traditional caching and RC2 had lower hit rates. However, RC2 retained its performance advantage. With an eight hour separation between the initial visit and the reload, RC2 saved a median of 1.1% less bandwidth than in the immediate reload scenario; traditional caching saved 36.7% less.

As Figure 5 demonstrates, an RC2 proxy achieves 99.1% of the maximum possible savings in the delayed reload case. In the immediate reload case, RC2 achieves 96.1% of the optimal savings. Traditional caching only enables 47.5% of the optimal savings for delayed reloads, and only 71.9% for immediate reloads.

3.5   Analysis of Bandwidth Savings

In Section 2, we described four reasons why traditional caching logic often leads to unnecessary cache misses. Figure 6 uses that taxonomy to explain why RC2-based caching outperformed traditional caching. Each of the four reasons was impactful, but surprisingly, misspecified caching headers ("Req match, resp uncached") were the most popular reason for cache misses with traditional caching logic. In the median page, 33.1% of newly cacheable objects had been fetched during the initial page load, but marked as uncacheable by the server, such that, during a reload, requests for those objects would generate cache misses, even though the bits in the objects had already been fetched.

Modified domain names were the second most popular reason for cache misses, causing 29.9% of the misses for the median page. Modified query strings caused 20.8% of the misses for the median

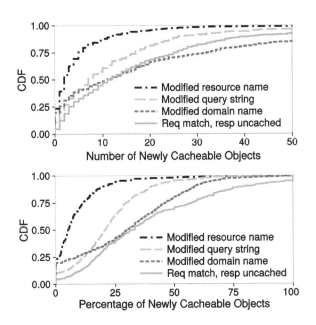

Figure 6: The reasons why traditional caching generated misses for objects that would hit in an RC2-managed cache. These results came from the immediate reload experiments.

Object Type	% newly cacheable objects	% newly cacheable bytes
JavaScript	29.8%	26.6
CSS	5.0%	3.3
Images	46.3%	63.4
Fonts	1.2%	2.1
JSON	13.8%	3.9
Other	3.9%	0.7

Figure 7: The types of newly cacheable objects that RC2 found. Recall that RC2 marks HTML as uncacheable (§3.3).

page. Modified resource names were the least common reason for misses, causing only 5.4% of misses for the median page.

Every page in our corpus suffered from at least one of the four types of unnecessary cache misses. Additionally, 89% of pages contained at least one object that was named by multiple URLs which only differed in their query strings. 95% of pages contained at least one object that was marked uncacheable by a server, but whose bits did not change across reloads. These statistics remained stable for both immediate reloads and delayed reloads.

Figure 7 lists the MIME types for the newly cacheable objects that RC2 caching discovered. Images were the most common type, both in terms of object count (46.3%) and bytes saved (63.4%). JavaScript files provided the second-largest amount of bytes saved (26.6%).

3.6 Page Load Time

Prior studies of mobile caching found that page load times (PLTs) are only moderately affected by cache hits—warm cache PLTs decrease by only 13% relative to cold cache PLTs [24]. The reason is that a traditional cache stores few objects that reside on the critical path for a page load [17]. Since RC2 improves cache hit rates, RC2 should

Scenario	Median PLT	95th-percentile PLT
Traditional	5.23 seconds	14.66 seconds
RC2	5.27 seconds	14.54 seconds

(a) Cold caches.

Scenario	Median PLT	95th-percentile PLT
Traditional	4.31 seconds	9.95 seconds
RC2	3.62 seconds	7.69 seconds

(b) Warm caches, immediate reload.

Scenario	Median PLT	95th-percentile PLT
Traditional	4.68 seconds	10.83 seconds
RC2	3.70 seconds	5.62 seconds

(c) Warm caches, 8-hour-delayed reload.

Figure 8: Page load times for traditional caching and RC2.

increase the likelihood that critical path objects will hit in the cache. Thus, RC2 should lower PLTs as well as bandwidth consumption.

To empirically measure the PLT benefits, we USB-tethered a Nexus 5 phone to a Linux desktop machine. The desktop machine ran an RC2 proxy which treated Mahimahi servers [18] as the origin servers for all web content. The phone/proxy connection was an emulated Verizon LTE link which used packet delivery schedules driven by an empirical trace [26]. The proxy/Mahimahi link used an emulated RTT of 5 ms, and an emulated bandwidth of 25 Mbps. We also evaluated traditional caching by having the phone directly contact the Mahimahi servers over an emulated LTE link.

In all warm cache experiments, we warmed the cache (and RC2 proxy) by simulating a user with a 100-day old browser cache. At the beginning of simulated day 1, the browser cache was empty. During each simulated day, the simulated user loaded 10 pages drawn from a Zipfian distribution over the Alexa Top 500 pages. For each page PLT to examine, we then ensured that the cache had objects from either a recent or an 8-hour-old version of the page. Using this methodology, we could measure the expected size of the per-client data structures kept by a proxy—the final size of such a structure on the 100th simulated day was roughly 636 KB.

Figure 8 shows the PLT results. In the cold cache case, median PLTs are slightly higher (0.76%) with RC2 because of proxy overheads for manipulating per-client data structures and loading pages inside of a headless browser. However, RC2 provides significant PLT reductions in warm cache scenarios; compared to baseline PLTs that used cold caches, RC2 reduces warm cache PLTs by 30.8% for immediate reloads, and 29.3% for 8-hour-delayed reloads.

4   OPEN CHALLENGES AND FUTURE WORK

Web traffic is increasingly shifting from HTTP to HTTPS [15]. The transition is beneficial for security, but detrimental to proxy-based solutions for reducing load times or decreasing bandwidth costs. Compression proxies like Flywheel [1], and RDR proxies like Amazon Silk [3], require access to cleartext HTTP traffic; however, to gain access to that traffic, proxies would have to spoof HTTPS origin servers and break TLS's end-to-end security guarantees. Flywheel and Amazon Silk choose not to break those guarantees, thereby eschewing acceleration for HTTPS traffic. In contrast, Opera Mini does perform man-in-the-middle TLS mediation, such that end-to-end integrity is broken, but both HTTP and HTTPS pages can be accelerated. The results in Section 3 used Opera Mini-style proxying; RC2's performance would obviously be worse if only HTTP traffic could be proxied. For example, in delayed reload scenarios, RC2 provides 99.1% of the optimal benefits if all traffic can be proxied, but only 81.2% of those benefits if HTTPS traffic must be ignored. RC2 still outperforms traditional caching (which only provides 47.5% of the optimal benefits), but proxy-based web acceleration in general is threatened by the increasing ubiquity of HTTPS. Researchers have begun to investigate secure mechanisms for TLS introspection by middleboxes [16, 22]; further work is needed to apply such techniques to web acceleration proxies.

An RC2 proxy stores a per-client data structure that represents the proxy's view of the client-side browser cache. In our unoptimized RC2 prototype, the data structure for a client with a 100-day-old cache is roughly 636 KB in size. The data structure contains hash values (which are random-looking and thus incompressible), as well as URLs and dates (which are more promising candidates for compression). To maximize proxy scalability, future work should investigate concrete approaches for shrinking per-client data structures.

Using HTML rewriting, an RC2 proxy takes control of a phone's browser cache. We believe that rewriting can enable other proxy-managed optimizations. For example, proxies receive HTTP requests from a large set of phones. By observing cross-request correlations (e.g., "requests for page X are typically followed by requests for page Y"), a proxy can inject <link> prefetch tags [25] for Y into X, so that a mobile browser will proactively fetch Y before the local user requests Y.

5   RELATED WORK

Ma et al. examined mobile caching behavior [11], but ignored HTTPS content. Their survey also did not consider cross-site aliasing relationships (as considered in Section 3.6). Additionally, their survey considered a cache hit to be a false hit if, at the time of the cache hit, the server-side version of an object differed from the client-side version retrieved from the cache. This definition is problematic, since sites can define cross-object consistency semantics which Ma et al.'s methodology would flag as leading to false cache hits.

Prior systems have explored client/server protocols for implementing content-based caching. For example, in CZIP [20], a client fetches a page using two HTTP-level RTTs: one to fetch the list of hashes for objects in the page, and another to fetch the raw data for objects that are not client-resident. In Silo [12], a web server inlines all of the external content referenced by an HTML file, and then splits the inlined HTML into chunks. The server returns the chunks to the client, who stores the chunks in DOM storage; in a subsequent request for the HTML, the client indicates which chunks are locally resident, so that the server only has to return the new ones (plus a list of old chunks that are no longer contained in the page's inlined HTML). These prior systems for content-based caching are either incompatible with standard web browsers [20, 21], or cannot track aliasing relationships for the same object across different sites [12]. In contrast, RC2 works on commodity browsers, and can track aliasing relationships across all sites that a client visits.

6   CONCLUSION

Bandwidth is precious on mobile phones. In this paper, we quantify the amount of bandwidth that is needlessly consumed by HTTP fetches that miss in a traditional browser cache, but would have hit in a content-based one. We then propose a new content-based caching scheme, called RC2. RC2 leverages a proxy that rewrites HTML to avoid unnecessary cache misses. Experiments with 500 popular sites demonstrate that RC2 eliminates 99.1% of unnecessary cache misses, while requiring no changes to mobile browsers.

REFERENCES

[1] Victor Agababov, Michael Buettner, Victor Chudnovsky, Mark Cogan, Ben Greenstein, Shane McDaniel, Michael Piatek, Colin Scott, Matt Welsh, and Bolian Yin. 2015. Flywheel: Google's Data Compression Proxy for the Mobile Web. In *Proceedings of NSDI*.
[2] Alexa. 2018. Alexa Top 500 Global Sites. http://www.alexa.com/topsites. (2018).
[3] Amazon. 2018. Silk Browser. http://amazonsilk.wordpress.com/. (2018).
[4] Apple. 2018. https://developer.apple.com/documentation/webkit/wkwebview. (2018).
[5] Google. 2018. Android Developer Reference: WebView. https://developer.android.com/reference/android/webkit/WebView.html. (2018).
[6] Ariya Hidayat. 2018. PhantomJS. http://phantomjs.org/. (2018).
[7] HTTP Archive. 2018. Desktop Trends. http://httparchive.org/interesting.php#bytesperpage. (2018).
[8] HTTP Archive. 2018. Mobile Trends. http://mobile.httparchive.org/interesting.php#bytesperpage. (2018).
[9] Sunghwan Ihm and Vivek Pai. 2011. Towards Understanding Modern Web Traffic. In *Proceedings of IMC*.
[10] Terence Kelly and Jeffrey Mogul. 2002. Aliasing on the World Wide Web: Prevalence and Performance Implications. In *Proceedings of WWW*.
[11] Yun Ma, Xuanzhe Liu, Shuhui Zhang, Ruirui Xiang, Yunxin Liu, and Tao Xie. 2015. Measurement and Analysis of Mobile Web Cache Performance. In *Proceedings of WWW*.
[12] James Mickens. 2010. Silo: Exploiting JavaScript and DOM Storage for Faster Page Loads. In *Proceedings of USENIX WebApps*.
[13] James Mickens, Jeremy Elson, and Jon Howell. 2010. Mugshot: Deterministic Capture and Replay for Javascript Applications. In *Proceedings of NSDI*.
[14] Jeffrey Mogul, Yee Man Chan, and Terence Kelly. 2004. Design, Implementation, and Evaluation of Duplicate Transfer Detection in HTTP. In *Proceedings of NSDI*.
[15] David Naylor, Alessandro Finamore, Ilias Leontiadis, Yan Grunenberger, Marco Mellia, Maurizio Munafò, Konstantina Papagiannaki, and Peter Steenkiste. 2014. The Cost of the "S" in HTTPS. In *Proceedings of the CoNEXT*.
[16] David Naylor, Kyle Schomp, Matteo Varvello, Ilias Leontiadis, Jeremy Blackburn, Diego R. López, Konstantina Papagiannaki, Pablo Rodriguez Rodriguez, and Peter Steenkiste. 2015. Multi-Context TLS (mcTLS): Enabling Secure In-Network Functionality in TLS. In *Proceedings of SIGCOMM*.
[17] Ravi Netravali, Ameesh Goyal, James Mickens, and Hari Balakrishnan. 2016. Polaris: Faster Page Loads Using Fine-grained Dependency Tracking. In *Proceedings of NSDI*.
[18] Ravi Netravali, Anirudh Sivaraman, Somak Das, Ameesh Goyal, Keith Winstein, James Mickens, and Hari Balakrishnan. 2015. Mahimahi: Accurate Record-and-Replay for HTTP. In *Proceedings of USENIX ATC*.
[19] Opera. 2018. Opera Mini. http://www.opera.com/mobile/mini. (2018).
[20] KyoungSoo Park, Sunghwan Ihm, Mic Bowman, and Vivek S. Pai. 2007. Supporting Practical Content-addressable Caching with CZIP Compression. In *Proceedings of USENIX ATC*.
[21] Sean Rhea, Kevin Liang, and Eric Brewer. 2003. Value-Based Web Caching. In *Proceedings of WWW*.
[22] Justine Sherry, Chang Lan, Raluca Ada Popa, and Sylvia Ratnasamy. 2015. BlindBox: Deep Packet Inspection over Encrypted Traffic. In *Proceedings of SIGCOMM*.
[23] Ashiwan Sivakumar, Shankaranarayanan Puzhavakath Narayanan, Vijay Gopalakrishnan, Seungjoon Lee, Sanjay Rao, and Subhabrata Sen. 2014. PARCEL: Proxy Assisted BRowsing in Cellular Networks for Energy and Latency Reduction. In *Proceedings of CoNEXT*.
[24] Jamshed Vesuna, Colin Scott, Michael Buettner, Michael Piatek, Arvind Krishnamurthy, and Scott Shenker. 2016. Caching Doesn't Improve Mobile Web Performance (Much). In *Proceedings of USENIX ATC*.
[25] W3C. 2017. Resource Hints. https://w3c.github.io/resource-hints/. (May 4, 2017).
[26] Keith Winstein, Anirudh Sivaraman, and Hari Balakrishnan. 2013. Stochastic Forecasts Achieve High Throughput and Low Delay over Cellular Networks. In *Proceedings of NSDI*.

Just Do It: Fast and Easy Mobilization of *Spot Tasks* in Web-based Enterprise Applications

Uma Parthavi Moravapalle and Raghupathy Sivakumar
Georgia Institute of Technology, Atlanta, GA

ABSTRACT

In this paper, we consider the problem of mobilizing *Spot Tasks*, a special category of workflows within web-based enterprise applications. Spot tasks are simple workflows that can be finished by interacting with only one page of the application. We present *Taskr*, a do-it-yourself mobilization solution that users, regardless of their skills, can rely on to mobilize their spot tasks in a robust fashion. *Taskr* uses remote computing with application refactoring to achieve code-less mobilization and allows for flexible mobile delivery wherein users can execute their spot tasks through Twitter, Email or a native mobile app. We implement a prototype of *Taskr* and show through user studies that it has the potential to reduce task burden significantly.

ACM Reference Format:
Uma Parthavi Moravapalle and Raghupathy Sivakumar Georgia Institute of Technology, Atlanta, GA. 2018. *Just Do It:* Fast and Easy Mobilization of *Spot Tasks* in Web-based Enterprise Applications. In *Proceedings of 19th International Workshop on Mobile Computing Systems and Applications (HotMobile'18)*. ACM, New York, NY, USA, 6 pages. https://doi.org/10.1145/3177102.3177117

1 INTRODUCTION

The adoption of mobile devices, and in particular smartphones, has grown steadily over the last decade. Fifty-one percent of enterprise workers today use mandated apps for their business on their phones [2]. Seventy-seven percent of the workers rely on their personal smartphones to perform their work [4]. One of the key drivers of the adoption and use of smartphones is the self-perceived increase in productivity. Employees self-reported getting an hour of time back by relying on smartphone apps for their work. Intriguingly, employees were relying as much on company-issued mobile apps as they were on *bring your own application* apps [7].

Now consider an enterprise worker, Alice, who is a field salesperson. An average enterprise runs 400+ applications for its business operations. Alice is likely to interact with many of these applications, with examples ranging from Oracle HR, SAP ERP, Microsoft

Sharepoint, and Salesforce CRM. If Alice desires to do some of her Salesforce tasks on her smartphone when she is away from her desk, she currently has to be dependent on either Salesforce releasing a mobile app or her employer building a custom mobile app that taps into the Salesforce APIs. In both cases, not only does the mobile app for Salesforce need to exist, but her specific task also has to make the cut through the de-featurization process necessary for mobilization, and has to be achievable with minimal burden within the design of the mobile app.

Interestingly, in spite of the increasing adoption of mobility in enterprises, studies show that over eighty percent of enterprise mobile apps are abandoned after the first use [1]. In this context, we identify a category of tasks called *Spot Tasks*, and present a strategy wherein Alice can perform the desired mobilization *herself* and *without requiring any support from either the application vendor or the enterprise.*

We define spot tasks as tasks that can be accomplished by the users interacting substantively with the desktop application *only on a single page*. The interaction on that page could be in the form of read, act, and navigate actions. Also, that specific page could be arbitrarily anywhere within the application's navigation tree. While we relax these definitions in subtle ways later in the paper, we also show how even such a constrained definition can support a wide variety of enterprise task profiles. For example, consider a purchase approval task on a typical SAP SRM (supplier relationship management) application. This could require the user to login and authenticate herself, navigate to "My Work", navigate to "Purchase Management", navigate to "Requisition Approvals", see a list of approval requests, check on those requests that need to be approved, click on the "Approve" button, and finally logout of the application. In this example, the first sequence of pages visited is for navigational purposes while the purchase request review and approval are done on a single page. Thus, we categorize such a task as a spot task.

Spot tasks are limited in capabilities, but have several critical advantages that make them an interesting candidate for a mobilization strategy. We present a mobilization solution called *Taskr* to mobilize spot tasks that exploits these advantages and delivers the following properties: (i) Configuration by doing: *Taskr* allows the user to perform the mobilization herself regardless of the user's technical skills. All *Taskr* requires for the mobilization of a spot task is for the user to be able to *perform the spot task* on the desktop application; (ii) Programmatic APIfication: Once the user configures what needs to be mobilized, *Taskr* programmatically creates the necessary APIs using purely a front-end strategy[1] that requires no access to source code from the application vendor, or even special provisions by the enterprise; (iii) Flexible mobile delivery: Since

---

Corresponding author: Uma Parthavi Moravapalle (parthavi@gatech.edu)

This work was funded in part by National Science Foundation grants IIP-1701115, CNS-1513884, and CNS-1319455, and the Wayne J. Holman Endowed Chair.

HotMobile'18, February 12–13, 2018, Tempe, AZ, USA
© 2018 Association for Computing Machinery.
ACM ISBN 978-1-4503-5630-5/18/02...$15.00
https://doi.org/10.1145/3177102.3177117

---

[1]We elaborate later in the paper, but at a high level this involves relying on a remote-computing based approach to create the APIs.

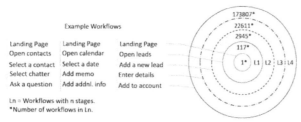

Figure 1: Complexity of the Salesforce desktop application

spot tasks are restricted to a single interaction page, and *Taskr* further imposes limits on the amount of content and actions mobilized on the interaction page, it allows for flexible delivery mechanisms on the smartphone. *Taskr*, specifically, allows the user to consume the mobilized tasks through Twitter (direct messaging), Email, and a Native Mobile App.

We implement *Taskr* on an AWS backend and an Android frontend, and conduct preliminary user experiments to evaluate its performance. The results are promising and show that not only does *Taskr* reduce the actions required to complete tasks (by over 35%) but also that users are more satisfied completing spot tasks with *Taskr* compared to the desktop or the mobile browser (by over 7*x*). The rest of the paper is organized as follows: We define spot tasks in Section 2 and introduce *Taskr*'s design in Section 3. We then evaluate it in Section 4 and discuss related work in Section 5. Finally, we discuss some issues with *Taskr* and conclude in Section 6.

2 MOBILIZATION AND SPOT TASKS

2.1 Mobilization and Defeaturization

Enterprise desktop applications are complex and allow a wide variety of business functions. These applications support a large number of workflows - wherein each workflow represents a goal-oriented series of actions taken by the user[2]. Considering the constraints of the smartphone, it is not feasible for a mobile app to support all the desktop workflows. Therefore, the desktop application has to be *defeaturized* before it can be mobilized. For example, The Salesforce CRM web application has over a 180K navigational workflows at a depth of 4 levels (see Figure 1). On the other hand, in Salesforce1 mobile app (the mobile version of Salesforce CRM), there are only 48 navigational workflows at the first level (as opposed to 117 in the desktop version).

Enterprises typically defeaturize at the following granularities: (i) *The entire web application along with all the features are retained in the mobile app.* Considering the desktop application as a large collection of pages, the structure of the pages within the application is largely maintained. This granularity is chosen when all the features within the application are heavily used; (ii) *A subset of features from the original application, carefully chosen either by the enterprise or the vendor, are mobilized.* The features to be mobilized are chosen based on how heavily they are used and the requirements of the user's job functions. With this strategy, the structure of the pages among the application is largely maintained, while reducing the number of features on any given page; (iii) *A mobile-first approach*

---

[2]For example, Salesforce has about 180K navigational workflows with just 4 navigational steps

that uses APIs provided by the application to build the mobile app ground up. This approach can only mobilize those features that have been exposed as APIs; (iv) *A sequence of features that constitute different steps of a single workflow are mobilized.* In this case, once the user starts the workflow on the mobile device, only the features relating to this workflow are presented, thereby decreasing the effort of finding a feature.

2.2 Spot Tasks

In this paper, we identify another potential defeaturization granularity - *Spot Tasks*. A spot task is a simple linear workflow within an enterprise application where-in all the user interactions are only performed on one page of the application. However, this page can be buried deep within the complex application and the navigational effort required to reach that particular page may be high.

UI elements within an application page can be classified as: (i) READ: elements that carry content that is only consumed by the user (e.g., text content of an article); (ii) ACT: elements through which the user writes some parameters in the web application (e.g., text boxes to enter values, dropdown lists, etc.); and (iii) NAV: elements that progress the workflow to the next stage (e.g., links, submit buttons, etc.); For a spot task, each stage of the workflow, except the last stage, has only one NAV element and the final stage of the workflow can have READ/ACT/NAV elements. In other words, if the presence of READ, ACT, and NAV elements in a stage is denoted as R, A, and N, respectively, and the end of a stage is denoted as X, the spot task can be described using a regular expression as follows:

$$ST = [NX] * R?A?N?X$$

Note that even such a constraining definition of spot tasks still covers a substantial number of workflows within enterprise applications. We identify 45 spot tasks within 9 enterprise applications in Section 4. For example, checking the revenue on Salesforce, adding a vendor on Quickbooks, and viewing the available vacation days on Oracle Peoplesoft are all spot tasks (assuming the user is logged in).

Spot task variations: In this paper, we further expand the definition of spot tasks to also account for workflows with fixed (non-variable) inputs along all the stages except the last stage. The non-variable inputs allow for the hard coding of the ACT actions needed to reach the final screen where the user actions are performed. If the user is required to enter a username and password before executing a workflow, then all of the previous examples are still spot tasks under this definition (username and password are fixed values)[3].

2.3 Mobilizing Spot Tasks

The granularities at which mobilization has traditionally been performed necessitate the enterprises to invest significant resources and employ developers with specialized skill sets. Further, the resultant mobile apps are constructed in a one-size-fits-all fashion and are unlikely to address the needs of the entire user base within an enterprise. Thus, for many users, there will exist workflows that the resultant mobile app (i) will not support at all; or (ii) have a considerably increased task burden to perform.

---

[3]We provide more examples of spot tasks in Section 4

However, if there exists a mobilization solution that the users themselves rely on to create an app that is custom built for their workflows, these issues could indeed be addressed. The challenge though is how to enable such configuration of the mobile app regardless of the skills possessed by the user, and also, how the resultant mobile app can be made user-friendly. In this paper, the only skill that we assume from the user is the ability to *perform the workflows (to be mobilized) on the desktop*. Since the user performs the workflows on the desktop anyway, this is a reliable assumption.

The simplicity of the spot tasks allows for the design of such a mobilization solution to be possible. Since the spot tasks have a limited number of UI elements from within only one screen of the application, easy configuration of the apps (and the layouts) can be achieved, without requiring the user to have coding and design skills. Also, the linear non-parametric nature of spot tasks allows for the creation of robust mobile apps. Since the value of ACT and NAV elements are fixed for spot tasks, the sequence of stages in the workflow will always be the same. This eliminates the need for the user to anticipate any branches that may depend on the value of ACT/NAV elements and configure them. Furthermore, even if these tasks are already mobilized under other granularities, the users still might have to experience navigational burden just to perform these simple tasks.

Scope and Goals: The scope of our work is limited to the mobilization of spot tasks within enterprise web applications. We primarily consider HTML/JS compatible web applications due to their dominance [5]. The solution needs to support all major smartphone OSs (Android, iOS, Microsoft). The solution also needs to be usable by all users regardless of their skills.

3 *TASKR*: A DO-IT-YOURSELF APPROACH TO SPOT TASK MOBILIZATION

In this section, we present *Taskr*, a framework that allows for mobilization of spot tasks within enterprise applications by all users. The *Taskr* infrastructure consists of three components - *Taskr-recorder*, *Taskr-server* and *Taskr-client* (Figure 1). The *Taskr-server* is hosted on a cloud platform. When the enterprise wants to allow DIY mobilization for a particular application, it hosts the corresponding application client (for web applications, this would mean a browser pointing to the appropriate URL) on the infrastructure. When a user wants to mobilize her workflows, she uses the *Taskr-recorder* configuration tool to configure the mobile app simply by *performing the workflow that needs to be mobilized*. The infrastructure generates a *Taskr-client* mobile app (.ipa, .apk, and URL) for the user to download and install onto her smartphone. When the user launches the *Taskr-client* app, a computing slice is set-up on the fly to service that specific user session. The slice automatically loads the corresponding desktop application and user configuration. The infrastructure delivers the mobile view as configured to the smartphone. The user interacts with the *Taskr-client* app, and the actions are shipped to the cloud infrastructure where they are performed on the desktop client. In addition to the mobile app, the user can also start the spot tasks by sending a command to the *Taskr* over Email, Twitter, SMS, Slack, etc. The server replies to the user with any configured READ elements and asks the user to send the values of the configured

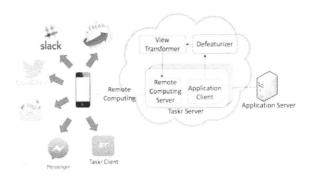

Figure 2: *Taskr* architecture

ACT elements. The user can then reply to this message with the ACT values. We now delve into the key design elements of *Taskr*.

3.1 Key Design Elements

Remote Computing with Refactoring: *Taskr* uses remote computing [8, 17] to mobilize applications while requiring no development and minimal deployment effort from the enterprise or the end-user. To mobilize any given application, enterprises can host a remote computing server and the application client on a Virtual Machine in the cloud. The application client's view is then streamed to the remote computing client on the user's smartphone. The user interacts with the application locally on her smartphone. It is indeed an interesting candidate to solve the mobilization problem. However, the key limitation of remote computing is that the entire application is streamed to the smartphone as-is.

Taskr optimizes the remote view for the client device through *Application Refactoring*, wherein the desktop application UI is dynamically transformed into an appropriate UI for the smartphone. Refactoring restructures the view for the target platform without changing the underlying application behavior via two steps - (i) reducing the number of features available (*Defeaturization*) and (ii) optimizing the application view (*Transformation*). The benefit of this approach stems from the fact that the UI elements of the desktop application can be selectively chosen and transformed into highly optimized versions for usability on the smartphone.

Do-It-Yourself Configuration: Users of an enterprise application best know what features are required to be present in the mobile app, in order to perform their job functions easily. *Taskr* leverages this fact and allows the users to configure defeaturization and transformation within remote computing themselves. For configuration, the users are only required to perform the workflows on the Desktop application in the presence of a configuration tool - *Taskr-recorder*. This tool observes the user's interactions with the application to know what UI elements are necessary for the completion of the task and defeaturizes the application to include only these elements. The tool also allows the users to fine-tune the configuration through an intuitive user interface.

Flexible Mobile Delivery: The result of the configuration process is a mobile app through which the users can view all their spot tasks and execute them. Note that a key goal of *Taskr* is to reduce the task burden of performing the tasks for all users irrespective of their skill levels. Therefore, *Taskr* does not restrict the users to use the mobile app to execute the tasks. Smartphone users use certain apps extensively throughout their day (e.g., Twitter, SMS, Email, Slack,

Messenger, etc.). *Taskr* leverages the users' familiarity with these modalities and allows them to execute their tasks within them. This saves the user the burden of learning to use the interface of a new mobile app - *Taskr* client. *Taskr* transforms the UI of the desktop application to suit these usage modalities i.e. smartphone native UI for the *Taskr-client* app and text blurbs for the other modalities.

Single Screen Transaction: The ideal candidates for DIY mobilization are the workflows that can be performed easily with the limited screen real estate of a smartphone. The workflows should not only require little user interaction but also be simple enough to be configurable by users of all skill ranges. Therefore, in order to maintain usability while at the same time requiring minimal intervention from the user, *Taskr* restricts the users to configure only a limited number of UI elements within one spot task. In this paper, we set the limit to 140 characters each for the total character count of READ elements and the labels of ACT elements[4].

3.2 Challenges and Design Choices

How is the configuration done? The user configures a spot task by simply performing that particular task in the presence of *Taskr-recorder*. For all the stages except the last stage of the task, the tool automatically tracks the UI elements that are acted upon by the user and records the action parameters - ACT elements, their values and NAV elements. For the last stage, the tool has an interface through which users can select any elements that may have been missed and assign a category to them - READ/ACT/NAV. As the user is selecting the elements, the tool records the number of characters of READ elements and the labels of ACT elements. Once the total number of characters in each category reaches the limit defined in Section 3.1, the user is notified and a further selection of elements is disabled.

How are UI elements identified reliably? If the actions performed by the user on the refactored view have to be correctly executed by the server, the UI elements involved in a workflow need to be reliably identified among all the other elements in that application, even when the application changes. Identification of UI element involves extracting a set of parameters (say, the *fingerprint*) unique to that element in the entire application view. Graphical coordinates cannot be used as a fingerprint, as minor changes on the page can easily break the element's fingerprint. Given that web applications are structured as a tree, called the document object model (DOM), the position of the element from an anchor element (nearest ancestor with an HTML attribute *id*) in the DOM can be considered as a fingerprint. However, it is susceptible to failure due to changes along the path from the anchor to the element. Therefore *Taskr*, instead of statically extracting an element's fingerprint, observes an element's features across multiple instances of the application over a period of time to determine what features remain stable and uses only these features as a fingerprint. Specifically, the features tracked by *Taskr* are: (i) Tag name, (ii) All HTML tag attributes, (iii) Path from the root node in the DOM , (iv) Path from the nearest ancestor on the DOM with an *id*, (v) Path from the nearest ancestor on the DOM with more than one children, (vi) Graphical coordinates with respect to the top left corner of the

page, (vii) Graphical coordinates from the nearest ancestor with an *id*, and (viii) Graphical coordinates from the nearest ancestor with more than one children. A subset of features that are the most stable (the same in at least 80% of all instances) is then used as the fingerprint.

How is data extraction done? Once the UI elements are identified, extracting the (i) nature of the UI element (e.g., textbox/button etc.) and any (ii) associated context (e.g., label) is crucial so that the user can understand and execute its function on the mobile device as intended. This information cannot always be inferred from the HTML source of the element. This problem is further aggravated by the presence of complex third-party UI frameworks. For example, a button drop-down menu from Bootstrap with source < a class='btn' > would be incorrectly classified as a link (from the 'a' tag). Therefore, *Taskr* uses a hybrid approach that not only obtains data from the source but also from the other surrounding tags, and by taking the user's help where such extraction is not possible. Using tag and attribute definitions from the HTML5 standard and from the complex UI frameworks, a list of rules for extraction is first created manually. For e.g., to get a label for an <input> element, the text within that element's tags is processed. When no text is found, the page source is be parsed to see if a 'label' tag for that input is present. At the configuration step, the extracted nature and context are displayed to the user. Whenever extraction using rules fails, the user is prompted to specify the nature and the context. Note that this is tractable as it only needs to be done once for every new UI element encountered.

Translation to a mobile view: Every UI element in the workflow selected by the user needs to be translated into the desired usage modality on the smartphone - native UI element for the smartphone app client and text for email, twitter, SMS, slack, etc. *Taskr* uses a translation table that maps each UI element (including the ones from the third-party UI frameworks) to a corresponding native UI element (for the app) and also a text version for the other modalities. The result of the translation is presented to the user during configuration. When the translation table does not contain a mapping for the selected UI element or if the result of the translation is not satisfactory, the user can manually specify the translation by selecting a type (e.g., text box, radio button, etc.) and a corresponding label. For every new element encountered this step needs to be done only once[5].

Mobile delivery and presentation: For every workflow stage, the translated versions of these elements have to be displayed on the mobile screen in a manner that enables the user to finish the task with minimal effort. Taking into account the simplicity of spot tasks and the inherent limits on the number of characters allowed in the final stage of the task, *Taskr* follows a fixed display template for every spot task. For the mobile app modality, *Taskr* divides the screen into three panes, and populates the READ elements in the first pane, the translated versions of the ACT elements in the second pane and two buttons 'SUBMIT' and 'CANCEL' in the final pane. The elements are displayed in a list within the respective panes and in the order of their selection during the configuration phase to preserve the logical sequence of actions in the workflow. For the

---

[4]This restriction is arbitrary and is imposed to allow all transactions to mostly fit within a few text messages

[5]Note that, the current version of the translation table covers most of the input elements from HTML5 standard.

Application	Workflows	Application	Workflows
AWS	1. Create a security group 2. View service status 3.View instance status 4. View account balance 5. Create new volume	Peoplesoft	1. View the latest salary amount 2. Add direct deposit account 3. View year to date earnings 4. Get balance vacation hours 5. Update contact information
Sharepoint	1. Get the next task deadline 2. Create a task and assign it 3. Edit a wiki page 4. Sync the website 5. Share a project	Salesforce	1. Get Quarterly net performance 2. Create a poll for followers 3. Get information on the top deal 4. Create a new campaign 5. Create an open lead

Figure 3: List of Worflows configured on enterprise applications

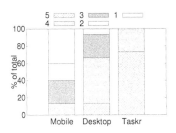

Figure 4: Likert responses from volunteers

other usage modalities, a text blurb is constructed with the text version of the READ elements in the final stage followed by the labels of the ACT elements (one in each line) and sent to the user. To execute the workflow, the user can reply to this blurb with values for the ACT elements (one in each line and in the same order).

4 EVALUATION

Prototype: We implement a proof of concept prototype of *Taskr* with which users can easily mobilize spot tasks and execute them through three different usage modalities - app, Twitter and Email (see Figure 4). Within this prototype, the *Taskr-recorder* is a Javascript browser extension for Google Chrome. The *Taskr-server* is written in python and deployed in the Amazon EC2 cloud. When the user selects a spot task, it instantiates a headless Chrome browser and attaches a Selenium automation driver to it. Upon receiving any user actions performed on the *Taskr-client*, it executes them on the browser through selenium. For the Twitter usage modality, the server uses Twitter Direct Messaging APIs to filter out appropriate commands from its Twitter stream and to send responses to the user. For the Email usage modality, the server monitors its email mailbox for any emails with commands using Python's imaplib. Any response to be sent to the user is handled by smtplib. Finally, the *Taskr-client* is implemented as an app for Android OS.

User Study: We mobilize spot tasks in 9 enterprise applications using *Taskr* in the following categories - Learning Management System (Sakai [9]), Human Resources Management (Oracle Peoplesoft), Collaboration (Sharepoint), Customer Relationship Management (Salesforce CRM), Accounting (Quickbooks [6]), Cloud Management (Amazon Web Services), Billing portal (A utility company website - name anonymized), Electronic Health Record (AtlasMD) and Fleet Management (Element Fleet). We configure five workflows from each of these applications representing typical daily usage patterns of employees. For brevity, we only show workflows from four of these applications in Table 3. We then start the *Taskr-client* on a Google Pixel smartphone (Android 7 Nougat) and the *Taskr-server* on an Ubuntu Server hosted on Amazon EC2 cloud instance. We subsequently execute each of the workflows on the *Taskr-client*, Chrome browser on the smartphone, and a Chrome browser on a desktop. Whenever the workflow cannot be performed using the mobile web version of the application, we load the desktop page of the application on the mobile browser to complete the workflow. We observed that, on an average, the workflows on *Taskr-client*

take 40.67% fewer actions compared to the desktop browser and 38.19% fewer actions compared to the mobile browser.

We also evaluate *Taskr* using subjective experiments on 15 volunteers[6]. We selected the following 5 workflows from 3 applications - Sakai (editing a wiki page, changing permissions of a site and adding a participant to a site), Amazon AWS (#4), and Peoplesoft (#2). Each volunteer performed the workflows on three platforms (*Taskr* client, Desktop and Mobile browser) in a random order. The volunteers were then asked to answer 7 questions rating each of the platforms. Each question had 5 Likert-type [13] responses from which the user could choose one. Each option has a score corresponding to it (from 1:worst to 5:best). Figure 4 shows the % of total responses across the scores from the users in a stacked graph for one of the questions - *How satisfied are you with the application?* The responses to other questions follow similar trends. The users consistently rated *Taskr-client* better than the other two platforms for all the questions. For example, 100% of the users were satisfied (score > 3) for *Taskr*. On the other hand, only 66.67% of users were satisfied with the desktop experience and 13.33% with the mobile experience. The desktop was rated the better in general than the mobile, due to the user's familiarity with the application on the desktop.

5 RELATED WORK

In [3, 19], the content of a website is rearranged or enlarged to improve the readability on a small screen . [15, 16] allow users to access web applications from mobile phones. However, these solutions are designed for static web applications; [18] is a remote computing solution that reduces the task burden by creating macros for repeated tasks. However, this solution does not rely on smartphone native UI, and rather relies on the Desktop UI as-is and does not defaturize. [11, 14] create application mashups that allow users to define a smaller subset of UI elements to be visible from a smartphone. However, complex image recognition is required to identify the user intent automatically. PageTailor [10] introduces reusable customization wherein the users can select the components of a web page to be rendered on the smartphone. However, this is only applicable to read content-centric web pages and not complex enterprise applications that require user interactions. [12] deconstructs PC applications to graphical primitives and reconstructs them on the mobile browser. However, it retains all features of the original

---

[6]The volunteers were mostly university students within 22-30 year age group

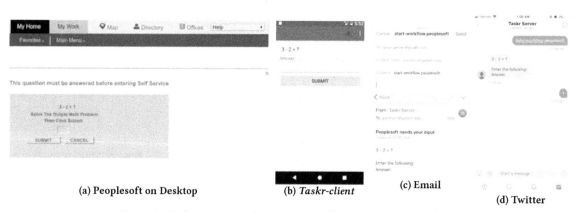

(a) Peoplesoft on Desktop   (b) *Taskr-client*   (c) Email

(d) Twitter

Figure 5: *Taskr* **prototype for a test workflow on Oracle Peoplesoft**

application, thereby reducing the usability when rendered on a small screen.

6 DISCUSSION

Security: Most enterprise applications require the user to log in (either explicitly or through a single sign-on service) before any workflow can be executed. The requirement of log in usually does not restrict the number of workflows that qualify as spot tasks as the username and password can be treated as fixed parameters. The login username and password required are required by *Taskr* to execute workflows on most enterprise applications. The login parameters constitute sensitive information and can be encrypted and stored on the local device using services like keychain API for iOS. When the spot task has to be executed, these parameters can be encrypted and sent to the server using transport security such as SSL. Alternately, this sensitive data can be stored in the cloud isolated within enterprise network and hence be protected by enterprise firewalls. The user can then be restricted to using *Taskr* within the enterprise network. If the application server allows it, a continuous login session can be maintained at the *Taskr-server* using the stored username and password.

Evaluation: *Taskr* requires accurate fingerprinting of UI elements to execute the workflow. While we discuss the fingerprint technique used by *Taskr* in Section 3 and implement it in the prototype, we do not evaluate it for correctness. We plan to investigate this in the future. We implemented *Taskr-client* and server for twitter, email and native app usage modalities. However, we only conduct subjective tests on the native mobile app modality. We plan to implement a few other modalities and extend the testing in the future.

Extraction rules and Translation tables: *Taskr* relies on manually constructed rules for information extraction and fixed translation tables. For the prototype, we constructed these rules for most elements defined by the HTML5 standard. However, many web applications use elements defined by third party UI frameworks. We plan to extend these rules for some popular UI frameworks used by web applications.

Extension to other workflows: *Taskr* helps users mobilize simple workflows that can be described as spot tasks. This restriction limits the number of workflows that can be mobilized. We plan to relax these restrictions to include workflows that can be described

as a sequence of spot tasks, and also other general workflows in the future.

7 CONCLUSION

In this paper, we identify a new granularity of mobilization - spot tasks, and argue that it empowers the users to drive the mobilization efforts themselves. We present *Taskr* a do-it-yourself mobilization infrastructure and implement a prototype through which users can mobilize spot tasks and execute them through a mobile app, Twitter or Email. We then evaluate it with users and show its benefits.

REFERENCES

[1] 2017 trends in enterprise mobility. https://goo.gl/3M2Ruv.
[2] Employees say smartphones boost productivity by 34 percent. https://goo.gl/PmEUys.
[3] Feed circuit. http://feedcircuit.garage.maemo.org/.
[4] Gartner survey shows that mobile device adoption in the workplace is not yet mature. https://www.gartner.com/newsroom/id/3528217.
[5] Google trends on web platforms. https://goo.gl/qqy558.
[6] Intuit quickbooks. https://quickbooks.intuit.com/.
[7] Mobile workforce to drive further enterprise change in 2017. https://goo.gl/uWHqGm.
[8] Remote desktop protocol. http://msdn.microsoft.com/en-us/library/aa383015(VS.85).aspx.
[9] Sakai. https://sakaiproject.org/.
[10] N. Bila, T. Ronda, I. Mohomed, K. N. Truong, and E. de Lara. Pagetailor: Reusable end-user customization for the mobile web. In *Proceedings of the 5th International Conference on Mobile Systems, Applications and Services*, MobiSys '07, New York, NY, USA, 2007.
[11] F. Lamberti and A. Sanna. Extensible guis for remote application control on mobile devices. *IEEE Computer Graphics and Applications*, 28(4):50–57, July 2008.
[12] H. Li, P. Li, S. Guo, X. Liao, and H. Jin. Modeap: Moving desktop application to mobile cloud service. *Mobile Networks and Applications*, 19(4):563–571, 2014.
[13] R. Likert. A technique for the measurement of attitudes. *Archives of Psychology*, 22(140):1–55, 1932.
[14] I. Mohomed. Enabling mobile application mashups with merlion. In *Proceedings of the Eleventh Workshop on Mobile Computing Systems & Applications*, HotMobile '10, New York, NY, USA, 2010.
[15] A. Moshchuk, S. D. Gribble, and H. M. Levy. Flashproxy: Transparently enabling rich web content via remote execution. In *Proceedings of the 6th International Conference on Mobile Systems, Applications, and Services*, pages 81–93, New York, NY, USA, 2008.
[16] J. Nichols and T. Lau. Mobilization by demonstration: Using traces to re-author existing web sites. In *Proceedings of the 13th International Conference on Intelligent User Interfaces*, IUI '08, pages 149–158, New York, NY, USA, 2008. ACM.
[17] T. Richardson and J. Levine. The remote framebuffer protocol. 2011.
[18] C.-L. Tsao, S. Kakumanu, and R. Sivakumar. Smartvnc: An effective remote computing solution for smartphones. In *Proceedings of the 17th Annual International Conference on Mobile Computing and Networking*, pages 13–24, New York, NY, USA, 2011.
[19] D. Zhang. Web content adaptation for mobile handheld devices. *Commun. ACM*, 50(2):75–79, Feb. 2007.

How do Mobile Apps Violate the Behavioral Policy of Advertisement Libraries?

Feng Dong[1], Haoyu Wang[1,2], Li Li[3], Yao Guo[4,5], Guoai Xu[1], Shaodong Zhang[1]

[1] Beijing University of Posts and Telecommunications, Beijing, China
[2] Beijing Key Laboratory of Intelligent Telecommunication Software and Multimedia
[3] Faculty of Information Technology, Monash University
[4] Key Laboratory of High-Confidence Software Technologies (Ministry of Education)
[5] School of Electronics Engineering and Computer Science, Peking University, Beijing, China
{dongfeng,haoyuwang,xga,zhangsd}@bupt.edu.cn,li.li@monash.edu,yaoguo@pku.edu.cn

ABSTRACT

Advertisement libraries are used in almost two-thirds of apps in Google Play. To increase economic revenue, some app developers tend to entice mobile users to unexpectedly click ad views during their interaction with the app, resulting in kinds of ad fraud. Despite some popular ad providers have published behavioral policies to prevent inappropriate behaviors/practices, no previous work has studied whether mobile apps comply with those policies. In this paper, we take Google Admob as the starting point to study policy-violation apps. We first analyze the behavioral policies of Admob and create a taxonomy of policy violations. Then we propose an automated approach to detect policy-violation apps, which takes advantage of two key artifacts: an automated model-based Android GUI testing technique and a set of heuristic rules summarized from the behavior policies of Google Admob. We have applied our approach to 3,631 popular apps that have used the Admob library, and we could achieve a precision of 86% in detecting policy-violation apps. The results further show that roughly 2.5% of apps violate the policies, suggesting that behavioral policy violation is indeed a real issue in the Android advertising ecosystem.

KEYWORDS

Ad library; Admob; behavior policy; Ad fraud; Android

ACM Reference Format:
Feng Dong[1], Haoyu Wang[1,2], Li Li[3], Yao Guo[4,5], Guoai Xu[1], Shaodong Zhang[1] . 2018. How do Mobile Apps Violate the Behavioral Policy of Advertisement Libraries?. In *HotMobile '18: 19th International Workshop on Mobile Computing Systems & Applications, February 12–13, 2018, Tempe , AZ, USA*. ACM, New York, NY, USA, 6 pages. https://doi.org/10.1145/3177102.3177113

1 INTRODUCTION

Mobile apps have seen widespread adoption in recent years, with more than 3.3 million apps available in Google Play [7]. More than 85% of the apps are free [25], and ad libraries (e.g., Admob) are commonly used by app developers to monetize their apps by showing ads to mobile users.

A significant number of studies focused on the topic of ad libraries in various directions. LibRadar [17] and WuKong [23] were proposed to identify third-party libraries used in Android apps. Meng et al. [18] focused on privacy leakage detection of ad libraries. Shekhar et al. [20] proposed to separate the privilege of ad libraries from the host apps to prevent permission escalation. Cho et al.[8] and Nath et al.[10] proposed to detect click fraud of advertisements in Android apps.

Although mobile ad libraries have been extensively studied, no previous work has been proposed to analyze **whether Android apps comply with the usage and behavioral guidelines defined by ad networks**. Some popular ad libraries (e.g., Admob and DoubleClick) have released policies to regulate the behaviors of apps that use them [4, 13], including how the ads should be placed and how they interact with users. Some policies are mandatory and are meant to avoid kinds of ad fraud, which might affect user experiences significantly. Moreover, breaking the policies can also impact the reputation of ad networks and advertisers, as in the end, the displayed ads are from those ad companies.

In this paper, *we propose an exploratory study on how Android apps violate the behavioral policy of ad library*. To the best of our knowledge, this work is the first attempt in our community towards checking whether ad libraries are properly used by Android apps. We choose the Google Admob library [5] as the starting point because it is a quite popular ad network [21] provided by Google, the official maintainer of Android, and it has defined clear guidelines and policies for its users to follow, which eases implementing and checking for instances in which ads violate those guidelines and policies.

Practically, we summarize a taxonomy of policy violations based on the behavior policy provided by Google Admob [4]. Based on this taxonomy, we then propose an automated approach to detect policy-violated apps. We introduce an automated test input generation technique to traverse the user interface (UI) states (i.e., a running page of apps) and construct a UI state transition graph. Each state has been associated with a set of visual views (e.g., buttons), where the metadata such as the position of each view is included. The ad-related transitions are then located based on the UI state graph and are consequently checked against a set of heuristic rules characterized based on the Admob policies.

We have implemented a prototype system to detect policy violations and applied it to 3,631 popular Android apps. The experimental results show that we could achieve a precision of 86% in violation detection, which counts for roughly 2.5% of apps violated Admob's behavior policies, demonstrating that policy violation is indeed a real issue in the Android ecosystem. We have released the dataset and experiment results to the mobile app research community at: *https://github.com/BUPT-privacy-research/ad-policy-violation*.

2 BACKGROUND & RELATED WORK

2.1 The Behavior Policy of Admob

Mobile ads are usually displayed in three common ways: 1) **Banner ad**, which is a rectangular image or text ad that occupies a spot within apps; 2) **Interstitial ad**, which is a square and locates in the center of the screen; 3) **Full Screen ad**, which fills the whole screen. These types of ads are integrated into an app by either specifying it in the layout XML file or embedding it in the source code[1].

Google Admob has released a series of policies (including content policies, behavioral policies, etc.) to guide and regulate the usage of Admob library [4]. Once an app developer fails to comply with these policies, Admob will disable ad serving or disable his/her Admob account, although Admob does not explicitly provide how they perform policy-violation detection. In this paper, *we only focus on behavioral policies*, because other policies are either non-mandatory or hard to detect due to the vague standard. For example, Admob does not permit monetization of dangerous content, while it is hard to define which content is dangerous. As a result, we consider in this work six Admob behavioral policies that are summarized, along with their key behaviors, in Table 1.

2.2 Related Work

Here, we discuss some closely related work relating to general ad library and automated Android UI testing.

Ad libraries. A significant number of studies focused on the topic of ad libraries in various directions such as on discovering ad libraries [14, 17, 22], on detecting privacy leaks within ad libraries [11, 16], on separating the privilege of ad libraries from host apps [20, 24], and on pinpointing click frauds [8, 10]. We believe all the aforementioned approaches can be leveraged to supplement our work towards providing a better characterization of violated ad policies.

Automated Android GUI Testing. Automated app testing has been recurrently adopted to address various challenges [6, 9]. The testing part of our approach is in line with those work but have a different focus. Because automated Android GUI testing is known to be time-consuming, we

have conducted several customizations on our model-based approach to improve the overall efficiency in Section 3.2.

3 POLICY-VIOLATION DETECTION

3.1 Overview

The overall process of our approach is shown in Figure 1. We first use LibRadar [3, 17], an obfuscation-resilient tool to identify apps that use Admob library with simple static analysis and feature comparison. Then we propose an automated test input generation technique to run apps that embed the Admob library on smartphones. We preserve the attribute information of visual views (i.e., controls) and state (i.e., a running page of apps) transition information in the *UI state transition graph*. By leveraging properties such as resource strings, view types preserved in the attribute information, we can identify Admob ad views accurately. Finally, we apply a set of heuristic rules to detect policy violations.

3.2 UI State Transition Graph Generation

Automated Test Input Generation. Monkey [2] is the most popular and lightweight tool to perform Android GUI testing, but the inputs generated by Monkey are *completely random*, which is not effective for us to explore the ad-contained states and generate the UI state transition graph.

In our approach, we generate inputs based on the current UI state to simulate real user behaviors. As Android apps are event-driven, inputs are mostly in the form of events. In our implementation, we simulate both UI events (e.g., touch, click, etc.) and system events (e.g., BOOT_COMPLETED intent). Note that **we generate UI-guided events according to the position and type of UI elements instead of sending random events and clicks like Monkey [2] does**. We take advantage of Accessibility [12] to understand the layout of the UI state, and obtain exhaustive information from each view such as name, size and class name, which could be used to build a view tree that can accurately describe current state. Our automation technique gets the view list from the current state and chooses the event input for the next view based on a systematic exploration strategy.

Exploration Strategy. Previous work suggested that traversing all the UI states of an app takes several hours [15]. By manually labeling 1,963 UI states that generated from 180 apps [1], **we find that 89.3% of the UI states (1,752) do not contain any ad views and more than 90% of ad views are displayed in either the main UI state or exit state**. Thus we take a breadth first traversal exploration strategy to explore the states for more effective results in terms of ad coverage and efficiency. To achieve the balance between time efficiency and coverage, we explore each state with maximal 50 events. The initial experiments on 180 apps suggested that the time efficiency increases by 17 times on average (7 minutes vs 120 minutes per app), while we could cover 90% of the UI states that contain ad views.

Generating UI State Transition Graph. Our automation technique runs apps automatically to generate the UI state

---

[1]https://developers.google.com/admob/android/quick-start

Table 1: Analysis of Google Admob Behavioral Policies.

Policy #	Policy Detail	Key Behaviors
Policy #1	Ads should not be placed very close to or underneath buttons or any other object which users may accidentally click while interacting with your application	Ads are overlapped with or hidden behind other views
Policy #2	Ads should not be placed in a location that covers up or hides any area that users have interest in viewing during typical interaction	Displaying ads during users' interaction with the app
Policy #3	There must be a way to exit a screen without clicking the ad	Ads cannot be closed unless clicked
Policy #4	Ads should not be placed in applications that are running in the background of the device or outside of the app environment	Displaying ads outside the host apps
Policy #5	Ads should not be placed in a way that prevents viewing the app's core content. Example: an interstitial ad triggered every time a user clicks within the app	Poping up ads frequently
Policy #6	Publishers are not permitted to place ads on any non-content-based pages such as thank you, error, log in, or exit screens	Placing ads on start, exit, login, or thank you screens

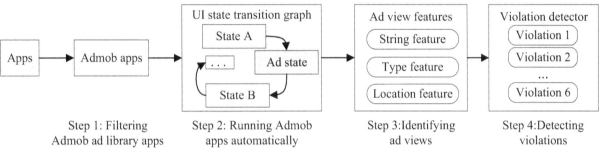

Step 1: Filtering Admob ad library apps   Step 2: Running Admob apps automatically   Step 3: Identifying ad views   Step 4: Detecting violations

Figure 1: Approach Overview.

transition graph, which is basically a directed graph. Each node of the graph represents a state and each edge between two nodes represents the input event that triggers the state transition. Figure 2 shows an example of the UI state transition graph. The app (*com.rcplatform.fontphoto*, version 4.0.7) is launched by event 1 with an intent event "am start", triggering transitions from state A to state B that contains an ad view (with resource_id "ad_container"). State B is a launch screen (i.e., the first screen after starting the app), thus the ad view is placed on the non-content-based page, which violates the Policy #6.

3.3 Identifying Ad Views

To differentiate the Admob ad views from a large number of normal views in a given UI state, we manually labeled many ad views and normal views, and compared them from various aspects (e.g., resource string, position, view type, etc.) to explore features that can distinguish them.

We randomly choose 180 apps from the 3,631 Admob apps and manually label 1,963 UI states generated from them. Overall, we obtain 1,752 ad-free states and 211 ad-contained states. Then we observe various features that could be used to identify ad views. As shown in Table 2, the features could be

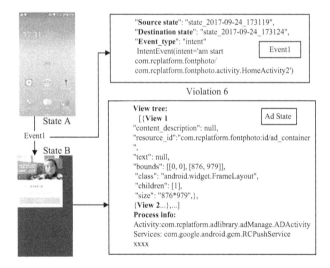

Figure 2: An example of UI state transition graph.

classified into three categories: string features, type features and location features.

For string features, we find that roughly 90% of Admob ad views (189 out of 211) in the labeled ad-contained states have special representative strings in "resource_id" field

Table 2: Features we used to identify Ad views.

Category (attribute)	Value
type (class)	ImageView, WebView
location (size)	620*800[Center],600*760[Center], 600*790[Center]
string (resource_id)	AdWebview, AdLayout, ad_container, fullscreenAdView, FullscreenAd, AdActivity, AppWallActivity, AppBrainActivity, OverlayActivity

of attribute information, such as *"AdWebview"*, *"AdLayout"* and *"ad_container"*, while other views in the 1,963 labeled UI states do not use these strings. Thus we have collected a list of 9 common strings to detect ad views. For example, view 1 in the ad state in Figure 2 has a "resource_id" named "id/ad_container", which indicates that it is an ad view.

For apps that have no explicit string features due to fully obfuscation (22 out of 211), we use a heuristic detection method based on the type and the position of the view. All the 211 Admob ad views in our labeled dataset are implemented by system views "ImageView" and "Webview". Furthermore, they usually have specific size and position features as shown in Table 2. For example, for "Webview" that locates in the center of the screen with the size of 620*800, we will identify it as an ad view.

3.4 Violation Detection

We now provide the practical rules that are, so far, implemented in our work to detect violations.

Violation 1: We consider that an ad view violates Policy #1 if and only if it has overlapped with or hidden behind other views. Note that we detect overlap and hiding by calculating the size, bounds and z-coordinates in the attribute information of the views.

Violation 2: Violation 2 can be found in either interstitial ads or full screen ads. Our violation detector first traverses all the UI states by checking the UI state transition graph to identify the states that contain interactive views (e.g., dialog and buttons). Then it will check the adjacent (previous or next) UI states to analyze whether an ad view exists. The UI state will be regarded as a violation if an ad view is placed on top of interactive views.

Violation 3: In general, the interstitial ads and full screen ads could be closed by either clicking the *close widget* or touching the back button. Since it is non-trivial to automatically identify the *close widget*, in this paper, we only consider the situation where interstitial or full screen ads cannot be closed by touching the back button.

Violation 4: Violation 4 is flagged when an ad view is displayed after its host app exits. Thus, for each state that contains ad views, we check the package name of the host app[2]. Note that the Android system default HOME app's

[2]Note that the host app of an ad view will be *system default HOME app* if the tested app exits.

Table 3: The experiment result of detection.

	Violation (prediction)	Normal (prediction)
Violation	TP(74)	FN(15)
Normal	FP(12)	TN(3530)

name varies according to different system version, the package name is "com.cyanogenmod.trebuchet" in our experiment smartphones.

Violation 5: This violation is flagged if and only if an ad state is triggered more than three times. To avoid repeated visits, which may cause inaccurate counts, we only count it once if a UI state is visited, although multiple times, via the same path.

Violation 6: This violation is flagged if and only if interstitial or full-screen ads are placed on the app launching, exiting and log in pages. The app launching and exiting states could be identified when we start or close the app. The log in state can be heuristically identified based on the view information. For example, if a state contains two *editviews* and has string features such as "username" and "password", we will regard it as a log in state.

4 EVALUATION

We study the prevalence of policy violation on a large scale of apps that embed the Admob library. Apps are running on a Nexus 5 smartphone instead of emulators, because previous work [19] suggested that some apps refuse to display ads when it detects the app is running in an emulator. Note that our automation GUI testing tool is running on a laptop, and it fetches app information from the device and sends input events to the device through Android Debug Bridge (ADB). Experiment results are available on GitHub [1].

4.1 Data Collection

We collected 5,981 popular Android apps from Google Play in July 2017. Take advantage of LibRadar [3], we could identify 3,631 apps (60.71% of the collected apps) that embed the Admob library. We get 39,702 states from these apps, among which 3,872 states contain ad views. Through a manual analysis, we found that the accuracy of ad view identifier reached 95%, which means that most of the Admob ad views in our dataset are identified correctly.

4.2 Experiment Results

Overall Result. First of all, to label the ground truth data, two experienced master students in our group check the graphs manually for five days. As a result, we label 89 policy-violation apps, which covers about 2.5% of the Admob apps in our dataset. We then use these apps to evaluate our automated violation detector, the detection results are shown in Table 3. Our violation detector identifies 86 policy-violation apps. Among them, 12 apps are false positives. Besides, 15 apps are false negatives. Thus the corresponding precision and recall of our detector are 86.05% and 83.15%, respectively.

Table 4: The distribution of violation apps.

Violation	#1	#2	#3	#4	#5	#6	Total
Number of apps	5	6	0	2	18	87	89

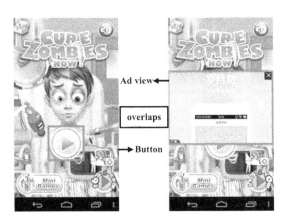

Figure 3: An example of Violation #1.

(1) Violation 2: Ad view pops up above the instruction dialog

(2) Violation 4: Ad view is placed in the home screen

Figure 4: Examples of Violation #2 and Violation #4.

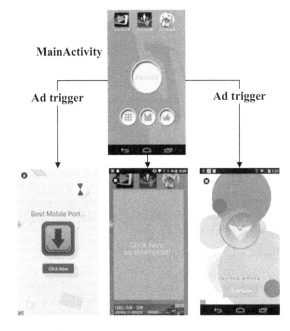

Figure 5: An example of Violation #5.

False Negatives. We inspected the 15 instances and found three reasons that could lead to false negatives. (1) **Lazy-loading of the ad views**. In some cases, it has a delay time to display the ad views, leading to the result that we cannot record it in the states. For example, the ad views in app *br.com.gtlsistemas.crosswords* (version 1.6.0) has a 5 seconds delay to be displayed before our automation technique records the state. (2) **Fully obfuscation**. We find some apps are fully obfuscated, making it hard to extract representative string features to identify ad views. For example, we extract no useful features to identify ad views in app *bubbleshooter.blaze.pop* (version 1.0.1). (3) **Some ad views are not displayed when the app is used for the first time**. For example, ad views in app *com.tp.android.waxspa* (version 1.0.1) appear only after the app is started at the second time.

False Positives. Our violation detector caused false positives because some normal views had the same size and location features as ad views, which could mislead our detector. We will discuss the limitations in the Section 5.1.

Violation Distribution. The distribution of the 89 policy-violation apps is shown in Table 4. Note that some apps have violated more than one policy. For example, app *com.spiderapps. redhotfruits* (version 1.2) violates type 4, type 5 and type 6. More than 97% of the policy-violation apps break Policy #6, that is to say, these apps pop up ads upon launching or before potentially leaving the app. One possible reason is that placing ads on these pages could potentially increase the impression (i.e., the number of ads displayed) and clicks. Note that we do not identify apps that violate Policy #3. One possible reason is that Violation #3 could greatly decrease user experience, which will lead to the uninstallation of the app. Thus this type of violation is uncommon.

Case Study. Fig. 3 shows an example of Violation #1. The app (*com.tp.android.curezombie2nd*, version 1.0.0) has more than 1 million downloads in Google Play. The *game button* is overlapped with the ad view, which could cause accidentally click. Fig. 4 (1) shows an example of Violation #2 (*com.heaven.thermo*, version 1.3). The ad view pops up above the instruction dialog, causing undesirable click on the ad instead of the *OK button*. Fig. 4 (2) shows an example of Violation #4 (*com.HomeCleaningGames*, version 5.0). The ad view is placed on the home screen after exiting the host app. The example of Violation #5 (*com.sink.apps.girl.voice.changer*, version 1.0.4) is shown in Fig. 5. The ad view triggers every time after the main activity receives an event input. The app has 1,000,000 - 5,000,000 downloads. The example of Violation #6 is shown in Fig. 2. The policy-violation apps with high downloads may have already produced a huge negative impact on a lot of mobile users.

5 DISCUSSION

5.1 Method Limitations

Ad Coverage. To improve the time efficiency, we use an optimized UI-guided automation technique with the BFS exploration strategy, which is able to traverse more than 90% of the ad-contained states. However, it is quite possible that we cannot traverse all the states that contain ad views, e.g., it has a delay time to display the ad views in some cases as discussed in Section 4.2. Note that many apps abuse the notification bar to display ads, we did not study this kind of ads in this paper.

Ad View Identification. We use a heuristic approach to detect ad views. However, our experiment results show that some ad views have no obvious features due to code obfuscation, which could cause false positives. To mitigate this, one possible solution is to apply advanced program analysis (e.g., mapping ad views to the decompiled code) or machine learning techniques to build a more accurate ad view identifier.

5.2 Implications

Our experiment results show that behavioral policy violation is indeed a real issue in the Android ecosystem. Profit-driven app developers may break the behavioral policies of ad networks in order to increase economic revenue. However, *inappropriate usage of ad libraries may impact the success of mobile apps as it gives a bad impression to app users.* Furthermore, app markets and ad networks should take efforts to identify/prevent policy violation apps. Ad networks should also consider how to prevent/check certain policy violations when designing ad libraries, e.g., requiring app developers to implement a *close function* for each ad view in the ad libraries to prevent Violation #3.

6 CONCLUSIONS

In this paper, we propose an exploratory study of ad behavioral policy violation in Android apps. We first design a set of violation rules based on the characteristics observed from the Admob behavioral policies. Then, we propose an automated approach (via automated GUI testing) to detect ad behavior policy violations. By applying our approach to 3,632 apps that have embedded with Admob library, our approach achieves a precision of 86.05% in detecting policy violations. The experiment results further show that 2.5% of apps have violated the Admob policies, suggesting that behavior policy violation is a real problem in Android ecosystem and hence is necessary to be highlighted and subsequently avoided.

ACKNOWLEDGMENT

This work is supported by the National Natural Science Foundation of China (No.61702045, No.61401038 and No.61772042), the 2016 Frontier and Key Technology Innovation Project of Guangdong Province Science and Technology Department (No.2016B010110002), the National Key Research and Development Program (No.2017YFB0801901), and the BUPT Youth Research and Innovation Program (No.2017RC40). *Haoyu Wang* is the corresponding author. We would like to thank our shepherd Dr. *Narseo Vallina-Rodriguez* and the anonymous reviewers for their helpful comments.

REFERENCES

[1] 2017. admob-behavioral-policy-violation. (2017). Retrieved October 16, 2017 from https://github.com/admob-behavioral-policy-violation/violation-detector.git
[2] 2017. MonkeyRunner. (2017). https://developer.android.com/studio/test/monkeyrunner/index.html
[3] 2018. LibRadar. (2018). Retrieved January 9, 2018 from https://github.com/pkumza/LibRadar
[4] Google Admob. 2017. AdMob & AdSense policies. (2017). Retrieved October 17, 2017 from https://support.google.com/admob/answer/6128543?hl=en&ref_topic=2745287
[5] Google Admob. 2017. AdMob by Google. (2017). Retrieved October 21, 2017 from http://www.google.cn/admob/
[6] D. Amalfitano, A. R. Fasolino, P. Tramontana, B. D. Ta, and A. M. Memon. 2015. MobiGUITAR: Automated Model-Based Testing of Mobile Apps. *IEEE Software* 32, 5 (2015), 53–59.
[7] AppBrain. 2017. Number of Android applications. (2017). https://www.appbrain.com/stats/number-of-android-apps
[8] Geumhwan Cho, Junsung Cho, Youngbae Song, and Hyoungshick Kim. 2015. An empirical study of click fraud in mobile advertising networks. In *ARES*. IEEE, 382–388.
[9] Shauvik Roy Choudhary, Alessandra Gorla, and Alessandro Orso. 2015. Automated Test Input Generation for Android: Are We There Yet? (E). In *ASE*. 429–440.
[10] Jonathan Crussell, Ryan Stevens, and Hao Chen. 2014. Madfraud: Investigating ad fraud in android applications. In *MobiSys*. ACM, 123–134.
[11] Soteris Demetriou, Whitney Merrill, Wei Yang, Aston Zhang, and Carl A Gunter. 2016. Free for All! Assessing User Data Exposure to Advertising Libraries on Android.. In *NDSS*.
[12] Android Developers. 2018. Accessibility Overview. (2018). Retrieved January 9, 2018 from https://developer.android.com/guide/topics/ui/accessibility/index.html
[13] DoubleClick. 2017. DoubleClick program policies. (2017). Retrieved October 21, 2017 from https://support.google.com/adxseller/topic/7316904?hl=en&ref_topic=6321576
[14] Li Li, Tegawendé F Bissyandé, Jacques Klein, and Yves Le Traon. 2016. An Investigation into the Use of Common Libraries in Android Apps. In *SANER 2016*. 403–414.
[15] Bin Liu, Suman Nath, Ramesh Govindan, and Jie Liu. 2014. DECAF: Detecting and Characterizing Ad Fraud in Mobile Apps.. In *NSDI*. 57–70.
[16] Minxing Liu, Haoyu Wang, Yao Guo, and Jason Hong. 2016. Identifying and Analyzing the Privacy of Apps for Kids. In *HotMobile '16*. 105–110.
[17] Ziang Ma, Haoyu Wang, Yao Guo, and Xiangqun Chen. 2016. Libradar: Fast and accurate detection of third-party libraries in android apps. In *ICSE*. ACM, 653–656.
[18] Wei Meng, Ren Ding, Simon P Chung, Steven Han, and Wenke Lee. 2016. The Price of Free: Privacy Leakage in Personalized Mobile In-Apps Ads.. In *NDSS*.
[19] Thanasis Petsas, Giannis Voyatzis, Elias Athanasopoulos, Michalis Polychronakis, and Sotiris Ioannidis. 2014. Rage Against the Virtual Machine: Hindering Dynamic Analysis of Android Malware. In *EuroSec '14*.
[20] Shashi Shekhar, Michael Dietz, and Dan S Wallach. 2012. AdSplit: Separating Smartphone Advertising from Applications.. In *USENIX Security Symposium*, Vol. 2012.
[21] Nicolas Viennot, Edward Garcia, and Jason Nieh. 2014. A measurement study of google play. In *IMC*. 221–233.
[22] Haoyu Wang and Yao Guo. 2017. Understanding Third-party Libraries in Mobile App Analysis. In *ICSE 2017*. 515–516.
[23] Haoyu Wang, Yao Guo, Ziang Ma, and Xiangqun Chen. 2015. WuKong: a scalable and accurate two-phase approach to Android app clone detection. In *ISSTA*. 71–82.
[24] Haoyu Wang, Yuanchun Li, Yao Guo, Yuvraj Agarwal, and Jason I. Hong. 2017. Understanding the Purpose of Permission Use in Mobile Apps. *ACM Trans. Inf. Syst.* 35, 4, Article 43 (July 2017), 43:1–43:40 pages.
[25] Haoyu Wang, Zhe Liu, Yao Guo, Xiangqun Chen, Miao Zhang, Guoai Xu, and Jason Hong. 2017. An Explorative Study of the Mobile App Ecosystem from App Developers' Perspective. In *WWW 2017*. 163–172.

Characterizing the Reconfiguration Latency of Image Sensor Resolution on Android Devices

Jinhan Hu, Jianan Yang, Vraj Delhivala, Robert LiKamWa

Arizona State University

Tempe, Arizona

jinhanhu@asu.edu,jyang168@asu.edu,vdelhiva@asu.edu,likamwa@asu.edu

ABSTRACT

Advances in vision processing have ignited a proliferation of mobile vision applications, including augmented reality. However, limited by the inability to rapidly reconfigure sensor operation for performance-efficiency tradeoffs, high power consumption causes vision applications to drain the device's battery. To explore the potential impact of enabling rapid reconfiguration, we use a case study around marker-based pose estimation to understand the relationship between image frame resolution, task accuracy, and energy efficiency. Our case study motivates that to balance energy efficiency and task accuracy, the application needs to dynamically and frequently reconfigure sensor resolution.

To explore the latency bottlenecks to sensor resolution reconfiguration, we define and profile the end-to-end reconfiguration latency and frame-to-frame latency of changing capture resolution on a Google LG Nexus 5X device. We identify three major sources of sensor resolution reconfiguration latency in current Android systems: (i) sequential configuration patterns, (ii) expensive system calls, and (iii) imaging pipeline delay. Based on our intuitions, we propose a redesign of the Android camera system to mitigate the sources of latency. Enabling smooth transitions between sensor configurations will unlock new classes of adaptive-resolution vision applications.

KEYWORDS

Image sensor; Camera System; Reconfiguration; Mobile devices; Operating system optimization

ACM Reference format:

Jinhan Hu, Jianan Yang, Vraj Delhivala, Robert LiKamWa. 2018. Characterizing the Reconfiguration Latency of Image Sensor Resolution on Android Devices. In *Proceedings of 19th International Workshop on Mobile Computing Systems and Applications, Tempe , AZ, USA, February 12–13, 2018 (HotMobile '18),* 6 pages.

https://doi.org/10.1145/3177102.3177109

1 INTRODUCTION

The accuracy and performance of vision processing on mobile devices promises a proliferation of vision-powered possibilities. For

HotMobile '18, February 12–13, 2018, Tempe , AZ, USA

© 2018 Association for Computing Machinery.

ACM ISBN 978-1-4503-5630-5/18/02...$15.00

https://doi.org/10.1145/3177102.3177109

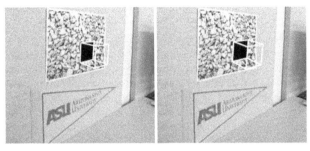

(a) At 1860x2480 resolution, estimated pose has L2-norm translation error 0.87 cm, rotation error 0.82°.

(b) At 720x960 resolution, estimated pose has L2-norm translation error 1.15 cm, rotation error 8.51°.

Figure 1: Low resolution frames cause slight errors in camera pose estimation, creating visible gaps in geometry.

example, real-time face recognition can identify faces to track interpersonal interactions [2], object recognition can observe road signs for navigation [4], and augmented reality (AR) can integrate virtual objects with the physical world for immersive user experiences. Combined with a wide adoption of strong computational and sensing hardware on mobile devices, the trend of algorithmic improvements for computer vision has led companies to issue broad development support through computer vision frameworks, e.g., Google Mobile Vision, OpenCV and AR frameworks, e.g., Apple ARKit, Google ARCore, PTC Vuforia.

However, the energy efficiency of vision applications is severely limited by the inability to rapidly configure sensor operation. Previous research has focused on improving the energy-efficiency of processing image data, such as bypassing traditional image signal processing stages [3], pushing neural network processing into the analog domain of the image sensor [11], and offloading sensor processing to the cloud [15]. However, it is well understood that the power consumption of *capturing* sensor data dominates system power consumption (the SONY IMX377 image sensor draws over 39% of Nexus 5X system power consumption [5]) and can vary significantly with spatiotemporal resolution [12].

Indeed, enabling an ability to tune a sensor's spatial resolution to downsample a field-of-view or focus on regions-of-interest would allow a system to balance energy efficiency and image fidelity for visual tasks [11]. For example, an application could briefly capture high resolution image frames to locate distant objects with high precision, while capturing low-resolution frames to display nearby information to the user with high energy efficiency. Unfortunately, the act of reconfiguring sensor operation for different resolutions is accompanied by long latency, dramatically dropping application performance as the operating system and sensor hardware coordinate to reconfigure sensor operation.

We define two types of sensor reconfiguration latency that detract from vision application performance in distinct ways. **End-to-end reconfiguration latency** is the time between an application's request to change configuration and the time the application receives a full frame of the new configuration. An increase in end-to-end latency creates an inflexibility to shift between modes of operation. An average end-to-end latency of 400 ms will prevent applications from smoothly transitioning the balance of energy efficiency and image fidelity. However, after the application issues a configuration request, frames of the prior configuration will continue to arrive at the application. Thus, we use **frame-to-frame latency** to indicate the interval between two frames being provided to the application (the latter frame being newly configured). An increase in frame-to-frame latency creates a perception that the system is "dropping frames". Compared to the typical frame-to-frame latency of 33 ms at 30 frames per second (FPS), an average frame-to-frame latency of 267 ms is equivalent to the system dropping 8 camera frames.

In this paper, we explore sources of sensor resolution reconfiguration latency in the Android system, comprehensively profiling a Google LG Nexus 5X. Our measurements indicate an average end-to-end reconfiguration latency of 400 ms and an average frame-to-frame latency of 267 ms. We identify OS bottlenecks in the software stack and sensor pipeline bottlenecks in the hardware system architecture. We observe three major sources of frame-to-frame latency in the Android system: (i) sequential configuration patterns, (ii) expensive system calls, and (iii) imaging pipeline delay.

Built on our understanding, we propose mechanisms to redesign mobile camera systems. Invoking principles of reusing allocated resources, parallelizing independent operations, and timely control of channel management, these mechanisms aim to provide responsive reconfigurability through minimizing end-to-end reconfiguration latency and high-quality user experience during reconfiguration by minimizing frame-to-frame latency.

Thus, in this paper, we contribute the following:
- We use an augmented reality case study to discuss the need for dynamic resolution reconfiguration.
- We profile sources of sensor reconfiguration latency to identify software and hardware bottlenecks.
- We propose mechanisms to redesign low-level operating systems to minimize sensor reconfiguration latency.

2 BACKGROUND

Reconfiguration in the operating system Camera resolution reconfiguration involves all layers of the Android system stack, including the application, the camera framework, the camera Hardware Abstraction Layer (HAL), and the kernel camera device drivers.

The procedure is as follows:

(1) The application sends a resolution request and creates a new camera capture session.
(2) The framework waits for the prior session to stop and calls the HAL to configure streams.

(3) The HAL deletes previous channels and streams.
(4) The framework issues a capture request to the HAL.
(5) The HAL initializes channels and streams, configuring sensor hardware with the capture settings of the output buffer.
(6) The HAL sends captured frames through pipeline stages for image signal processing. The HAL sends fully-processed frames to the framework.
(7) The framework delivers the frame to the application surface and calls a developer-defined callback function.

Reconfiguration in sensor hardware To better understand the reconfiguration from a sensor hardware perspective, we study datasheets provided by image sensor manufacturers [13][14]. In all cases, we find that at the sensor hardware level, the end-to-end hardware reconfiguration latency is one to two frame times after the register reconfiguration request is issued. For a frame time of 33 ms, corresponding to a frame rate of 30 FPS, this can be up to 66 ms. The sensor uses the following sequence of operations to reconfigure:

(1) When the sensor receives a request, the sensor waits for the current frame to capture. Depending on when the request arrives, this can be immediate, or take up to one frame time.
(2) While frame A is being read out, the sensor captures a new frame with the new configuration. This takes one frame time.
(3) The sensor reads out frame B while the next frame is being captured. This takes one frame time to complete.

3 CASE STUDY: ADAPTIVE RESOLUTION FOR POSE ESTIMATION

To examine the potential effectiveness of resolution reconfiguration, we present a case study around marker-based pose estimation to understand the relationship between frame resolution, task accuracy, and energy efficiency. Marker-based pose estimation visually locates a physical marker to geometrically register a physical environment with a virtual camera, allowing insertion of virtual objects alongside real environments for AR. User experience is sensitive to the precision of pose estimation; as shown in Fig. 1b, slight errors cause visible gaps in geometry, breaking user immersion. When streaming frames, errors become especially obvious, as the irregular variations cause a feeling of jitter.

Fortunately, by operating on frames with sufficiently high resolution, pose estimation can minimize errors. Unfortunately, capturing at high resolution draws substantial power, reducing the battery life of mobile devices. Indeed, per-frame system energy consumption scales with resolution, as charted in Fig. 2c. Appropriate frame resolutions will strike a balance between pose estimation accuracy and energy efficiency.

To study this tradeoff, we implement OpenCV's marker-based pose estimation tutorial [17], which extracts visual features from a frame, matches them with marker features using Flann-based matching, and estimates camera pose through a Perspective-n-Point algorithm[1]. This reports the rotation and translation vectors of the camera against a physical marker.

---

[1]We use SIFT features to optimize for accuracy. Access code and results at https://github.com/hujinhan12/MeteorStudioReconfigurationLatencyHotMobile

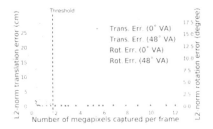

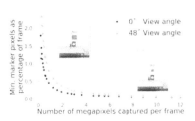

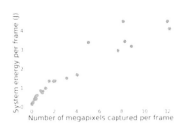

(a) At fixed marker distance of 2 m, reducing pixels per frame and increasing viewing angle (VA) will increase L2-norm translation/rotation error.

(b) For error below threshold, reducing pixels per frame and increasing VA requires the marker (in red) to occupy a larger percentage of FOV.

(c) Reducing pixels per frame will reduce system energy consumption for capturing and processing each frame.

Figure 2: Relationship between frame resolution, viewing angle, accuracy, minimum marker pixels, and energy efficiency

Our case study uses a Google Nexus 5X to capture 12 Mp images at different angles and distances from a 7.5 in. by 10 in. marker. We use bilinear downsampling to simulate low-resolution captures from the same pose. This allows us to quantify estimation precision by comparing the estimated rotation and translation vectors of downsampled images against "ground truth" vectors processed from high resolution images.

3.1 Number of marker pixels influences pose estimation accuracy

We find that pose estimation accuracy is dependent upon the percentage of field-of-view (FOV) occupied by marker pixels. As shown in Fig. 2a, at a fixed distance of 2 m, with the camera pointed at the marker, where the marker occupies approximately 1.3% of the field-of-view, the L2-norm estimation error sharply increases as frame resolution is lowered to 480x640, after which the marker cannot be located. This worsens when the camera views the marker at an angle; at a 48° viewing angle, the estimation error sharply increases as resolution is lowered at and below 810x1080. The marker cannot be located in a frame below 600x800 resolution.

Thus, to keep pose estimation error below a threshold, the frame resolution must be large enough that the marker occupies enough pixels for the algorithm to extract features. For small and/or distant markers, high resolution is required, whereas for larger and/or closer markers, lower resolution may suffice. Fig. 2b charts necessary marker coverage as a percentage of the field-of-view for different image resolutions and different viewing angles. As a consequence, depending on (i) the physical distance between the camera and the marker, (ii) the viewing angle between the camera and the marker, and (iii) the size of the marker, the system needs a sufficient frame resolution to precisely locate markers.

3.2 Frame resolution should flexibly adapt to user movement

While energy efficiency motivates the use of minimal resolutions, the implications of Section 3.1 denote a lower limit of acceptable resolution for estimation, given the distance and angle from a marker. This limit of acceptable resolution will change – users will continuously move, changing the camera position with respect to the marker. Moreover, without knowing the location of markers in an environment, the pose estimation application will need to occasionally obtain high resolution frames to locate markers in a scene before using lower resolution captures that suffice to continually estimate the pose of the camera with respect to visible markers.

Thus, to balance energy efficiency and task accuracy, *marker-based pose estimation applications need the ability to dynamically reconfigure sensor operation*. Of course, marker-based pose estimation is just one class of many that would benefit from dynamic sensor reconfiguration; markerless augmented reality, object recognition, and face recognition could all use resolution-based tradeoffs between efficiency and accuracy.

Unfortunately, dynamic reconfiguration is not currently possible without a drop in performance – changing resolution results in hundreds of milliseconds of latency, during which no new frames are provided to the application. In this paper, our goal is to characterize sources of this latency in order to propose mechanisms to overcome the latency.

4 CHARACTERIZE RECONFIGURATION LATENCY IN THE OPERATING SYSTEM

To better understand the sensor resolution reconfiguration latency, we perform an in-depth characterization of the camera library, HAL, and service of the Android OS. In this section, we measure the influence of various configuration functions upon end-to-end and frame-to-frame latency.

Measurement methodology We profile reconfiguration latency on a Google LG Nexus 5X, with a rear-facing 12Mp Sony IMX377 image sensor, loaded with Android Open Source Project, v. 7.1.2. On this device, we instrument an Android test application to request a frame resolution configuration when an on-screen button is clicked. The application cycles through a set of resolutions from 3024x4032 to 120x160.

We inject timing code into Android's camera library framework layer and the camera HAL. Our code prints system timestamps at the beginning and end of each library function and HAL function. These timestamps track the resolution configuration workflow across the Android system stack.

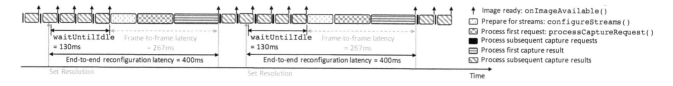

Figure 3: Current sequential configuration patterns incur significant end-to-end and frame-to-frame latency. Shortly after a configuration request, the application continues to receive frames of the previous configuration.

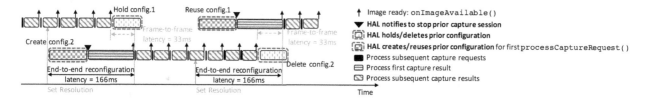

Figure 4: Our proposed alternative introduces parallelizing configuration procedures, reusing configurations, and timely HAL control of channel management, that will reduce the end-to-end and frame-to-frame latency.

Function	Layer	Latency	E-t-E	F-t-F
waitUntilIdle()	Library	130 ms	33%	0%
configureStreams()	Library	60 ms	15%	22%
processCaptureRequest()	Library	84 ms	21%	31%
process_capture_result()	HAL	102 ms	26%	38%

Table 1: Latency breakdown, including proportion of end-to-end (E-t-E) and frame-to-frame (F-t-F) latency

4.1 Measuring reconfiguration latency

The operating system implements sensor reconfiguration through interactions between the application camera library, service, and HAL layers. To instrument interactions, we breakdown reconfiguration into critical functional stages, as shown in Table 1. In doing so, we find latency culprits: waitUntilIdle(), configureStreams(), processCaptureRequest(), and process_capture_result().

4.1.1 waitUntilIdle(). After preparing buffers for the new configuration, waitUntilIdle forces the process to wait until the system clears the pending request queue from the previous configuration. This waitUntilIdle latency forces the HAL to process one stream at a time, only configuring new streams after completing and deleting previous streams.

waitUntilIdle latency varies, depending on the number of pending requests in the queue. According to our measurements, end-to-end waitUntilIdle latency averages around 130 ms, which contributes almost 33% of the end-to-end reconfiguration latency, as shown in Table 1. Though this end-to-end latency is large, it will not affect frame-to-frame performance since the system still returns frames to the application during idle time, as shown in Fig. 3.

4.1.2 configureStreams(). After clearing the pending request queue for the previous configuration, the framework library invokes configureStreams to create the new capture session for the new configuration. Upon invocation, the HAL will stop and release

previous channels, streams, and buffers. Subsequently, the HAL will reallocate buffers, reconfigure new streams, and add them to new channels. This sequence involves several system calls. When turning off streams, the HAL invokes 3 VIDIOC_STREAMOFF ioctl calls to disable hardware. These ioctl calls consume around 20 ms. Adding to the latency, using 18 IPC sockets to release buffers uses 10 ms.

This procedure for deleting old configurations and issuing new configurations occurs when creating any new capture session. The average amount of end-to-end latency for configureStreams is around 60 ms, which contributes to 15% of the end-to-end reconfiguration latency. As this operation takes place after previous frames have stopped streaming to the application, configureStreams also contributes 22% to frame-to-frame latency.

4.1.3 processCaptureRequest(). After the HAL creates the capture session, the framework layer sends repeated capture requests to the HAL, using processCaptureRequest to form each request. As discussed in the background, the HAL must read capture settings and buffer addresses and activate all channels and streams. This invokes several system calls, including IPC socket communication that consumes 14 ms in total, one SensorService JNI library call for sensor hardware configuration that takes 25 ms, and one updating stream information call that consumes 10 ms.

Altogether, the latency of processCaptureRequest is around 84 ms, contributing 31% to frame-to-frame latency and 21% to end-to-end reconfiguration latency. Notably, after the first capture request for a given configuration setting, calls to processCaptureRequest do not need to initialize channels and streams, and only use 2 ms latency.

4.1.4 process_capture_result(). As the HAL directs frame capture and processing, it uses process_capture_result to communicate capture progress to the library framework. A captured frame undergoes several transformation stages in a processing pipeline that can include per-channel white balancing, Bayer pattern demosaicing, and RGB transformations [8]. process_capture_result indicates the remaining pipeline stages for a frame. After a frame leaves the pipeline, the HAL returns the result to the framework.

In steady state, the pipeline returns results every 33 ms. However, the initial time it takes to fill the pipeline creates latency between the capture request and the first result returned. This latency amounts to around 102 ms, which contributes 38% to the frame-to-frame latency and the 26% to the end-to-end reconfiguration latency.

Along with other miscellaneous reconfiguration latencies, amounting to 24 ms, these reconfiguration stages incur 400 ms of end-to-end latency and 267 ms of frame-to-frame latency.

5 IDENTIFY SOURCES OF LATENCY IN THE OPERATING SYSTEM

A deeper look into our characterization exposes three critical sources of latency: *(i)* sequential configuration patterns, *(ii)* expensive system calls, and *(iii)* imaging pipeline delay. Here, we discuss these sources of latency and propose mechanisms to mitigate their influence.

5.1 Sequential configuration patterns

The current Android camera system executes configuration through a step-by-step sequence, outlined in Section 4.1. The execution of one function blocks the next function, which contributes to reconfiguration latency. As an example, the current framework returns pending request frames to the application before deleting channels, streams, and buffers, using `waitUntilIdle` as a synchronization barrier, preserving previous resources while they are being used. As channel deletion and creation are grouped into the subsequent call to `configureStreams`, the HAL cannot create channels until after the HAL fully deletes previous channels. Thus, sequential configuration prevents new capture requests until completing previous pending requests.

5.1.1 Proposed alternative: Parallelize configuration procedures. Towards reducing the sequential bottleneck of reconfiguration, we propose to parallelize the deletion and creation of channels, streams, and buffers. While deletion must happen after pending requests return, *channel creation* does not need to wait for channel deletion or for the return of pending requests. Thus, we can parallelize the channel creation with the handling of previous requests, including the deletion of previous channels. This will allow channel creation and configuration to continue during `waitUntilIdle`.

5.2 Expensive system calls

The Android camera HAL invokes system calls to request kernel services, especially to delete, create, and initiate streams. Previous research shows that system calls are time consuming, due to context switches and I/O wait time [16][7]. Across the reconfiguration sequence, 79 ms is consumed by system calls, which contributes 29% to the frame-to-frame latency.

5.2.1 Proposed alternative: Reuse prior configurations to avoid system calls. We propose to give the HAL the controllability to hold and reuse prior channel configurations, especially for scenarios that repeatedly reuse configurations, e.g., toggling between low and high resolutions. This will avoid repeated use of system calls

to delete and create channels. The proposed mechanism requires a rearchitecture of the HAL to maintain multiple configuration resources to swap them in as needed. We will study the memory implications of holding buffers and plan to devise low memory strategies, e.g., releasing unused buffers under memory pressure.

5.3 Imaging pipeline delay

The camera system uses a pipeline to capture and process image frames. This parallelizes several operations, including frame readout, white balancing, demosaicing, and RGB transformation. As these operations occur simultaneously, the pipeline exports frames at high frame rates.

However, there is substantial latency from capture request to frame return. For a 4-stage pipeline, this amounts to 132 ms of end-to-end latency. Moreover, as discussed in Section 5.1, sequential operation forbids requests from loading into the pipeline until the previous pipeline has been cleared. Thus, pipeline latency also contributes to frame-to-frame latency.

5.3.1 Proposed alternative: Timely HAL control of channel management. To keep the pipeline fully occupied, the previous session should continue capturing and processing frames until the camera hardware and processing stages have been configured for the new session. To provision for this, we propose to give the HAL precise timing control to issue system calls, rather than having the library dictate the scheduling. Enabled by our proposed parallel channel management (Section 5.1), the HAL can allow the previous session to continue while preparing new channel resources. After the HAL prepares the new channel, the HAL will trigger sensor drivers to capture at the new resolution, while simultaneously releasing the previous request channel. This will fully remove any influence of reconfiguration on frame-to-frame latency.

Potential impact of proposed mechanisms Our mechanisms will involve a redesign of the camera HAL and the camera framework library. However, as shown in Fig. 4, successful implementation will reduce end-to-end reconfiguration latency from 400 ms to 166 ms, allowing applications to flexibly adapt capture resolution to balance energy efficiency and task accuracy. More importantly, because our system preserves frame-to-frame latency, e.g., 33 ms for 30 FPS, applications will be able to reconfigure resolution without dropping frames. This ability will advance new classes of vision algorithms that use resolution-based tradeoffs to improve performance and efficiency in a variety of visual tasks.

6 RELATED WORK

Optimizing sensor hardware efficiency Sensor hardware efficiency limits vision applications. Jayasuriya et al. have presented a configurable hardware imaging signal processing pipeline [3]. RedEye proposes to push neural network processing to the sensor [11]. [9] has presented a novel framework to monitor and reduce sensors' contexts. Our work can interoperate with such optimizations, hiding the configuration delay of using these systems.

Operating systems optimization Prior work, such as RTDroid [18], has explored the deficiency of the Android system for providing real-time services. Others have proposed an energy optimization framework enabling energy manager to utilize information provided by the application [10] . Inspired by them, we examine and characterize the capability of current systems for providing responsive and continuous service to sensor reconfiguration requests.

Exposing camera control Previous researchers have recognized the significance of programmability for camera operation, such as through Frankencamera [1] and OpenKCam [6]. Our proposed system integrates the idea of exposing low-level camera control to applications for providing a fine-grained camera control. We focus on reducing the latency for providing such configuration services.

7 CONCLUSION

To balance the energy efficiency of vision applications, the system should continuously reconfigure sensor operation. However, we observe that sensor resolution reconfiguration takes substantial latency during which no frame is returned to the application. We define and profile end-to-end and frame-to-frame latency caused by reconfiguring resolution. We identify three sources of latency: sequential configuration patterns, expensive system calls, and imaging pipeline delay. Built on these understandings, we propose a redesign of the camera system which will overcome the latency barrier caused by reconfiguring sensor resolution. We envision that our work will enable a future of adaptive vision on mobile devices.

Acknowledgement This material is based upon work supported by the National Science Foundation under Grant No. 1657602.

REFERENCES

[1] Andrew Adams, Eino-Ville Talvala, Sung Hee Park, David E. Jacobs, Boris Ajdin, Natasha Gelfand, Jennifer Dolson, Daniel Vaquero, Jongmin Baek, Marius Tico, Hendrik P. A. Lensch, Wojciech Matusik, Kari Pulli, Mark Horowitz, and Marc Levoy. 2010. The Frankencamera: An Experimental Platform for Computational Photography. In *Proceedings of the 37th International Conference and Exhibition on Computer Graphics and Interactive Techniques*.

[2] Brandon Amos, Bartosz Ludwiczuk, and Mahadev Satyanarayanan. 2016. *OpenFace: A general-purpose face recognition library with mobile applications*. Technical Report. CMU-CS-16-118, CMU School of Computer Science.

[3] Mark Buckler, Suren Jayasuriya, and Adrian Sampson. 2017. Reconfiguring the Imaging Pipeline for Computer Vision. *CoRR* (2017).

[4] Tiffany Yu-Han Chen, Lenin S. Ravindranath, Shuo Deng, Paramvir Victor Bahl, and Hari Balakrishnan. 2015. Glimpse: Continuous, Real-Time Object Recognition on Mobile Devices. In *Proceedings of the 13th ACM Conference on Embedded Networked Sensor Systems*.

[5] Sony Semiconductor Solutions Corporation. 2017. IMX377CQT ProductSummary v1.5. (2017).

[6] KHRONOS Group. 2013. Camera BOF. (2013). https://www.khronos.org/assets/uploads/developers/library/2013-siggraph-camera-bof/Camera-BOF_SIGGRAPH-2013.pdf

[7] Tomas Hruby, Teodor Crivat, Herbert Bos, and Andrew S. Tanenbaum. 2014. On Sockets and System Calls Minimizing Context Switches for the Socket API. In *Proceedings of the 2014 International Conference on Timely Results in Operating Systems*.

[8] Google Inc. 2017. Android Developers: CaptureResult. (2017). https://developer.android.com/reference/android/hardware/camera2/CaptureResult.html

[9] Seungwoo Kang, Jinwon Lee, Hyukjae Jang, Hyonik Lee, Youngki Lee, Souneil Park, Taiwoo Park, and Junehwa Song. 2008. SeeMon: Scalable and Energy-efficient Context Monitoring Framework for Sensor-rich Mobile Environments. In *Proceedings of the 6th International Conference on Mobile Systems, Applications, and Services*.

[10] L. Li, J. Wang, X. Wang, H. Ye, and Z. Hu. 2017. SceneMan: Bridging mobile apps with system energy manager by scenario notification. In *Proceedings of the 2017 IEEE/ACM International Symposium on Low Power Electronics and Design*.

[11] Robert LiKamWa, Yunhui Hou, Julian Gao, Mia Polansky, and Lin Zhong. 2016. RedEye: Analog ConvNet Image Sensor Architecture for Continuous Mobile Vision. In *Proceedings of the 43rd International Symposium on Computer Architecture*.

[12] Robert LiKamWa, Bodhi Priyantha, Matthai Philipose, Lin Zhong, and Paramvir Bahl. 2013. Energy Characterization and Optimization of Image Sensing Toward Continuous Mobile Vision. In *Proceedings of the 11th Annual International Conference on Mobile Systems, Applications, and Services*.

[13] ON Semiconductor 2017. *AR0330 1/3-inch CMOS Digital Image Sensor*. ON Semiconductor. Rev. 18.

[14] ON Semiconductor 2017. *MT9P031 1/2.5-Inch 5 Mp CMOS Digital Image Sensor*. ON Semiconductor. Rev. 10.

[15] Mahadev Satyanarayanan. 2015. A Brief History of Cloud Offload: A Personal Journey from Odyssey Through Cyber Foraging to Cloudlets. *GetMobile: Mobile Comp. and Comm.* 18 (2015).

[16] Livio Soares and Michael Stumm. 2010. FlexSC: Flexible System Call Scheduling with Exception-less System Calls. In *Proceedings of the 9th USENIX Conference on Operating Systems Design and Implementation*.

[17] Open Source Computer Vision. 2016. Real Time pose estimation of a textured object. (2016). http://docs.opencv.org/3.2.0/dc/d2c/tutorial_real_time_pose.html

[18] Yin Yan, Shaun Cosgrove, Varun Anand, Amit Kulkarni, Sree Harsha Konduri, Steven Y. Ko, and Lukasz Ziarek. 2014. Real-time Android with RTDroid. In *Proceedings of the 12th Annual International Conference on Mobile Systems, Applications, and Services*.

Adversarial Localization against Wireless Cameras

Zhijing Li*, Zhujun Xiao+, Yanzi Zhu*, Irene Pattarachanyakul*,
Ben Y. Zhao+ and Haitao Zheng+

{zhijing,yanzi}@cs.ucsb.edu,ireneeypatt@hotmail.com,{zhujunxiao,ravenben,htzheng}@cs.uchicago.edu
*UC Santa Barbara, + University of Chicago

ABSTRACT

This paper identifies and empirically evaluates the effectiveness of adversarial localization attacks against wireless IoT devices, *e.g.*, wireless security cameras in the home. We use experiments in home and office settings to show that attackers can accurately pinpoint the location of WiFi cameras, using a small amount of stealthy, passive, exterior measurements coupled with unsupervised learning techniques. We also show that current defenses have minimal impact against these attacks, and are also easily circumvented via countermeasures. Thus significant work is needed to develop robust defenses against these attacks.

ACM Reference Format:
Zhijing Li*, Zhujun Xiao+, Yanzi Zhu*, Irene Pattarachanyakul*, Ben Y. Zhao+ and Haitao Zheng+. 2018. Adversarial Localization against Wireless Cameras. In *Proceedings of 19th International Workshop on Mobile Computing Systems & Applications (HotMobile '18)*. ACM, New York, NY, USA, 6 pages. https://doi.org/10.1145/3177102.3177106

1 INTRODUCTION

Digital homes are becoming increasingly commonplace. Some of the most popular products today are for home security. Companies like Ring and Google Nest offer cheap, high quality wireless video devices for surveillance and intruder detection. They offer users a sense of security, especially when homeowners are away from home.

As these devices gain in popularity, their widespread deployment means any security vulnerability in their design will have large-scale impact across a large user population. For wireless home cameras, one key vulnerability comes in the form of signal leakage and remote localization by external attackers[1]. From outside the home, a burglar can use wireless measurements to detect the likely location of wireless security cameras, and can then plan their intrusion to avoid detection. Studies have shown that nearly 60% of home burglars will consider the presence of cameras or other video equipment when selecting targets [1]. Others show that burglars (even shoplifters) are adept at identifying and leveraging cameras'

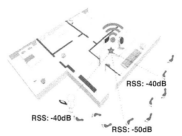

Figure 1: An example scenario of adversarial localization on behind-the-wall wireless camera.

blind spots to evade detection [2, 3]. This type of attack is sometimes called *adversarial localization*[2], where an attacker applies localization techniques to locate third party wireless transmitters.

The goal of this paper is to understand the practical effectiveness of adversarial localization in a realistic setting. We are particularly interested in *stealthy* attacks against wireless cameras, given the direct implications on home security systems. We consider the attack model shown in Figure 1. An adversary, a human or a robot, travels outside the home, passively collects received signal strength (RSS) data of a WiFi camera, then uses the RSS data to estimate the camera location. The key features of this attack model are stealthiness and simplicity. Being passive, the adversary does not need to communicate with the target; only requiring RSS measurements, the attack can be easily carried out by walking (normally) pass the home with a compact COTS WiFi receiver and applying existing RSS-based localization algorithms [5, 9]. Note that while more advanced localization algorithms (*e.g.* time, fingerprinting, AoA based) may lead to higher accuracy, they either require active communications with the target [15, 20, 28, 32][3] or bulky/specialized hardware with multiple antennas [31, 32]. These requirements largely reduce the attack stealthiness.

We perform numerous experiments using COTS video cameras in different home and office settings. In each case, the attacker and the camera are fully separated by walls. We show that despite significant noise in WiFi signals through the walls, localization attacks can be effective but the accuracy varies significantly across measurement instances. We propose unsupervised learning techniques an attacker can use to isolate high-quality measurement instances from noisy instances. For example, the attacker can determine on the fly whether the current measurement is sufficient to produce an accurate result, and use this information to terminate or continue the current effort, or plan a different route. Doing so dramatically improves efficacy of these attacks.

---

[1]Other extensions of this attack include jamming or even modifying the camera's wireless signal. In this paper, we focus on the attack to localize the camera rather than changing its signal.

---

[2]Our version of the adversarial localization differs from those proposed for wireless sensor networks [10, 13, 22, 30], which involve multiple sensors and focus on sensor routing mechanism design.
[3]Today's WiFi cards cannot report CSI/AoA in the monitor mode.

WiFi Camera	TX Power (dBm)	Avg. Packet Size (bytes)	Packet Rate (pkt/s)
Yi Home Camera (720p, 2.4GHz)	16–18	650	60
Yi Home Camera2 (1080p, 2.4GHz)	16–18	645	75
Amcrest ProHD (1080p, 2.4GHz)	~19	1190	80
Samsung SmartCam (1080p, 5GHz)	~19	900	50

Table 1: WiFi cameras used in our experiments.

Environment	Adversary Behavior
Apartment	Adversary walks on the outdoor hallway.
House	Adversary walks on the lawn and sidewalk.
Office-a	Adversary walks on the indoor hallway.
Office-b	Adversary walks both inside & outside the building.

Table 2: Environments where we performed the attacks.

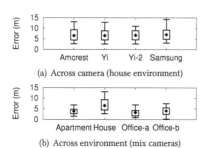

(a) Across camera (house environment)

(b) Across environment (mix cameras)

Figure 2: Localization performance in terms of quantile (5%, 25%, 50%, 75%, 95%).

We then study possible defenses against these attacks, which add noise to RSS signals in both temporal and spatial domains. We find that these defenses are moderately effective against the basic attack, but have minimum impact when the attacker uses advanced ML techniques. Further, a more sophisticated attacker deploys countermeasures in the form of additional stationary receivers, which help remove the impact of noise in the temporal domain. Overall, current defenses fall short against these localization attacks.

Our work seeks to bring attention to the practical dangers of widespread deployment of IoT devices like home video cameras. By taking a brief walk with today's COTS WiFi receivers, our simple attacks can already achieve 2.7 meters in median localization error and minimum variance in four common home/office environments. The efficacy will further improve as the adversary uses more advanced algorithms or hardware. We need to quickly develop effective defenses against these attacks to improve the security of wireless IoT devices in the home/office.

2 ADVERSARIAL LOCALIZATION

Our goal is to understand the effectiveness of adversarial localization on behind-the-wall wireless cameras. We performed actual attacks on popular COTS WiFi cameras in typical home and office scenarios. We now describe the attack model, our experiment configuration and dataset, and our findings.

2.1 Adversarial Model

We consider an adversary who physically moves outside the target house/apartment/office, seeking to localize WiFi cameras behind the walls (Figure 1). While moving, the adversary uses a standard WiFi receiver, *e.g.* a laptop or a smartphone, to *passively* sniff transmissions from nearby WiFi devices [25]. From the sniffed data, the adversary extracts non-payload information like MAC address, RSS and frame length. With these information, the adversary can identify WiFi cameras by directly matching their MAC addresses if she is knowledgeable enough or by analyzing traffic patterns, *e.g.* traffic volume and packet types [27]. After recognizing each target

camera, the adversary builds a signal trace per target, *i.e.* a set of tuples (time, position, RSS) along a moving trajectory, and applies TX localization to estimate the target's position.

TX Localization. We consider RSS based passive TX localization, which does not require the adversary to communicate with the victim (for stealthiness). After de-noising RSS trace using window-based averaging, we apply the log-distance path loss model to estimate the camera location. We chose this method because it is simple, widely used, and has been shown to be robust against biased spatial coverage [17]. Thus our results provide a lower-bound on the accuracy of adversarial localization using COTS WiFi sniffers.

2.2 Measurements

We performed measurements on four WiFi security cameras with the highest ratings on Amazon (see Table 1). They use different WiFi chipsets and frequency bands (2.4GHz and 5GHz). We placed these cameras in rooms of resident houses, apartments and office buildings, and varied their locations (3 locations per room). In each experiment, the camera and the adversary were separated by walls (of different building materials). Table 2 summarizes the settings.

The adversary uses a laptop (Macbook Air) to sniff WiFi traffic and a smartphone (Samsung Galaxy SIII) to track moving trajectory. The adversary applies dead-reckoning on smartphone sensor data, using the accelerometer readings to track walking distance and the orientation readings to track angles. We performed experiments to confirm that the trajectory error has negligible impact on localization performance.

Our experiments were carried out by six people with different heights, weights and walking behaviors. Since they lead to consistent results, we did not differentiate them in our following discussions. Overall, our experiments produced more than 1.2k walking traces (each of 25-60 meters long), mapping to more than 2.6 million (time, position, RSS) tuples.

2.3 Attack Effectiveness

We quantify the accuracy of adversarial localization by *absolute localization error*, *i.e.* the distance between the estimated transmitter location and the ground truth. Figure 2(a) plots the quantiles (5%, 25%, 50%, 75%, 95%) of the localization error for each camera across all the walking traces. We see that the localization performance is similar across the four cameras (who use different WiFi chipsets and carrier frequencies). The median error is around 4-5 meters, which is within the room level. Yet the variance is significant, and the error can reach 12 meters. This is as expected since previous works have shown that transmitter localization is highly sensitive to measurement coverage, environmental dynamics, noises and RF interference [17, 19].

Figure 2(b) then plots the localization error quantiles for different environments, mixing all the camera results. Interestingly, the accuracy varies across the environments. The error is particularly large for "house" due to more complex fading profiles and longer distance between the camera and the adversary compared to the other environments. In this case, the median error rises to 6.8 meters, while the rest three environments remain 4 meters. But a consistent trend is that the variance of localization error is large.

3 MINIMIZING VARIANCE

Given the large variance in localization accuracy, the basic adversarial localization faces heavy uncertainty on its effectiveness. To reduce variance, the most intuitive method is to perform multiple rounds of measurements[4] and aggregate the raw data or the localization results. We tested this approach on our dataset and found that the improvement is limited and often saturates after three rounds. Furthermore, repeatedly wandering around the target home will easily raise red flags.

Instead, we propose a method to predict the localization accuracy or *fidelity* of any measurement instance, using unsupervised learning analysis. It allows the attacker to separate high-quality measurements from noises and carry out the attack more effectively.

3.1 Predicting Localization Accuracy

Given a measurement instance (*i.e.* a round of sniffing), the adversary first quantifies the accuracy of the localization result produced from the data (referred as *fidelity*), and only uses the localization result if the predicted accuracy is high.

To estimate fidelity, the adversary uses *unsupervised feature clustering* [19]. Feature clustering groups data instances together based on their *similarity* across a small group of key features. It assumes that a specific combination of data features tends to coexist in measurement instances that produce accurate localization results. If this assumption holds, such clusters will be easily identifiable, and will reveal the key features that strongly correlate with fidelity. Using these key features, the adversary can determine whether a measurement instance is of high fidelity or not. While our recent work has used this approach to prune crowdsourced cellular measurements [19], we seek to use it to analyze behind-the-wall WiFi signals, which have different propagation properties.

We applied this feature clustering approach on our dataset. The detailed procedure is similar to [19], thus omitted for brevity. We start from four groups of features extracted from the raw measurement data: *packet* features on traffic statistics, *spatial* features used by common spatial analysis [26], *RSS* features on RSS statistics, and *combined* features that capture the fitting error of the localization model and the joint distribution of packet/RSS and spatial properties. We also included the environment type as a feature.

The feature clustering results are shown in Figure 3. We obtained two key findings.

1. Natural Clusters on Localization Accuracy. Our results confirm the strong tie between feature clusters and localization accuracy. Figure 3(a) shows that the measurement instances in our dataset are divided into 3 clusters. Cluster A (49% of instances) produces fairly accurate localization results (2.5 meters and 5.5

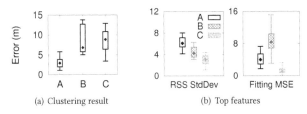

(a) Clustering result   (b) Top features

Figure 3: Feature clustering performance.

meters for median and 95%-tile, respectively). Cluster B (35%) and C (16%) have relatively high localization errors (almost all > 5 meters).

Figure 3(b) shows that two key features, *RSS standard deviation* and *fitting mean squared error (MSE)*, can be used to distinguish cluster A from the others. Measurement instances in cluster A display large RSS standard deviation but low model-fitting MSE. This is because RSS standard deviation increases as the adversary moves closer to the transmitter (camera). In this case, RSS measurements become more reliable in the presence of environmental artifacts. The next key feature is model-fitting MSE. Intuitively, this value should be small to have desirable localization accuracy. The exception is cluster C which has low values and yet bad localization results. This is because cluster C mainly consists of measurements that are far away from the transmitter and the RSS readings are *flat* across the trajectory. This type of data leads to a good model-fit, but is unsuitable for localization (since they do not capture the distance-RSS relationship).

2. Consistency across Environments/Cameras. We also observe that the clustering results and feature properties are *consistent* across all environments, cameras types and locations. This aligns with that of [19] on outdoor cellular localization. Such consistency greatly facilitates the attack. An adversary can use offline, local measurements to build clusters and determine the key features used to identify high quality measurement instances. It can then derive the fidelity level instantaneously during the actual attack.

Based on this observation, we configure the feature thresholds to identify a high-fidelity measurement instance (*i.e.* those in cluster A) as RSS standard deviation above 5 and fitting MSE lower than 6. These feature thresholds do not change when we only use data from any individual environment or camera.

3.2 Advanced Attack Performance

We now show the localization performance when the adversarial uses fidelity estimation to *prune* the data, *i.e.* only using a measurement instance if its fidelity value is sufficient. As baselines, we also include results of the basic attack and *data combining* where we aggregate three rounds of measurements since the performance saturates at this point.

Gain of Pruning. We first look at the "house" environment, which has the *worst* localization performance of the four environments. Figure 4(a) shows the localization performance for basic attack, after combining, and after pruning. Consistently across all four cameras, pruning offers significant performance improvement, reducing the median error from more than 6.8 meters to 4.2 meters, and bounding the error by 6 meters (compared to 15 meters in the basic attack). Next, Figure 4(b) plots results of the four environments while mixing results of all four cameras. Again pruning

---

[4]We assume that the attacker walks in the same area across measurement rounds, since his moving space within the camera's WiFi signal coverage is often limited, *e.g.* sidewalks, hallways etc.

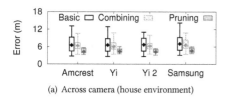
(a) Across camera (house environment)

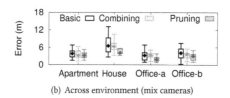
(b) Across environment (mix cameras)

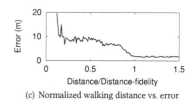
(c) Normalized walking distance vs. error

Figure 4: Localization performance of advanced localization attacks.

leads to significant improvement in localization accuracy, reducing variance from 6.4 to 1.8. This shows that identifying useful data is much more effective than blindly adding data.

Cost of Pruning. While effectively reducing the variance of localization accuracy, pruning comes at the cost of often requiring extra rounds of measurements until a high-fidelity instance is reached. Since we carried out 15 rounds of measurements per environment/camera/camera location configuration, we were able to compute the number of extra rounds required. Overall, 64% of measurement instances were determined as high fidelity by our pruning tool. For 17% of cases, no useable instance was found after 15 rounds of measurements, meaning that the attacker was unable to localize the camera with reasonable accuracy. For the rest, it takes an average of 3.25 rounds to reach a high-fidelity instance.

Minimizing Measurement Distance. The attacker can continuously monitor the fidelity level of the current measurement. After a sufficient level of fidelity is reached, he can terminate the measurement (for stealthiness and efficiency). Figure 4(c) plots the localization accuracy with the moving distance. We normalize the x-axis by the distance where the required fidelity level is achieved (Distance-fidelity). We see that our fidelity estimation can accurately identify the "stopping point". Across all the high-fidelity instances (766), the min, median, max of Distance-fidelity are 6.1, 23.9, and 53.2 meters, respectively. Similarly, the attacker can use fidelity to terminate "unsuccessful" measurements.

Together, our experiments on the advanced attacks show that adversarial localization is highly effective against WiFi cameras (behind the walls). By walking around the building/house briefly, the attacker can estimate the locations of indoor WiFi cameras with room-level accuracy (median of 2.7 meters), and identify unreliable measurements.

4 PRACTICAL DEFENSES

In term of defense, ideally, one can reconfigure WiFi hardware or install signal reflectors to prevent signal coverage beyond the wall/room [8, 14, 29]. Yet in practice, such approach incurs high cost, limits the camera's connection to the AP, and is often infeasible to deploy. Instead, we consider a suite of practical defenses that add noise to RSS signals in both the temporal and spatial domains, by modifying the camera WiFi transmit power or adding extra "cameras".

- *Temporal Obfuscation* – The camera adjusts its WiFi transmit power randomly over time, creating random noise on RSS values observed by the adversary. This idea originated from the power adjustment scheme in [12].

- *Spatial Obfuscation* – Extra WiFi transmitters, *e.g.* cameras, are placed away from the victim (in neighboring rooms). They coordinate with the victim to produce transmissions that are well mixed into the victim's transmissions so that the attacker cannot separate them during sniffing[5]. The design was inspired by recent works on anti-sensing using full duplex radios [24] and device cooperation [23].

Next, we describe both defenses, our experiments to validate them, and potential countermeasures by the adversary.

Key Findings. Current defenses fall short against adversarial localization attacks. While moderately effective against the basic attack, they have minimum impact when the attacker uses advanced ML techniques like pruning. The attacker can also deploy countermeasures in the form of additional stationary receivers, which help remove the impact of noise in the temporal domain.

4.1 Defense 1: Temporal Obfuscation

When the victim camera changes its transmit power randomly, the attacker will observe noisy RSS values that could degrade the localization results. The power variation needs to be large enough to create RSS distortion, and yet stealthy enough to avoid being predicted or removed.

Randomization Configuration. Three factors matter when configuring power randomization: *variation range*, *pattern*, and *frequency*. The range depends on the hardware capability, *e.g.* the dynamic range of power amplifier, and the required transmission range of the camera to reach its AP at a specific rate. The choice of the randomization pattern is non-trivial since there are many options. We consider *distribution-based*, *e.g.* Beta, Uniform, Exponential, Gaussian, and *pseudo-random number generators*. Among them, Beta provides the opportunity to maximize variance while *Uniform* (a special case of Beta) maximizes the entropy.

We first used trace-driven emulation to narrow down our choices before implementing them on our testbeds. Leveraging our RSS datasets, we emulate transmit power randomization by adding the instantaneous offset in transmit power (in dB) directly onto the attacker's RSS value (in dB). While making an ideal assumption that there's no packet loss and interference, this effort allows us to study the choice of variation range, pattern and frequency using repeatable experiments. For all our experiments, the average and maximum transmit power levels remain the same.

Our results show that the variation range needs to be larger than 10dB to make any visible change in localization results. Also the variation frequency needs to be carefully chosen. Rapid changes

---
[5]They use the same MAC address of the victim, and synchronize their packet sequence numbers for WiFi transmissions.

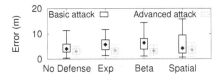

Figure 5: Localization performance of no defense, temporal obfuscation (Exponential (Exp), Beta distribution), and spatial obfuscation.

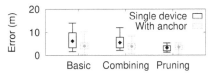

Figure 6: Attack performance w/ and w/o anchor. The victim uses power randomization (Beta).

can be easily mitigated via de-noising, and slow changes lead to little impact within each measurement round. Overall a frequency of one per 200 packets is desirable assuming the adversary moves at a walking speed. Finally, we narrowed down to the Beta ($\alpha=\beta=0.5$) and Exponential distributions since they lead to the heaviest degradation in localization accuracy while holding large entropy values.

Testbed Experiments.   While today's WiFi APs support power adaptation, this feature is not yet available on WiFi cameras. Thus we implement power randomization using USRP-GNU radios. Using the IEEE 802.11 implementation [7], we configure each USRP N210 node (XCVR2450 daughterboard) to mimic the camera operations in Table 1. We modify the automatic gain adaptation to enable 0-20dB gain variation at a granularity of 0.5dB. For each experiment, we configure the USRP transmitter to operate on three modes sequentially: fixed power (with 10dB gain), Beta randomization, and Exponential randomization. Overall, our dataset includes 0.9K walking traces in all four environments, with 4.2 million (time, position, RSS) tuples.

Results.   We compare the efficacy of both basic and advanced attacks with and without the defense. We mix the results across all experiments since they are consistent. Figure 5 shows that power randomization is moderately effective against the basic attack, but has minimum impact when the attacker uses pruning. Here we assume the adversary is aware of the use of power randomization, and can adjust the feature thresholds properly. We verified that the clustering results and key features under power randomization are consistent with those under fixed power. The exact feature thresholds depend on the randomization pattern and range, which can be easily estimated by sniffing signals at a fixed location over a short period of time (<8 minutes shown by our experiments).

On the other hand, we do observe that power randomization increases the cost of data pruning. Now only 32% of measurement instances can offer high fidelity results (compared to 63% under fixed power). And in average it now takes 12 measurement rounds to obtain a high-fidelity localization outcome (compared to 3 rounds under fixed power). Therefore, temporal obfuscation by power randomization can increase the cost of localization attacks. However,

later in §4.3 we show that such advantage can be easily diminished by attackers deploying additional stationary receivers.

Impact on Cameras.   By lowering the camera's transmit power, power randomization could lead to undesirable packet losses and throughput drop. While we did not observe this artifact in our experiments, it can become a limiting factor when the link between the camera and the AP is already weak.

4.2   Spatial Obfuscation

In this defense, we place another camera (USRP with fixed power) in the neighboring room of the victim camera (USRP with fixed power), and repeat our experiments. The distance between the two is between 3-22 meters (with median of 8 meters). To avoid implementing coordination between the two cameras, we simply mix their RSS traces as a single one. Note that given the tight coordination requirement, this defense is much harder to implement in practice compared to power randomization.

Results.   Figure 5 shows the defense is moderately effective against the basic attack. It raises the variance of localization error beyond that of power randomization. However, the attacker can overcome the defense by applying feature clustering to identify high-quality measurement instances, using the same feature thresholds of single camera scenarios. With pruning, the measurement overhead is slightly worse than that under single camera case: 47% of the measurement instances are now useable (compared to 63%); it takes an average of 3.67 rounds of measurements to reach a high-fidelity result.

Another interesting finding is that the location of the second camera is an important factor but hard to optimize. It should be away from the victim to create large noise on RSS, and yet close to the attacker (of unknown location) to produce strong WiFi signals that will be used in localization. Overall, this defense is difficult to optimize and costly to implement.

4.3   Countermeasure by Adversaries

Defenses via power randomization can also be countered. In theory, the RSS contribution from power randomization can be removed by using a stationary WiFi sniffer (referred to as anchor) to measure RSS continuously in the attack area [16, 18]. Subtracting the RSS change seen by the anchor from its own RSS, the attacker can remove the randomization contribution. Of course, this assumes that the anchor and the receiver face similar channel conditions.

To validate this countermeasure, in each of our previous USRP measurements, we also deployed three stationary anchors to collect RSS. We find that the performance depends heavily on the anchor choice. A good anchor will capture the majority of the victim's packets to build a comprehensive RSS trace for power subtraction. Thus in each experiment, we picked the anchor with the lowest packet loss rate.

Figure 6 compares the localization error of the basic and advanced attacks with and without the use of anchors, when the victim uses power randomization (Beta). We see that the use of anchors largely improves localization accuracy under the basic attack. When the attacker uses data pruning, the accuracy improvement becomes negligible, but the pruning overhead reduces significantly. 52% of measurement traces are useable (compared to 32%) and the average number of measurement rounds reduces from 12 to 3.8. Thus the countermeasure is effective.

5 RELATED WORK

Indoor WiFi TX Localization. Existing works can be classified into *fingerprinting, time, AoA,* and *RSS*. We use RSS based methods because they do not require active communication with the target, and can be easily carried out via compact, COTS WiFi receivers/sniffers. Our goal in this work is not to minimize localization error (which we leave to future work), but to demonstrate the practicality and effectiveness of adversarial localization attacks.

TX Location Privacy. Researchers have developed multiple mechanisms to protect TX location privacy. Device anonymization [12] prevents the adversary from recognizing a device by its ID, but traffic and signal analysis [27] can still recognize devices like cameras. Others use antenna arrays [14, 29], directional antenna [6] or signal reflectors [8] to limit transmission coverage, but suffer from high cost and limited effectiveness due to environment constraints. Similar to our work, [4, 11] applied power randomization to prevent untrusted users from localizing themselves, but only drew conclusions from simulations. [24] designs full-duplex obfuscator to jam or obfuscate signals, but the high hardware cost prevents its adoption by IoT devices. [23] creates ghost locations from synchronized transmissions of devices in close proximity, but only targets fingerprinting-based localization. Our work is not to invent new defenses, but to show that existing defenses are inadequate. Finally, our work differs from adversarial localization in wireless sensor networks [10, 13, 22], which design routing protocols across a group of sensors to avoid localization of source nodes.

6 OPEN CHALLENGES

Our work highlights the dangers of reliance on IoT devices in a security context. Using commodity devices, attackers today can perform highly effective localization attacks against WiFi cameras inside the home/office. Significant work is needed to develop robust defenses against these attacks.

Adversarial localization for mobile devices. While this work targets stationary WiFi cameras, an open question is how adversarial localization attacks apply to other IoT devices in the current (and future) market. An example is the commercial mobile surveillance robots that survey a home while streaming videos. The camera movements and rotations certainly introduce new challenges in launching adversarial localization attacks. To locate and track a moving WiFi camera, the attacker will likely need more information beyond RSSI values.

Identifying and tracking multiple devices. Each home/room will likely deploy multiple (WiFi-based) IoT devices. Thus the attacker needs to separate and identify various target devices before localization. A straightforward solution is to use MAC addresses as the unique identifiers for each device. But some of today's devices already employ MAC address randomization to prevent being tracked constantly. Although existing works have proposed methods to reverse engineer MAC randomization via traffic analysis [21], its impact on adversarial localization remains unclear and needs investigation. Aside from MAC address based identification, the attacker can also perform traffic analysis to separate IoT devices if they have different traffic patterns. There are interesting follow-up works for our study.

ACKNOWLEDGEMENT

We thank the anonymous reviewers for their feedback. This work was supported by NSF grants AST-1443956 and CNS 1705042.

REFERENCES

[1] 2013. *Burglars Confess: Why Your Home is a Target.* http://www.alarm.org/HomeSafety/BurglarsSpillAboutSecuritySystems.aspx.
[2] 2016. *Minimize Blind Spots.* http://www.vivint.com/neighborhood/tech-neighbor/minimize-blind-spots-for-your-security-camera-system/.
[3] 2016. *Security Camera Blind Spots: How to Find and Avoid Them.* https://reolink.com/find-and-avoid-security-blind-spots.
[4] F. Anjum, S. Pandey, and P. Agrawal. 2005. Secure Localization in Sensor Networks Using Transmission Range Variation. In *Proc. of MASS.*
[5] P. Bahl and V.N. Padmanabhan. 2000. RADAR: An in-building RF-based User Location and Tracking System. In *Proc. of INFOCOM.*
[6] K. Bauer and et al. 2009. The Directional Attack on Wireless Localization. In *Proc. of GLOBECOM.*
[7] B. Bloessl, M. Segata, C. Sommer, and F. Dressler. 2013. An IEEE 802.11 a/g/p OFDM Receiver for GNU Radio. In *SRIF.*
[8] J. Chan, C. Zheng, and X. Zhou. 2015. 3d Printing Your Wireless Coverage. In *Proc. of HotWireless.*
[9] K. Chintalapudi, A.P. Iyer, and V.N. Padmanabhan. 2010. Indoor localization without the pain. In *Proc. of MobiCom.*
[10] N. Dutta, A. Saxena, and S. Chellappan. 2010. Defending Wireless Sensor Networks against Adversarial Localization. In *Proc. of MDM.*
[11] R. El-Badry, A. Sultan, and M. Youssef. 2010. Hyberloc: Providing Physical Layer Location Privacy in Hybrid Sensor Networks. In *Proc. of ICC.*
[12] T. Jiang, H.J. Wang, and Y. Hu. 2007. Preserving Location Privacy in Wireless LANs. In *Proc. of MobiSys.*
[13] P. Kamat, Y. Zhang, W. Trappe, and C. Ozturk. 2005. Enhancing Source-Location Privacy in Sensor Network Routing. In *Proc. of ICDCS.*
[14] Y.S. Kim, P. Tague, H. Lee, and H. Kim. 2012. Carving Secure Wi-Fi Zones with Defensive Jamming. In *Proc. of Asia CCS.*
[15] M. Kotaru, K. Joshi, D. Bharadia, and S. Katti. 2015. Spotfi: Decimeter Level Localization Using Wifi. In *Proc. of SIGCOMM.*
[16] J.H. Lee and R.M. Buehrer. 2009. Location Estimation using Differential RSS with Spatially Correlated Shadowing. In *Proc. of GLOBECOM.*
[17] L. Li and et al. 2014. Experiencing and Handling the Diversity in Data Density and Environmental Locality in an Indoor Positioning Service. In *Proc. of MobiCom.*
[18] X. Li, Y. Chen, J. Yang, and X. Zheng. 2011. Designing Localization Algorithms Robust to Signal Strength Attacks. In *Proc. of INFOCOM.*
[19] Z. Li, A. Nika, X. Zhang, Y. Zhu, Y. Yao, B. Zhao, and H. Zheng. 2017. Identifying Value in Crowdsourced Wireless Signal Measurements. In *Proc. of WWW.*
[20] A.T. Mariakakis, S. Sen, J. Lee, and K. Kim. 2014. Sail: Single Access Point-based Indoor Localization. In *Proc. of MobiSys.*
[21] J. Martin and et al. 2017. A Study of MAC Address Randomization in Mobile Devices and When it Fails. *arXiv preprint arXiv:1703.02874* (2017).
[22] K. Mehta, D. Liu, and M. Wright. 2012. Protecting Location Privacy in Sensor Networks against a Global Eavesdropper. *IEEE Transactions on Mobile Computing* 11, 2 (2012).
[23] S. Oh, T. Vu, M. Gruteser, and S. Banerjee. 2012. Phantom: Physical Layer Cooperation for Location Privacy Protection. In *Proc. of INFOCOM.*
[24] Y. Qiao and et al. 2016. PhyCloak: Obfuscating Sensing from Communication Signals. In *Proc. of NSDI.*
[25] C. Sanders. 2011. *Practical Packet Analysis: Using Wireshark to Solve Real-World Network Problems.* No Starch Press.
[26] S. Shekhar and S. Chawla. 2003. *Spatial Databases: A Tour. Introduction to Spatial Data Mining.* Pearson.
[27] S. Siby, R.R. Maiti, and N.O. Tippenhauer. 2017. IoTScanner: Detecting Privacy Threats in IoT Neighborhoods. In *IoTPTS.*
[28] J. Wang and et al. 2016. Lifs: Low Human-effort, Device-free Localization with Fine-grained Subcarrier Information. In *Proc. of MobiCom.*
[29] T. Wang and Y. Yang. 2011. Location Privacy Protection from RSS Localization System using Antenna Pattern Synthesis. In *Proc. of INFOCOM.*
[30] Y. Xi, L. Schwiebert, and W. Shi. 2006. Preserving Source Location Privacy in Monitoring-based Wireless Sensor Networks. In *Proc. of IPDPS.*
[31] J. Xiong and K. Jamieson. 2013. ArrayTrack: A Fine-Grained Indoor Location System.. In *Proc. of NSDI.*
[32] M. Youssef and et al. 2006. Pinpoint: An Asynchronous Time-based Location Determination System. In *Proc. of MobiCom.*

A Case for Temperature-Driven Task Migration to Balance Energy Efficiency and Image Quality of Vision Processing Workloads

Venkatesh Kodukula, Sai Bharadwaj Medapuram, Britton Jones, Robert LiKamWa

Arizona State University, Tempe, AZ

vkoduku1@asu.edu,bmedapur@asu.edu,bsjones7@asu.edu,likamwa@asu.edu

ABSTRACT

Many researchers in academia and industry [4, 8] advocate shifting processing near the image sensor through near-sensor accelerators to reduce data movement across energy-expensive interfaces. However, near-sensor processing also heats the sensor, increasing thermal noise and hot pixels, which degrades image quality. To understand these implications, we perform an energy and thermal characterization in the context of an augmented reality case study around visual marker detection. Our characterization results show that for a near-sensor accelerator consuming 1 W of power, dynamic range drops by 16 dB, image noise increases by 3 times, and the number of hot pixels multiplies by 16, degrading image quality. Such degradation impairs the task accuracy of interactive perceptual applications that require high accuracy. The marker-detection fails for 12% of frames when degraded by 1 minute of 1 W near-sensor power consumption.

To this end, we propose temperature-driven task migration, a system-level technique that partitions processing between the thermally-coupled near-sensor accelerator and the thermally-isolated CPU host. Leveraging the sensor's current temperature and application-driven image fidelity requirements, this technique mitigates task accuracy issues while providing gains in energy-efficiency. We discuss challenges pertaining to effective, seamless migration decisions at runtime, and propose potential solutions.

CCS CONCEPTS

• **Computer systems organization** → **Heterogeneous (hybrid) systems**;

KEYWORDS

continuous sensing, mobile systems, task migration

ACM Reference Format:
Venkatesh Kodukula, Sai Bharadwaj Medapuram, Britton Jones, Robert LiKamWa. 2018. A Case for Temperature-Driven Task Migration to Balance Energy Efficiency and Image Quality of Vision Processing Workloads. In *Proceedings of 19th International Workshop on Mobile Computing Systems*

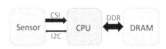

(a) Traditional vision pipeline has energy-expensive camera and memory interfaces.

(b) Near-sensor processing greatly reduces data traffic, relieving energy-expensive interfaces.

Figure 1: Traditional and near-sensor vision pipelines

& Applications (HotMobile '18). ACM, New York, NY, USA, 6 pages. https://doi.org/10.1145/3177102.3177111

1 INTRODUCTION

With rapid advances in computer vision, vision-based workloads are increasingly compute- and memory-intensive. Processing such workloads on traditional CPU/GPU based systems (Fig. 1a) is energy-inefficient and slow, due to limited spatial parallelism and energy-expensive DRAM transactions. This has motivated a significant trend towards shifting processing nearer to the image sensor to reduce the overhead of transferring imaging data from the sensor to the application processor. Some works propose streaming DRAM-less vision accelerators [8], while others propose mixed-signal processing [2, 15] to reduce the data size of the imaging output. Advances in 3D stacked fabrication have opened further possibilities for near-sensor processing with minimal footprint, integrating pixel arrays, memory, and processing circuits in different layers. The smaller interconnects and fine-grained parallel processing of stacked architectures raises performance and energy-efficiency, while maintaining small physical area. Due to these factors, commercial devices have employed stacked technology to integrate image signal processing, e.g., demosaicing and white balance, inside compact sensor modules. Whether stacked or non-stacked, the envisioned near-sensor processing architecture would resemble Fig. 1b.

However, near-sensor processing raises sensor temperature, especially for stacked sensor solutions. This is particularly problematic for image sensors, whose quality degrades at raised temperatures. This limitation has blocked the potential expressiveness and performance of near-sensor accelerator implementations from coming to fruition. In § 3, we characterize that after 1 minute of 1 W of near-sensor power draw, sensor temperature rises by 24 °C, which increases the standard deviation of thermal noise by 3X, drops dynamic range by 16 dB, and multiples the number of hot pixels by 16. In addition to degrading user experience, low quality negatively affects the task accuracy of vision applications. In the above conditions, our pose estimation study fails to detect markers in 12% of frames when images are subject to the thermal noise of near-sensor processing. Under normal noise conditions, i.e., when processing far from the sensor, the same pose estimation detects markers on all frames.

To this end, we propose a balance of near-sensor processing and far-sensor processing through temperature-driven task migration. The migration will shift processing nearer to the sensor to promote energy-efficiency by reducing data traffic. As the sensor heats up, the migration shifts processing far from the sensor to promote image fidelity by allowing the sensor to cool down. This strategy will maintain image quality and task accuracy while providing energy-efficiency gains of near-sensor processing. In § 4, we discuss system-level challenges towards temperature-driven task migration.

2 BACKGROUND AND RELATED WORK

Thermal noise in image sensors Image sensors are susceptible to thermal issues, as an increase in temperature reduces signal fidelity of the sensor output due to thermal noise [10]. Thermal noise is fundamentally present across any carrier of charge. For sensors, the mean-square thermal noise voltage is characterized as kT/C, i.e., proportionally related to temperature and inversely proportional to capacitance. Image sensors are particularly susceptible to thermal noise in low light environments, where the image signal is weak, due to fewer photon arrivals.

Furthermore, the dark current of a photodetector creates another temperature-dependent source of noise, which doubles with every 7 K rise in temperature [9]. Dark current manifests as "hot pixels" in the image frame, abnormally bright pixels in otherwise dark scenes. As disclosed in datasheets, many sensors are designed with 60 °C - 70 °C as a hard limit for guaranteed fidelity, but image quality degrades on approach to the limit.

Task migration for the mobile cloud Due to limited energy budgets on mobile systems, many works explore offloading the computation to the cloud. These works are fundamentally different in terms of application partitioning strategy, offloading decision, framework mechanisms, i.e., virtual machine cloning and code offloading. In Mirror Server [20], the entire application is offloaded to a virtual machine. In CloneCloud [6], partitioning is done at a thread-level granularity, based on static program analysis. The offloading decision is taken dynamically based on application status. In MAUI [7], partitioning is done at method-level granularity and the MAUI profiler and solver dynamically make offloading decisions for remote-able methods. These techniques inform our understanding of potential task migration strategies for heterogeneous distributed systems.

Thermal-driven migration for processor Thermal management techniques for microprocessors aim to quell concerns related to hardware reliability and cooling cost. Dynamic voltage and frequency scaling trades energy savings for performance. To reduce performance loss, dynamic thermal management can use trigger,

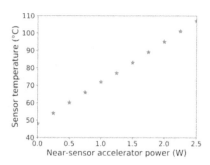

Figure 2: Sensor steady state temperature increases with near-sensor processing power. 1 W raises temp. by 24 °C for an ambient temperature of 27 °C.

response, and initiation mechanisms [5], hybridized thermal stress-aware adaptation [18], and stochastic techniques for thermal safety [12].

Many OS and compiler-based thermal-aware task scheduling techniques also serve to manage temperature through software-hardware cooperation of thermal-aware priority queues [14], passive load balancing and active migration techniques [16], and mechanisms around task queues [3].

These techniques inspire investigation towards thermal-aware migration for sensors, augmented by the sensor's sensitivity to thermal coupling from near-sensor processing.

3 IMPLICATIONS OF NEAR-SENSOR PROCESSING

Here we present a characterization to understand the energy and thermal implications of near-sensor processing. In particular, we examine the potential effectiveness of near-sensor processing around a marker-based pose estimation application to understand the relationship between energy-efficiency, image fidelity, and task accuracy.

We have three objectives. First, we investigate the potential energy-efficiency of near-sensor processing. Second, we identify image artifacts generated by the heat of near-sensor processing. Finally, we study how these artifacts affect the task accuracy of an application.

3.1 Proximity for energy-efficiency

Near-sensor processing increases energy-efficiency by reducing expensive data movement across memory and camera interfaces. Here, we discuss these interfaces and their influence on a case study: visual marker-based pose estimation.

3.1.1 Traditional vision pipelines are energy-inefficient due to expensive interfaces. There are three main components in an imaging pipeline: image sensors, processing units, and memory. The physical interfaces between these components consume substantial power. Transmitter and receiver buffers of high speed interfaces use power-hungry operational amplifiers, whose power consumption linearly increases with data rate. Furthermore, to maintain high speeds without increasing voltage, differential interfaces use complementary signals to reduce the influence of noise, drawing more power than their single-ended interface counterparts. Altogether,

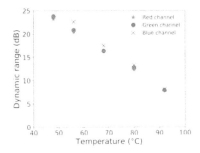
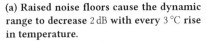

(a) Raised noise floors cause the dynamic range to decrease 2 dB with every 3 °C rise in temperature.

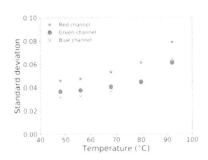

(b) Increased influence of thermally sensitive image noises increases the standard deviation of an image.

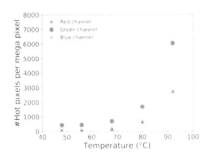

(c) Raised dark current triggers twice as many hot pixel aberrations with every 6 °C rise in temperature.

Figure 3: Raised temperatures degrade image quality due to thermal noise and hot pixel generation.

this results in energy-expensive high-speed interfaces; common LVDS interfaces consumes approximately 30 pJ/bit.

As shown in Fig. 1a, an image sensor and application processor communicate with each other via camera serial interface (CSI) for frame data and I^2C bus for camera control and configuration. Meanwhile, DRAM and CPU communicate via a DDR interface for read/write/control operations. In vision applications, e.g., marker-based pose estimation, these interfaces consume substantial power dissipation, which we examine using Microsemi's power estimator [1]. For high precision, the application may need to process frames at high resolutions when visual markers are small and/or far from the camera. Streaming at 4K resolution at 60 frames per second will result in data rates on the order of Gbps.

For the camera interface, we evaluate a common CSI interface with 1 clock and 4 data lanes; we find that this consumes 135 mW of power. Since I^2C is used only for control/configuration, it operates at low frequency – 400 kHz – and consumes only 12 mW of power. For the DRAM interface, a common DDR3 configuration will use a width of 32 bits, ECC, and on-die 120 Ω termination. In this configuration, the DDR interface consumes around 600 mW of power. While CSI and DDR interfaces are active throughout the runtime of the application, the I^2C bus stays active just before the start of the application. Consequently, the camera and memory interfaces sum up to 835 mW of substantial power. Thus, interfaces cause traditional vision pipelines to be energy expensive, motivating a pursuit of optimization.

3.1.2 Near-sensor processing reduces the burden of energy-expensive interfaces. To avoid the burden of energy-expensive interfaces, near-sensor processing units should process vision workloads. This will reduce – and in some cases, eliminate – the use of energy-expensive DDR and CSI interfaces.

Near-sensor processing pipelines architecturally differ from traditional vision pipelines in that in-sensor memory replaces off-sensor DRAM. This allows the vision accelerator to operate on image data before the data crosses the off-sensor interface. The accelerator could be fixed-function hardware or a general-purpose processing unit, as long as it satisfies the computational needs of the near-sensor processing. With recent advances towards commercial in-sensor accelerators [13], such an architecture is practically realistic.

The near-sensor processing unit would substantially reduce interface data rate. In the case of marker-based pose estimation application, the output from the accelerator would need only be the translational and rotational estimates of a pose, whose 6 floating point numbers would occupy 24 bytes of data per frame. For optical see-through devices, the camera frame itself is not necessary. For video see-through devices, camera frames can be sent at lower resolutions and lower frame rates than those used for pose estimation. As opposed to the Gbps burden of camera frame data, which requires a CSI interface, the reduced data output would allow the use of the efficient I^2C interface for dramatically reduced energy consumption.

3.2 Proximity degrades task accuracy

While near-sensor processing is energy-efficient, it increases sensor temperature through thermal coupling. Higher temperatures significantly degrade image quality, due to thermal noise and hot pixel generation, impairing the task accuracy of vision applications. Here, we present a thermal characterization of near-sensor processing. Specifically, how does...

- ... near-sensor processing affect sensor temperature?
- ... sensor temperature affect image quality?
- ... image quality affect task accuracy?

3.2.1 Proximity generates heat. Any form of processing dissipates power, which creates heat. Due to their small, silent form factors, mobile devices use passive cooling to dissipate heat through conduction to the skin of the device. In smartphones, the sensor and CPU are separated via ribbon cable, which limits thermal coupling; CPU temperature does not substantially influence sensor temperature. However, the proximity of a near-sensor accelerator will generate strong thermal coupling of the sensor with accelerator power.

To characterize this temperature-power relationship, we use Therminator [19], a compact thermal simulator for smartphone hardware. The simulator uses a specification file to describe the device layout, comprising the size and location of different components, and a power trace file to profile component power. We modify the files to place the processor and sensor in close proximity, separated by 17 mm.

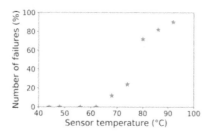

Figure 4: Degradation in image fidelity at higher temp. increases failure rate of marker detection.

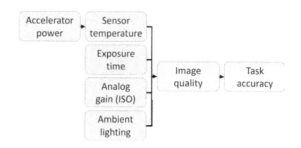

Figure 5: Dynamically changing sensor and environment conditions influence task accuracy. This poses a challenge to migration decisions.

In this placement, the steady state temperature of sensor linearly increases with the processing power of the near-sensor accelerator, as shown in Fig. 2. For every 1 W of near-sensor processing power, within 60 seconds, there is a 24 °C rise in sensor temperature. Stacked image sensor configurations will generate even greater temperature dependencies.

3.2.2 Heat degrades image fidelity. High temperatures degrade image quality, due to thermal noise and hot pixels. While denoising algorithms can remove some of these artifacts, their effectiveness needs to be weighed against their power consumption and performance overhead. We leave an extensive analysis of denoising solutions for near-sensor processing as future work. Here, to quantify noise, we perform experiments [1] to capture raw images under controlled lighting as we heat the sensor to different temperatures.

For our image capture platform, we use the AR0330, a Bayer-filtered 3.2 Mp image sensor, integrated with Microsemi Smart-Fusion2 advanced development kit. The solution uses DRAM for temporary image storage and an FPGA for processing. The FPGA hosts a Cortex-M3, which we use to configure the image sensor's registers, e.g., for 32 ms exposure time and 4X analog gain. We remove the camera lens to reduce temperature-related distortion in captured images.

We construct a platform to observe how reported pixel values change with temperature. To control lighting, we vary a pulse width modulated LED, adjusting its position for uniform sensor illumination. To control temperature, we use a Hitachi RH650V heat gun and a FLIR ONE thermal camera to raise and monitor temperature. We raise sensor temperature to 100 °C and capture frames as the sensor cools down. We cycle the temperature 10 times per lighting environment.

To generate a baseline "noiseless" image for comparison, we average 10 frames captured after the sensor settles to an ambient steady-state temperature of 44 °C. Using pixel-wise comparisons of captured frames against the baseline image, we characterize the effect of temperature on pixel value. To do this, we first group pixel locations by color channel and reported baseline pixel value. Then, for a given temperature, we treat each pixel of each captured frame as a sample of a distribution, grouped by the baseline pixel value of its pixel location. This characterization reports three important image degradations created by high temperatures.

Dynamic range reduction: Dynamic range measures a sensor's ability to capture dark and bright portions of a scene. As noise floor increases with temperature, the dynamic range of reported values shrinks. Our measurements show that high-temperature pixels report raised values, separated from the baseline value by a temperature-dependent offset. As this forces pixel values to start above zero and saturate at lower luminance, the effective range of reported pixel values shrinks. We measure that dynamic range drops by 2 dB for every 3 °C rise in temperature as shown in Fig. 3a.

Image noise increase: Thermally sensitive noise sources cause pixels to report deviated values. We quantify this by calculating the standard deviation of pixel values in our grouped distributions. Our measurements confirm that noise sharply increases with temperature, as shown in Fig. 3b.

Hot pixel generation: As discussed in the background, hot pixels appear where dark current is high. These aberrations increase with temperature, as dark current exponentially increases with temperature. We count abnormally large pixel values in dark images to measure the rate of hot pixel generation. Our measurements confirm that the number of hot pixels doubles for every 6 °C rise, as shown in Fig. 3c.

3.2.3 Degradation in image fidelity impairs task accuracy. Raised temperatures lead to pixel-level artifacts that degrade image quality, impairing the task accuracy of vision applications. To study the consequences of image quality on task accuracy, we insert noise into images around marker-based pose estimation, implemented around OpenCV's tutorial[2]. The code uses OpenCV calls to extract visual features and descriptors, to associate image features with reference template features through Flann-based matching, and estimate the pose of the camera through a Perspective-n-Point algorithm. This reports camera pose with respect to a physical marker.

For our characterization, we use our Microsemi imaging setup to capture images of a 7.5 in. x 10 in. marker from various perspectives. We then use noise models interpolated from our characterization, adding noise to captured images to simulate high temperature captures from the same camera pose. As shown in Fig. 4, at a fixed distance of 100 cm pointed at the target, the number of marker detection failures sharply increases with temperature. Thus, to keep estimation failures below a threshold, sensor temperature must remain low.

---

[1]Data available at https://github.com/kodukulav/research/thermal

[2]http://docs.opencv.org/3.2.0/dc/d2c/tutorial_real_time_pose.html

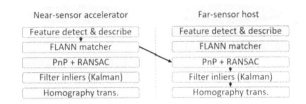

(a) All stages run on near-sensor accelerator, resulting in no communication overhead. This thermally strains the sensor.

(b) For thermal relief, we migrate three stages from near-sensor acc. to far-sensor host, using data transfer overhead.

Figure 6: Two different partition splits

Our measurements indicate: (*i*) processing far from the sensor is energy-inefficient, due to power-expensive interfaces, and (*ii*) processing close to the sensor degrades task accuracy due to image degradation. Thus, near-sensor processing and far-sensor processing schemes create a possibility for energy efficiency and task accuracy tradeoffs.

4 THERMAL-DRIVEN TASK MIGRATION

Our characterization reveals that near-sensor processing and far-sensor processing offer tradeoffs between energy-efficiency and image fidelity. This makes a strong case for thermal-driven task migration: shift workloads towards near-sensor processing for energy-efficiency and towards far-sensor processing for image fidelity.

Systems can partition workloads by different granularities: by programs, threads, classes, and methods. An effective granularity will allow the system to expressively and efficiently migrate tasks. In vision, as most processing can be represented using a connected graph [11], it is simplest to partition the task between operational stages, as in [17]. For example, as illustrated in Fig. 6b, for marker-based pose estimation, the system can run feature detection and FLANN stages on the near-sensor processing unit and the remainder of the stages on the far-sensor host. To allow the system to change the partition split at runtime, we assume the system architect will provision for flexible near-sensor operation. Whether the near-sensor operation consists of fixed-function units or general-purpose instructions, the system will need to be able to run different streams of operations on the near-sensor processing unit.

In the remainder of this section, we discuss thermal-driven task migration challenges related to decision-making and performance assurance for migrating between partition splits.

4.1 Situationally aware partition decisions

Determining an effective partition split must balance the thermal asymmetry of the distributed processing units and the costs of data transaction. For example, partitioning at an early stage grants thermal relief, but only at the expense of communication cost. On the other hand, partitioning at the latter stages of the pipeline ensures less thermal relief for less communication overhead.

To approach this challenge, we draw inspiration from related works that dynamically partition applications to offload mobile tasks to remote servers for energy efficiency [6, 7, 17]. Along similar lines, a dynamic partitioning of the connected graph could optimize workload placement for energy-efficiency and/or performance while still satisfying sufficient task accuracy. Thus, we plan to characterize the performance, energy, and communication overhead of partitioning in the context of processing vision workloads across near-sensor and far-sensor processing units. Such partitioning should also utilize local optimizations, e.g., dynamic voltage-frequency scaling on the accelerator or host.

As in prior offloading works, we envision a runtime that will dynamically decide which task stages should be offloaded, driven by inputs from a task profiler and an optimization solver. Unlike other migration works, however, partitioning between near- and far-sensor processing must be guided by several conditions that affect image quality and task accuracy, as illustrated in Fig. 5. Partitioning decisions will directly influence near-sensor processing activity, which raises sensor temperature over time. However, image quality also depends on the lighting environment; dark scenes require sensors to use large exposure times and high analog gains, increasing motion artifacts and noise sensitivity. Given the mobile nature of vision applications, the split decision will need to continually adapt to continuously changing conditions.

4.2 Seamless task migration

Vision processing can be pipelined to allow different stages to process in parallel at high performance. When the system opts to change the partition split, e.g., from Fig. 6a to Fig. 6b, the migration will need to shift stages to run on the far-sensor host. This presents a challenge: how will the system provide the pipeline data of previous stages to a newly migrated partitioning scheme? Ideally, this should be seamless; there should be no drop in pipelined processing performance.

To complete task migration to a different partitioning split, the system must synchronize computational states between the near-sensor processing unit and the far-sensor host. This includes any dependencies generated by previous operational stages. It also includes the output of the last stage before the partitioning split. In Fig. 6b, the latter three stages will not be able to run until they are provided with the output of the previous stages. In our case study, this constitutes 24 KB, which would take 17 ms to transfer from near-sensor to far-sensor. Thus, we will face the challenge of mitigating latency as the near-sensor accelerator communicates data and the far-sensor host fills the pipeline.

Efficient pipeline utilization has been well explored, e.g., in branch prediction. Along similar lines, to keep pipeline fully occupied, we can speculatively predict thermal emergencies and begin to fill the pipeline to minimize performance delays.

Future work: predictive scheduler for migration

We plan to study effective mechanisms towards a scheduler that uses sensor temperature, environment conditions, and application fidelity requirements to guide partitioning decisions between near-sensor and far-sensor processing. For smooth performance, our scheduler will predict migration points in advance, and use early communication to hide migration latency. Through this predictive scheduler, the system will implement thermal-driven task migration to balance energy efficiency and task accuracy for vision workloads.

5 CONCLUSION

Near-sensor processing is the key to energy-efficient imaging and vision, as evidenced by recent academic and industrial efforts towards stacked image sensors. However, we show that near-sensor processing degrades vision tasks due to thermal noise, placing hard limits on the adoption of near-sensor processing. Thus, to balance efficiency and accuracy, we propose thermal-driven task migration to dynamically shift tasks between the thermally coupled near-sensor accelerator and the far-sensor host, based on environmental conditions. We will build on our early work through a deeper implementation-based study of thermal-driven task migration mechanisms. We will also pursue a richer investigation into the broader implications of near-sensor processing on a wider variety of vision tasks. Thermal-driven task migration will enable a future of energy-efficient continuous mobile vision through powerful near-sensor processing.

ACKNOWLEDGMENTS

The authors are grateful for comments made by anonymous reviewers and the paper shepherd Dr. Nic Lane. The authors thank Microsemi for their generous support through SmartFusion2 hardware kit and software licenses. This material is based upon work supported by the National Science Foundation under Grant No. 1657602.

REFERENCES

[1] Microsemi power estimators and calculators. https://www.microsemi.com/products/fpga-soc/design-resources/power-calculator.

[2] A. Alaghi, C. Li, and J. P. Hayes. Stochastic circuits for real-time image-processing applications. In *Proc. of Design Automation Conference (DAC)*, 2013.

[3] A. S. Arani. Online thermal-aware scheduling for multiple clock domain CMPs. In *IEEE Int. SOC Conference*, 2007.

[4] B. Barry, C. Brick, F. Connor, D. Donohoe, D. Moloney, R. Richmond, M. O'Riordan, and V. Toma. Always-on vision processing unit for mobile applications. *IEEE Micro*, 2015.

[5] D. Brooks and M. Martonosi. Dynamic thermal management for high-performance microprocessors. In *Int. Symp. High-Performance Computer Architecture (HPCA)*, 2001.

[6] B.-G. Chun, S. Ihm, P. Maniatis, M. Naik, and A. Patti. Clonecloud: elastic execution between mobile device and cloud. In *Proc. ACM Conf. Computer systems*, 2011.

[7] E. Cuervo, A. Balasubramanian, D.-k. Cho, A. Wolman, S. Saroiu, R. Chandra, and P. Bahl. Maui: making smartphones last longer with code offload. In *Proc. ACM Int. Conf. on Mobile systems, applications, and services*, 2010.

[8] Z. Du, R. Fasthuber, T. Chen, P. Ienne, L. Li, X. Feng, Y. Chen, and O. Temam. ShiDianNao: Shifting vision processing closer to the sensor. In *Proc. Int. Symp. on Computer Architecture*.

[9] A. El Gamal and H. Eltoukhy. CMOS image sensors. *IEEE Circuits and Devices Magazine*, 21(3), 2005.

[10] J. Fraden. *Handbook of Modern Sensors: Physics, Designs, and Applications*. Springer New York, 2010.

[11] Itseez. OpenVX Computer Vision Acceleration Standard. https://www.khronos.org/openvx/.

[12] H. Jung and M. Pedram. Stochastic dynamic thermal management: A Markovian decision-based approach. In *Int. Conf. Computer Design*, 2007.

[13] Y. Kagawa, N. Fujii, K. Aoyagi, Y. Kobayashi, S. Nishi, N. Todaka, S. Takeshita, J. Taura, H. Takahashi, Y. Nishimura, et al. Novel stacked cmos image sensor with advanced cu2cu hybrid bonding. In *Proc. of Electron Devices Meeting (IEDM)*, 2016.

[14] A. Kumar, L. Shang, L.-S. Peh, and N. K. Jha. System-level dynamic thermal management for high-performance microprocessors. *IEEE Trans. Computer-Aided Design of Integrated Circuits and Systems*, 27, 2008.

[15] R. LiKamWa, Y. Hou, J. Gao, M. Polansky, and L. Zhong. Redeye: analog convnet image sensor architecture for continuous mobile vision. In *Proc. of Int. Symp. on Computer Architecture*, 2016.

[16] A. Merkel, F. Bellosa, and A. Weissel. Event-driven thermal management in SMP systems. In *Second Workshop on Temperature-Aware Computer Systems (TACS)*, 2005.

[17] M.-R. Ra, A. Sheth, L. Mummert, P. Pillai, D. Wetherall, and R. Govindan. Odessa: enabling interactive perception applications on mobile devices. In *Proc. ACM Int. Conf. Mobile systems, applications, and services*, 2011.

[18] K. Skadron. Hybrid architectural dynamic thermal management. 2004

[19] Q. Xie, M. J. Dousti, and M. Pedram. Therminator: a thermal simulator for smartphones producing accurate chip and skin temperature maps. In *ACM/IEEE Int. Symp. Low Power Electronics and Design (ISLPED)*, 2014.

[20] B. Zhao, Z. Xu, C. Chi, S. Zhu, and G. Cao. Mirroring smartphones for good: A feasibility study. In *Proc. Int. Conf. on Mobile and Ubiquitous Systems: Computing, Networking, and Services*, 2010.

Delivering the Mobile Web to the Next Billion Users

Ben Greenstein
Google
Seattle, Washington, U.S.A.
bengr@google.com

ABSTRACT

In many parts of the world, people have limited access to basic needs such as clean water, consistent electricity and healthcare. In these environments, having access to the web can be transformative for them and their communities, as it provides information on medical symptoms and treatments, opportunities for education and job training, and access to the arts and entertainment that often reaches far beyond the knowledge and output of the local community. Unfortunately, in these environments there are significant barriers to accessing that information on the web, including costs, connectivity, language, and an understanding of what the web provides. This talk will present an overview of the challenges and opportunities we face in making the mobile web useful and relevant for the next billion users who are coming online in the developing regions of the world. I'll present data on the current state of the mobile web, including usage patterns, as well as network and device constraints and web performance as seen in practice. I'll discuss several efforts at Google aimed at addressing the unique challenges of this population of users, and I'll conclude with thoughts on where we should focus going forward.

CCS Concepts/ACM Classifiers

• **Information systems~Browsers** • **Networks~Mobile networks** • **Networks~Network performance evaluation** • *Networks~Network protocol design* • *Human-centered computing~Web-based interaction*

Author Keywords

Mobile web; web performance; next billion users

BIOGRAPHY

Ben Greenstein is a software engineer at Google, where he leads an effort to improve mobile web performance and lower mobile data access costs by improving the efficiency of metered data use. Hundreds of millions of Chrome users worldwide benefit from this work. He's also affiliate faculty in the School of Computer Science and Engineering at the University of Washington. Previously, Ben was a researcher at Intel Labs Seattle, which focused on ubiquitous computing. There he worked to improve the privacy of wireless systems, and subsequently received best paper awards at MobiSys and Ubicomp. His research interests include web performance, mobile networking and systems, privacy, and embedded sensing. Ben received his Ph.D. in Computer Science from UCLA and B.A. from the University of Pennsylvania.

HotMobile'18, February 12–13, 2018, Tempe, AZ, USA.
© 2018 Copyright is held by the owner/author(s).
ACM ISBN 978-1-4503-5630-5/18/02.
DOI: https://doi.org/10.1145/3177102.3180277

Hermes: A Real Time Hypervisor for Mobile and IoT Systems

Neil Klingensmith
University of Wisconsin
naklingensmi@wisc.edu

Suman Banerjee
University of Wisconsin
suman@cs.wisc.edu

Workshop on Mobile Computing Systems & Applications, Tempe , AZ, USA, February 12–13, 2018 (HotMobile '18), 6 pages.
https://doi.org/10.1145/3177102.3177103

ABSTRACT

We present Hermes, a hypervisor for MMU-less microcontrollers. Hermes enables high-performance bare metal applications to coexist with RTOSes and other less time-critical software on a single CPU. We experimentally demonstrate that a real-time operating system scheduler does not always provide deterministic response times for I/O events, which can cause real-time workloads to be unschedulable. Hermes solves this problem by adding a layer of abstraction between the hardware I/O devices and the software that services them, making I/O transactions truly deterministic. Virtualization on low-power mobile and embedded systems also enables some interesting software capabilities like secure execution of third-party apps, software integrity attestation, and bare metal performance in a multitasking software environment. These features otherwise require additional hardware (i.e. multiple CPUs, hardware TPM, etc) or may not be available at all. In other projects, we have anecdotally noticed that real time operating systems are not always able to respond quickly and deterministically enough to time-sensitive operations, particularly under high I/O load. We validate this observed timing problem by measuring interrupt latency in an RTOS environment and comparing to an experimental implementation of Hermes. We find that not only is the interrupt latency lower in the virtualized environment, but it is also much more deterministic—a key figure of merit for real-time software systems. We discuss challenges of implementing a hypervisor on a CPU with no memory management unit, and we present some preliminary solutions and workarounds. We go on to explore some other applications of virtualization to mobile and IoT software.

CCS CONCEPTS

• **Software and its engineering** → *Virtual machines*; • **Computer systems organization** → **Real-time operating systems**; **Embedded systems**;

KEYWORDS

Real-time systems; hypervisor; virtualization

ACM Reference format:
Neil Klingensmith and Suman Banerjee. 2018. Hermes: A Real Time Hypervisor for Mobile and IoT Systems. In *Proceedings of 19th International*

1 INTRODUCTION

Modern embedded sensing and mobile applications increasingly perform diverse functions, including displaying user interfaces, managing networking, performing real-time data acquisition, and more. Some even allow third-party code to be downloaded and run alongside the factory firmware [17]. Such diversity in runtime requirements poses challenges to software architects, who must manage the often competing needs of different tasks.

To manage the diverse runtime requirements of embedded software, we have developed a lightweight embedded hypervisor we call Hermes[1], targeted to ARM Cortex-M microcontrollers. Other authors have proposed similar systems for mobile phone environments, but none that we are aware of on MMU-less processors [5, 9, 14].

IoT applications are frequently implemented on CPUs without an MMU in order to save cost and power. While the cost of MMU-ful Linux-capable processors is going down all the time, energy considerations (especially for mobile applications) are not likely to go away.

The problem we set out to solve is one of I/O latency in such a complex runtime environment. Real-time operating system (RTOS) scheduling algorithms cannot guarantee deadlines will be met under high I/O load. People usually solve this problem by running time-critical operations on a separate CPU [13]. For example, high-frequency signal sampling may be implemented in bare metal code running on an independent microcontroller while the user interface, networking, storage, etc. runs on the main device. This approach has a lot of obvious shortcomings: increased hardware and software complexity, power consumption, physical size, verification difficulty, etc.

Driver-level I/O processing has traditionally been assumed to be a negligible component of overall response time—an assumption that was valid 30 years ago as these real-time scheduling algorithms were being developed. At that time, embedded computers were single-purpose machines that largely performed the same task repetitively.

But that assumption of single-purposeness is becoming less valid. Modern microcontrollers are equipped with a diverse range of peripherals that was unimaginable in the 1980s.Network interfaces, high-speed data acquisition devices, touchscreens, and more all have a diverse range of requirements, but they are treated the same by the RTOS and CPU. Exception management for low-priority I/O

---

[1]HypErvisor for Real time MicrocontrollErS
http://hermes.wings.cs.wisc.edu

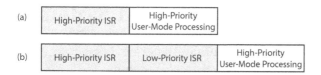

Figure 1: Timeline of (a) high-priority ISR followed by user-mode I/O processing and (b) low-priority ISR co-occuring with a high-priority ISR, delaying high-priority user mode processing.

Software Environment	Entropy of Latency
FreeRTOS, Serial Only	0.85
FreeRTOS, Serial + Ping Flood	1.78
Bare Metal Guest, Serial Only	0.27
Bare Metal Guest, Serial + Ping Flood	0.14

Table 1: Entropy of the distributions of latency measurements (distributions shown in Figure 2). Low values of entropy are more deterministic. The bare metal guest running in Hermes has much more predictable latency than tasks in FreeRTOS. Under Hermes, latency is still highly deterministic under high I/O load.

is always performed before user-mode code can respond to high-priority events, creating a kind of unintended priority inversion (depicted in Figure 1). Consequently, response times to latency-sensitive I/O events are not deterministic, which can result in failure (see an exploration of this in Section 2).

Conventional wisdom among real-time programmers is that ISRs should be as short as possible: clear the interrupt, maybe transfer a few bytes of data, and exit. Userland code should be responsible for responding to the event. In a crowded software environment with multiple drivers and tasks competing for CPU time, this programming method has the effect of delaying the actual response of all I/O events until all ISRs have finished executing. These delays break the assumptions that underlie real-time scheduling algorithms, which require the highest-priority task to always run first. Instead, we are running the driver code associated with low-priority tasks before the user code for high-priority tasks, and RTOSes do not have flexibility to change this behavior.

Hermes is a lightweight virtualization platform that lives between the hardware and the operating system. At its core, Hermes consists of some initialization code and a single interrupt service routine that catches and preprocesses all exceptions before dispatching them to the operating system. In its role as a mediator of exception processing, Hermes can allow multiple operating systems or bare metal applications to run side-by-side on an MMUless microcontroller, dispatching exception processing to the appropriate OS as necessary, much like a hypervisor running on a PC or server. We see several potential advantages to this software architecture:

(1) **Performance.** For time-critical applications, Hermes can provide a thin layer between the software and the hardware. Real time operating systems (RTOSs) on the other hand, often come with a lot of overhead in the form of system call latency for time-critical tasks. This may be unacceptable in applications where time-critical tasks need to coexist with other less critical code like networking or user interface software.

(2) **Security.** With Hermes, we can allow untrusted third party code to run in a sandboxed environment that protects mission critical software from attacks. Hermes, with the assistance of peripherals commonly available on commodity microcontrollers, can provide a root of trust for guests and remote agents.

(3) **Portability.** Hermes can provide a consistent virtual environment for all higher level software, regardless of the underlying hardware. This could enable, for example, edge

computing devices with heterogeneous hardware implementations to run user apps targeted to a common platform.

A diagram of the Hermes software architecture is shown in Figure 3. We are implementing Hermes on an ARM Cortex M7 CPU called the Atmel SAM E70 [6, 7] which has 2 Mbytes of flash and 384 kbytes of RAM. It also includes many advanced features of the latest ARM microcontrollers such as a floating point unit, a memory protection unit, separate instruction and data caches, and many peripherals. We have tested Hermes by running a FreeRTOS v9.0.0 [2] guest on top of the hypervisor. The contributions made by this work are the following:

- We measure the response time to interrupts in an RTOS environment, demonstrating that latencies can be nondeterministic under high I/O load.
- We propose the use of a hypervisor in real time software environments to ameliorate the determinism problem. The hypervisor can provide isolation between software tasks, which can improve timing predictability.
- We develop a rudimentary implementation of the hypervisor, and we study its performance. We discuss some of the difficulties of implementing a hypervisor on a microcontroller with no MMU.

2 PROBLEM VALIDATION

Using performance counters on the ARM Cortex M7 CPU, we measure the ISR-user space latency—the time between beginning of ISR execution to beginning of userspace data processing. This is a metric of how long it takes to respond to an I/O event. Ideally, for time sensitive I/O this time should be short and deterministic, meaning the same for each I/O event. We find that in the FreeRTOS environment, the ISR-user space latency is **less deterministic** under high I/O load, as expected. We have also experienced this problem when developing other systems, but we did not study it as carefully [12].

Experimental Setup

We measured the ISR-userspace latency for a serial port receive in FreeRTOS and Hermes. In FreeRTOS, we used an OS queue to transfer the data from an ISR to a user-mode task. In Hermes, we ran a FreeRTOS guest alongside a bare metal guest that transferred data between an ISR and userspace code using a memory buffer. In both runtime environments, we had two other periodic FreeRTOS tasks running alongside the latency test. In both cases, we ran the latency

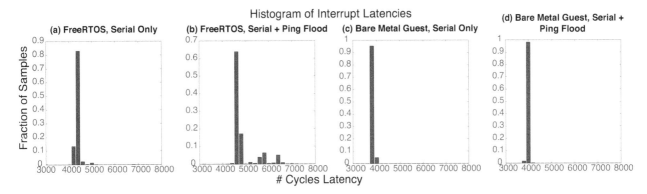

Figure 2: ISR-userspace latency histograms. Latency is measured as the number of cycles elapsed between executing the serial port receive ISR and beginning of userspace processing.

test in isolation as well as in the presence of high I/O load (a ping flood) to test how well each software environment could provide a deterministic runtime environment. The networking software that responded to the pings was implemented as a low-priority task in FreeRTOS for both environments.

FreeRTOS

FreeRTOS is a popular (if not the most popular) real-time operating system for embedded and IoT computers. It has been ported to CPUs manufactured by 20+ manufacturers representing every commonly used architecture (ARM, x86, etc.). FreeRTOS implements a rate monotonic scheduler in which each task has a fixed priority, and the highest priority task that is ready to run is executed first.

According to its development team, "FreeRTOS never performs a non-deterministic operation, such as walking a linked list, from inside a critical section or interrupt." Traditionally, its set of features—deterministic rate monotonic scheduler—is thought to provide deterministic event response times. This is true for CPU-intensive tasks, but, as we will see, that assumption of determinism breaks down under high I/O load.

Results

Figure 2 shows the results of our latency tests. Each subplot is a histogram of ISR-userspace latencies. Ideally, we would want these plots to have only one bar—a single response time for every I/O event. Figure 2 (a) and (b) show latency in FreeRTOS only, under low and high I/O load respectively. Under high I/O load, the latency histogram is more spread out because exceptions raised by unrelated I/O events delay execution of the user mode code in an unpredictable way. This happens when a serial port exception and a network port exception occur close in time. Both exceptions must be processed before the user mode code to handle the serial port receive can begin executing. We get shorter and more deterministic response times when the serial port exception occurs in isolation. If the network port exception occurs near the same time as the serial port exception, the network port ISR will have to execute before the CPU can return to user mode, delaying the response time. This is an inherent disadvantage of running multiple unrelated programs on a single processor which we are trying to correct with Hermes.

Figure 2 (c) and (d) show the latency of the same I/O operation running as a bare-metal guest inside Hermes. Determinism is higher

for histograms that are more clustered around a single value and lower for histograms that are more spread out.

Discussion

The reason that ISR-userspace latency is more deterministic in Hermes under high I/O load is that by design, Hermes can enable or disable different interrupt sources depending on which guest is active. In this test, we disabled the network port exception when the bare-metal serial port guest was running. This makes it impossible for the network port ISR to interrupt the user-mode code that handles the serial port receive. Operating systems in general do not support changing processor state for different threads[2], presumably because I/O transactions are assumed to be the domain of the operating system and mostly independent of user-mode software. That assumption was generally valid for early PCs and servers, whose job was primarily batch-mode processing with very little user interaction. Mobile and IoT devices have completely different set of requirements: they need to serve as a responsive user interface in which software works closely with I/O.

Uncertainty in scheduling can create real problems for these kinds of systems. For instance, if the same timing uncertainty in Figure 2 were imposed on ADC sampling in an IoT device, it could cause several decibels of harmonic distortion [3]. It is easy to imagine many situations in which timing errors could result in degraded system performance on mobile platforms.

We should be clear here that we do not have a full implementation of I/O prioritization in Hermes. The results in Figure 2 were obtained by forcing a context switch to the bare metal guest each time we took a serial port exception. We acknowledge that our implementation is not scalable, but the results give us some insight into what is possible with virtualization. Cleaning up the implementation should not significantly degrade performance of the hypervisor.

We considered several simpler alternative solutions that could be implemented in the RTOS to alleviate I/O latency:

(1) **Disable interrupts in user-level code.** This would allow us to process the I/O event in userspace without interruption. It does not solve the problem of ISR-userspace latency, since

---

[2]For example, we are not aware of any RTOS that allows the programmer to enable or disable different drivers while certain threads are running.

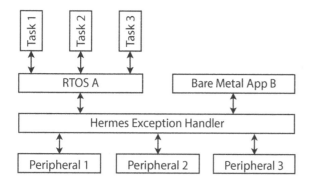

Figure 3: Architecture of the Hermes Hypervisor. The main component of Hermes, its monolithic exception handler, intercepts all exceptions before dispatching them to the guests.

more than one exception may execute sequentially before user code gets a chance to disable interrupts.

(2) **Process I/O events in the ISR.** This would allow us to ensure that our I/O events are processed in a timely fashion. This could be an acceptable solution for a single-purpose bare-metal app with no other tasks running concurrently. The problem with this approach in an RTOS is that it monopolizes the CPU during the entire I/O operation, likely causing other tasks to hang while the I/O event is handled.

(3) **Re-prioritize the interrupts.** We could use the CPU's interrupt prioritization circuits to execute the time-critical ISR first, before other ISRs. This wouldn't decrease latency in an RTOS environment because lower priority ISRs will always execute before the user space code.

None of these solutions is a viable alternative because they cannot reduce latency while maintaining a responsive runtime environment for other concurrent tasks.

3 ARCHITECTURE

In its current implementation, Hermes is a single monolithic interrupt service routine that intercepts all CPU exceptions before they can be processed by the operating system. Figure 3 shows a diagram of the interactions between the Hermes hypervisor and its guests. On boot, the Hermes initialization code sets up the CPU's exception table to point to the Hermes ISR. It then launches the guest operating systems in the ARM CPU's unprivileged execution mode[3].

3.1 Opportunities

Running a hypervisor on embedded IoT equipment enables some interesting possibilities for IoT software.

Distributed Processing on a Single Chip

Many embedded hardware designs use a distributed computation model to separate a complex task into several independent execution environments. For example, a board might have one network processor, one sampling processor, and a main CPU, each

performing its own specific task independently of the others. This type of design complicates the hardware and software and likely drives up the cost, size, and energy requirements of the equipment. With a hypervisor, we can run all software on a single CPU while maintaining isolation by running each independent application in its own VM. CPU and resource allocation can be strictly controlled by the hypervisor to ensure that deadlines are met. Our preliminary investigation into I/O latency in Section 2 suggests that we can use Hermes to isolate low-priority CPU time hogs (like the ping flood) from the rest of the system.

Security

Authenticating the software on an unattended embedded device is still an open problem. A few proposed solutions [4, 15] rely on measuring the timing of some arbitrary computational operation. The hypervisor may be able to serve as a root of trust for virtualized applications by implementing a virtualized trusted platform module (vTPM) [1] to be used by underlying software components. It may be possible to implement a virtual TPM in software using either ARM TrustZone [16] or an on-chip cryptographic accelerator [10].

3.2 Challenges

Implementing a virtualization environment on a platform with no hardware support has a unique set of challenges that we will discuss here.

Compile-Time Guest Setup

Since we are dealing with a system that has no MMU, we are required to compile all guests with the hypervisor into a single runtime binary. The practical challenge is that, for symmetric guests (more than one instance of a single guest OS), we must change the name of each function and variable in order to avoid linker errors. This can be mildly annoying because it makes the RTOS code harder to read. We have written a script to perform this task automatically.

Imprecise Bus Fault Exceptions

The ARM Cortex M line of CPUs throws bus fault exceptions for accesses to privileged memory regions that are mapped to certain control registers. Some of these exceptions can be imprecise, meaning that the CPU does not record the exact instruction that caused the exception. Instead, in response to an imprecise exception, the CPU will throw a bus fault as soon as possible (in our experience 2-10 instructions past the faulting instruction). This makes the job of the Hermes exception handler difficult since it does not know which privileged memory access needs to be emulated. The only thing we can be sure of is that the faulting instruction occurs earlier in the instruction stream than where the exception was thrown.

Fortunately for us, the ARM Cortex M7 device on which we implemented Hermes sometimes records the effective address of the instruction that caused the bus fault, even if the bus fault is imprecise[4].

We solve the problem of imprecise bus fault exceptions by tracing back through the instruction stream to look for a privileged instruction with the correct effective address that is likely to have caused the imprecise exception. Starting at the address of the instruction

---

[3]Normally, operating system code would run in privileged execution mode, but when the RTOS is running as a guest inside Hermes, it executes in unprivileged mode.

[4]Contrary to this fact, the ARM documentation indicates that the CPU *never* records the effective address of instructions that cause imprecise bus faults. We have either found an error in the documentation or a bug in the CPU, but this is good since it works to our advantage.

that caused the exception, we trace back through the last five instructions in order of memory address. We decode each instruction and compare its effective address to the address that caused the bus fault. If the instruction's effective address matches the offending effective address, then we assume a match and emulate that instruction.

Clearly, there are some pathological cases that could cause this approach to fail. So far, we have not encountered any code in a guest that causes this approach to fail to emulate the guest.

Some Special Register Accesses Don't Cause Exceptions

Two instructions on the ARM Cortex M7—mrs and msr—which write and read certain special-purpose registers in the ARM CPU do not cause privilege violation exceptions when executed by the guest. These instructions allow access to special CPU registers that control interrupt priority masking and accesses to the master stack pointer. The mrs and msr instructions are classified as privileged instructions, but when they are executed by code running in unprivileged mode, they fail silently: the register write is not committed, and the processor continues normal execution.

The problem is that if a guest OS tries to modify the processor state with one of these instructions, that state modification cannot be registered by Hermes since it does not cause an exception. The privileged instruction will complete like a nop instruction without modifying the CPU state. Critical CPU state changes like disabling interrupts will not work as intended.

We circumvent this problem by patching the OS kernel, adding an undefined instruction immediately following an mrs or msr. When the hypervisor encounters an undefined instruction exception, it will search backward in the instruction stream for an mrs or msr instruction. If we run an unpatched kernel inside the hypervisor, it will crash because the intended CPU state modifications will not happen as intended.

4 I/O VIRTUALIZATION

The main goal of the Hermes hypervisor is to provide a thinner layer between hardware and software than is possible with an RTOS. There are three general techniques for virtualizing I/O:

- **Passthrough** uses interrupt and DMA remapping to give guests direct access to hardware resources.
- **Partial emulation** implements a reduced-function virtual hardware device with a custom device driver for the guest.
- **Full emulation** implements full emulation of the physical hardware device, including the full complement of registers, FIFOs, etc available on the hardware.

In this work, we studied passthrough and partial emulation, using the network interface as the target I/O device. The network driver is convenient because it is easy to benchmark using ICMP echoes (pings), and it's easy to compare to other virtualization platforms.

Figure 4 shows a comparison of round trip times for three different Ethernet driver implementations. The bare metal implementation is the unmodified driver supplied by the chip manufacturer with no virtualization; it is our reference implementation.

The bridged implementation is a custom driver running in the guest. Ethernet device interrupts are handled by Hermes without being passed up to the guest. The hypervisor presents a virtualized network interface to the guest, and they hypervisor calls the chip

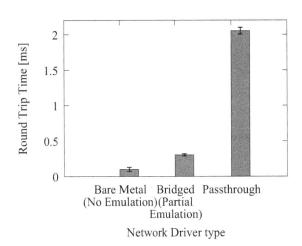

Figure 4: Comparison of ping round trip times for three Ethernet driver implementations on the ARM device.

manufacturer's driver functions to send and receive packets. The bridged driver allows multiple guests to share the same network interface by multiplexing incoming packets to the guests based on MAC address.

In the passthrough implementation, the guest runs the manufacturer's driver in raw form, emulated by Hermes. Ethernet device interrupts are caught by Hermes and passed to the guest, so all exception handling code is done in guest mode. The Ethernet device is not shared among multiple guests in this configuration.

Surprisingly, we find that the bridged (hypervisor-assisted) Ethernet driver performs far better than the passthrough. Since the passthrough driver runs all driver code in guest mode, all privileged instructions must be emulated by Hermes. This causes a significant slowdown in packet handling because the Ethernet driver has to invalidate a lot of data cache lines each time a packet is received, which requires many privileged instructions and memory accesses. In the bridged driver, the majority of privileged memory accesses and privileged instructions are done by the hypervisor, so they don't need to be emulated.

5 RELATED WORK

Other authors have explored real-time schedulers in hypervisors, in particular for Linux running in Xen [11, 18, 19]. None that we know of have been implemented on MMUless machines—even early hypervisors ran on machines with memory management units [8].

6 ACKNOWLEDGEMENTS

All authors are supported in part by the following grants from the US National Science Foundation: CNS-1345293, CNS-14055667, CNS-1525586, CNS-1555426, CNS-1629833, CNS-1647152, CNS-1719336.

REFERENCES

[1] Stefan Berger, Ramón Cáceres, Kenneth A. Goldman, Ronald Perez, Reiner Sailer, and Leendert van Doorn. 2006. vTPM: Virtualizing the Trusted Platform Module. In *Proceedings of the 15th Conference on USENIX Security Symposium - Volume*

15 (USENIX-SS'06). USENIX Association, Berkeley, CA, USA, Article 21. http://dl.acm.org/citation.cfm?id=1267336.1267357

[2] Richard Berry. 2017. FreeRTOS. (2017). http://www.freertos.org.

[3] Brad Brannon and Allen Barlow. 2006. Aperture uncertainty and ADC system performance. *Application Note AN501* (2006).

[4] Claude Castelluccia, Aurélien Francillon, Daniele Perito, and Claudio Soriente. 2009. On the Difficulty of Software-based Attestation of Embedded Devices. In *Proceedings of the 16th ACM Conference on Computer and Communications Security (CCS '09)*. ACM, New York, NY, USA, 400–409. https://doi.org/10.1145/1653662.1653711

[5] Yeongpil Cho, Junbum Shin, Donghyun Kwon, MyungJoo Ham, Yuna Kim, and Yunheung Paek. 2016. Hardware-Assisted On-Demand Hypervisor Activation for Efficient Security Critical Code Execution on Mobile Devices. In *2016 USENIX Annual Technical Conference (USENIX ATC 16)*. USENIX Association, Denver, CO, 565–578. https://www.usenix.org/conference/atc16/technical-sessions/presentation/cho

[6] Atmel Corporation. 2017. SAM E ARM Cortex-M7 Microcontrollers. (2017). http://www.atmel.com/products/microcontrollers/arm/sam-e.aspx.

[7] Atmel Corporation. 2017. SAM E70 Xplained Evaluation Kit. (2017). http://www.atmel.com/tools/atsame70-xpld.aspx.

[8] R. J. Creasy. 1981. The Origin of the VM/370 Time-sharing System. *IBM J. Res. Dev.* 25, 5 (Sept. 1981), 483–490. https://doi.org/10.1147/rd.255.0483

[9] Christoffer Dall and Jason Nieh. 2014. KVM/ARM: The Design and Implementation of the Linux ARM Hypervisor. In *Proceedings of the 19th International Conference on Architectural Support for Programming Languages and Operating Systems (ASPLOS '14)*. ACM, New York, NY, USA, 333–348. https://doi.org/10.1145/2541940.2541946

[10] Joan G. Dyer, Mark Lindemann, Ronald Perez, Reiner Sailer, Leendert van Doorn, Sean W. Smith, and Steve Weingart. 2001. Building the IBM 4758 Secure Coprocessor. *Computer* 34, 10 (Oct. 2001), 57–66. https://doi.org/10.1109/2.955100

[11] Marisol GarcÃĆÂa-Valls, Tommaso Cucinotta, and Chenyang Lu. 2014. Challenges in real-time virtualization and predictable cloud computing. *Journal of Systems Architecture* 60, 9 (2014), 726 – 740. https://doi.org/10.1016/j.sysarc.2014.07.004

[12] Neil Klingensmith, Dale Willis, and Suman Banerjee. 2013. A Distributed Energy Monitoring and Analytics Platform and Its Use Cases. In *Proceedings of the 5th ACM Workshop on Embedded Systems For Energy-Efficient Buildings (BuildSys'13)*. ACM, New York, NY, USA, Article 36, 2 pages. https://doi.org/10.1145/2528282.2534156

[13] Fabien Le Mentec. 2014. Using the Beaglebone PRU to achieve realtime at low cost. *Embedded Related* (April 2014). https://www.embeddedrelated.com/showarticle/586.php.

[14] Carlos Moratelli, Sergio Johann, and Fabiano Hessel. 2016. Exploring Embedded Systems Virtualization Using MIPS Virtualization Module. In *Proceedings of the ACM International Conference on Computing Frontiers (CF '16)*. ACM, New York, NY, USA, 214–221. https://doi.org/10.1145/2903150.2903179

[15] Bryan Parno, Jonathan M McCune, and Adrian Perrig. 2010. Bootstrapping trust in commodity computers. In *Security and privacy (SP), 2010 IEEE symposium on*. IEEE, 414–429.

[16] Himanshu Raj, Stefan Saroiu, Alec Wolman, Ronald Aigner, Jeremiah Cox, Paul England, Chris Fenner, Kinshuman Kinshumann, Jork Loeser, Dennis Mattoon, Magnus Nystrom, David Robinson, Rob Spiger, Stefan Thom, and David Wooten. 2016. fTPM: A Software-Only Implementation of a TPM Chip. In *25th USENIX Security Symposium (USENIX Security 16)*. USENIX Association, Austin, TX, 841–856. https://www.usenix.org/conference/usenixsecurity16/technical-sessions/presentation/raj

[17] Dale F. Willis, Arkodeb Dasgupta, and Suman Banerjee. 2014. ParaDrop: A Multi-tenant Platform for Dynamically Installed Third Party Services on Home Gateways. In *Proceedings of the 2014 ACM SIGCOMM Workshop on Distributed Cloud Computing (DCC '14)*. ACM, New York, NY, USA, 43–44. https://doi.org/10.1145/2627566.2627583

[18] Sisu Xi, Chong Li, Chenyang Lu, Christopher D Gill, Meng Xu, Linh TX Phan, Insup Lee, and Oleg Sokolsky. 2015. RT-Open Stack: CPU Resource Management for Real-Time Cloud Computing. In *Cloud Computing (CLOUD), 2015 IEEE 8th International Conference on*. IEEE, 179–186.

[19] Sisu Xi, Meng Xu, Chenyang Lu, Linh TX Phan, Christopher Gill, Oleg Sokolsky, and Insup Lee. 2014. Real-time multi-core virtual machine scheduling in xen. In *Embedded Software (EMSOFT), 2014 International Conference on*. IEEE, 1–10.

106

iTrack: Tracking Indicator LEDs on APs to Bootstrap mmWave Beam Acquisition and Steering

Muhammad Kumail Haider and Edward W. Knightly

Rice University, Houston TX

{kumail.haider,knightly}@rice.edu

ABSTRACT

We present iTrack, a system which steers mmWave beams at mobile devices by tracking the indicator LEDs on wireless APs to passively acquire direction estimates, and demonstrate that iTrack acquires and maintains beam alignment at the narrowest beamwidth level even in case of device mobility, without incurring any training overhead. Our implementation on custom dual-band hardware testbed shows that iTrack acquires direction estimates within 4.5 degrees of the ground truth and achieves beam steering accuracy of more than 97% while in tracking mode, without incurring any in-band training or feedback.

ACM Reference Format:

Muhammad Kumail Haider and Edward W. Knightly. 2018. iTrack: Tracking Indicator LEDs on APs to Bootstrap mmWave Beam Acquisition and Steering. In *Proceedings of 19th International Workshop on Mobile Computing Systems and Applications (HotMobile'18)*. ACM, New York, NY, USA, 6 pages. https://doi.org/10.1145/3177102.3177105

1 INTRODUCTION

The ever-increasing demand for high speed wireless connectivity to support applications like virtual and augmented reality, uncompressed video streaming and wireless docking is straining the capacity of current WiFi and cellular networks [1]. The wide GHz-scale bandwidth coupled with phased array antennas to realize high directionality in the mmWave spectrum, spanning a wide range of frequencies from 30 GHz to 300 GHz and beyond, can solve this problem by realizing data rates of up to 100 Gb/sec [8]. However, a key challenge in exploiting this expansive bandwidth and high data rates is that end nodes need to align their beams to establish a highly directional link, before any communication can happen.

To this end, existing commercial products [14, 19] and WLAN standards like 802.11ad [11] and 802.11ay [8] employ beam-search based training mechanisms, where one node sends training frames across all its beams while the other uses pseudo-omni antenna patterns to identify the strongest beam. Although this training, when repeated at both ends, discovers the strongest pair of beams with maximum data rates, the process may take 10's of *ms*. This overhead

represents missed opportunity to transmit 100's of Mb, severely degrading throughput and disrupting high-rate, low-latency applications. Moreover, the overhead worsens for multi-user transmissions [5, 8] and in Next-Gen THz networks with no pseudo-omni reception [10], increasing the order of beam-search space from $2N$ to N^2 for N beams at either end. Mobile nodes present an even greater challenge, where beam alignment may be repeatedly lost due to mobility, requiring more training epochs and incurring overhead each time.

We present iTrack, a system which steers mmWave beams at mobile devices by tracking indicator LEDs on wireless Access Points (APs) to passively acquire direction estimates, eliminating the need for beam search at the clients. Our design is motivated by the observation that most off-the-shelf wireless APs are equipped with light sources like notification LEDs, which are in close proximity to their phased array antennas. Therefore, by tracking this indicator LED at client devices using off-the-shelf light sensors (e.g., photodiodes), we can "point" the client's antenna beams towards the AP, without requiring any in-band training or beam search.

We demonstrate that iTrack acquires and maintains beam alignment at the narrowest beamwidth level at the clients even in case of device mobility, without incurring any training overhead. Moreover, our design is scalable with the number of clients, such that the AP can simultaneously align beams with multiple clients by performing a beam sweep only once at its end; client beams are selected via out-of-band light sensing.

For this, we exploit the pseudo-optical properties of mmWave channels; specifically the dominant Line of Sight (LOS) propagation, limited scattering and reduced multipath due to very short wavelength [2, 6]. Since visible light band exhibits similar dominant LOS propagation [3], our key idea is to estimate the Angle of Arrival (AOA) corresponding to the LOS path from the AP's indicator LED, and approximate it as the AOA in the mmWave band due to close proximity of AP's LED and its phased array antenna. Therefore, we select the client-side beam as the one with the highest gain along the AOA for the LOS path. We show that by passively tracking AP's indicator LED, an iTrack client continuously adapts its antenna beams without requiring any beam training.

The key challenge in exploiting the light source at the AP for this direction tracking is that, unlike lasers, light intensity from LEDs (or common light bulbs) is *incoherent*, and off-the-shelf light sensors can only measure the *intensity* of the incident light. Therefore, AOA estimation techniques in radio bands via antenna array phase difference (e.g., [21]) cannot be used. For this, we devise a novel method for incoherent-light Angle of Arrival (il-AOA) estimation by using an array of light sensors. Our key technique is to approximate the ratio of light intensities at adjacent sensors as a function of their AOA only by exploiting their angular separation on the

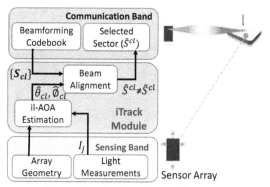

Figure 1: iTrack node architecture.

array. We then estimate the AOA of the LOS path without requiring any calibration or knowledge of the AP's position or client's orientation. Moreover, our method estimates il-AOA in both azimuth and elevation planes, allowing us to steer beams for both 2-D and 3-D beamforming codebooks.

We implement iTrack on a dual-band hardware platform and perform rigorous experiments to evaluate the key components of iTrack design. Our preliminary results are promising; showing that iTrack estimates il-AOA to within $4.5°$ without any knowledge of the AP or client's position. Moreover, in various rotational mobility scenarios, iTrack can steer beams correctly more than 97% of instances, without incurring any in-band training overhead or feedback. In the future, we plan to extend the experimental setup to include our wide-band platform with phased array antennas [14] and THz transceivers [10].

2 ITRACK DESIGN

In this section, we first present iTrack's system architecture. We then describe the beam alignment protocol and our novel method to estimate the il-AOA using light measurements from the AP's indicator LED.

2.1 System Architecture

The iTrack architecture is divided into two distinct bands; a *Communication Band* and a *Sensing Band*. The former comprises of mmWave band radios and phased array antennas at the AP and client nodes, over which data communication takes place. In most modern systems, the phases of antenna elements are defined via a 3-D beamforming codebook ({S}), such that by switching between codebook entries, beams can be electronically steered, discretizing the space around the array into virtual "sectors" [2]. While our design is compatible with any directional antenna design, for the rest of this section we assume phased array antenna system for both AP and clients. The Sensing Band comprises of an indicator LED at the AP and multiple light sensors at the client. We require that this LED be distinguishable from ambient light, which can be achieved by using RGB photodiodes for colored LEDs on the AP or by using recent solutions (e.g., [24]) to distinguish light sources. In any case, we do not require any data communication or signaling in the Sensing Band.

Fig. 1 depicts iTrack client node architecture. The client equips an array of J light sensors to measure light intensity (I) from the AP's LED. The set of intensities $\{I\} = I_j, j = 1, .., J$ is input to the iTrack software module (shown by the middle block), which has

two main components: *(i) il-AOA Estimation Block* which uses light measurements to estimate the azimuth and elevation components $(\hat{\theta}_{cl}, \hat{\phi}_{cl})$ of the il-AOA (Sec. 2.3); and *(ii) Beam Alignment Block* which estimates client's highest strength sector $\hat{S}_{cl}$ using the il-AOA estimates (Sec. 2.2). This estimated sector is then passed on to the Communication Band, and is used as the "selected sector" ($\tilde{S}_{cl}$) for directional transmission and reception.

2.2 Beam Alignment Protocol

Design Principle: Due to extremely small wavelength, mmWave channels are shown to have limited scattering, which is usually characterized using geometric channel models as follows [2, 6]:

$$\mathbf{H} = C \sum_{l=1}^{L} \alpha_l \, \mathbf{a}_T(\theta_{T,l}, \phi_{T,l}) \, \mathbf{a}_R(\theta_{R,l}, \phi_{R,l}), \qquad (1)$$

where C is a normalization constant, L is the number of physical paths, α_l is the path gain, $\mathbf{a}_T$ and $\mathbf{a}_R$ are the array response vectors at the transmitter and the receiver, and θ and ϕ denote the azimuth and elevation components of the corresponding Angle of Departure (AOD)/AOA respectively[1]. Due to dominant LOS propagation of mmWave channels shown in prior measurement studies and channel models [1, 22], we expect the LOS channel component to have the maximum gain. Therefore, our key idea is to exploit the AP's LED to estimate the il-AOA $(\hat{\theta}_{cl}, \hat{\phi}_{cl})$ of the LOS path at the client using light measurements only, and then select the client-side beam with maximum directivity gain (using known beam patterns) along the estimated AOA. As such, we avoid any mmWave in-band training or beam-search at the client. Note that we use the term il-AOA to specify the AOA of the physical LOS path between the AP and the client measured using light intensities. In particular, we use the client's codebook $\{S_{cl}\}$ to find the beam (or sector for discretized codebooks) $\hat{S}_{cl}$ which has maximum gain along $(\hat{\theta}_{cl}, \hat{\phi}_{cl})$, as follows:

$$\hat{S}_{cl} = \arg \min_{S_{cl,m}; m=1...N} \left| \angle (\Theta_{S_{cl,m}}, \Phi_{S_{cl,m}}) - (\hat{\theta}_{cl}, \hat{\phi}_{cl}) \right| \quad (2)$$

where $(\Theta_{S_{cl,m}}, \Phi_{S_{cl,m}})$ are the central azimuth and elevation angles of any client sector $S_{cl,m}$.

Using this estimation framework, we design iTrack to comprise of the following two phases.

Beam Acquisition: This is the initial phase where maximal strength sectors are not known at the AP or the clients e.g., at association or after link breakage. During this phase, an iTrack client estimates its maximal strength sector using light measurements as described above, and uses this sector to receive in mmWave band while the AP does a beam sweep at its end. The client then gives a feedback about AP's maximal strength sector to the AP. This may be followed by an optional beam refinement phase, as defined in 802.11ad [11], where the client can use the il-AOA estimate to do a local search in the neighboring sectors to refine beam selection. In any case, an exhaustive search is not required at the client end if il-AOA estimates are available.

In case of multi-user training, the AP can simultaneously train with any number of clients by doing a single beam sweep and getting feedback from the clients. As such, if the AP has N_{AP} sectors and trains with M clients, each with $N_{cl,m}$ sectors, then iTrack

---

[1]Due to channel reciprocity, only the AOA or the AOD needs to be estimated.

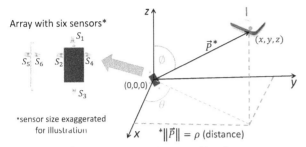

Figure 2: Indicator-LED sensing via client's sensor array.

requires beam search only over N_{AP} sectors during beam acquisition, compared to $N_{AP} \cdot \sum_{m=1}^{M} N_{cl,m}$ sector combinations in case of 802.11ad based pseudo-omni training or $(N_{AP})^M \cdot \prod_{m=1}^{M} N_{cl,m}$ in case of the optimal exhaustive search based training.

Beam Steering: After a directional link is established via Beam Acquisition, iTrack enters the Beam Steering phase, where it passively tracks the il-AOA from the AP's LED and continuously estimates the best client-side sector $\hat{S}_{cl}$ using the il-AOA estimates. Due to client mobility, if this best sector estimate becomes different from the selected sector $\tilde{S}_{cl}$ being used for communication, an interrupt ($\tilde{S}_{cl} \leftarrow \hat{S}_{cl}$) is passed to the MAC layer to adapt the current sector $\tilde{S}_{cl}$. As such, iTrack steers client-side beams without incurring any training or feedback overhead.

Moreover, the AP is oblivious to any changes in client-side sectors, making beam steering completely distributed. However, if beam alignment is lost due to unavailability of light estimates (e.g., due to self-blockage) or AP's sectors require adaptation, iTrack enters Beam Acquisition again.

2.3 il-AOA Estimation

Here we describe the visible light channel model and our method to estimate both azimuth and elevation components of the il-AOA for the LOS path using light measurements only.

Visible Light Channel Model: The intensity (I) of light received at a sensor is modeled by the Lambertian radiation pattern for LOS propagation [3] as follows:

$$I(\rho, \gamma, \psi) = T \cdot A \cdot g(\psi) \cdot \left(\frac{m+1}{2\pi}\right) \cdot cos^m(\psi) \cdot \frac{cos(\gamma)}{\rho^2} \quad (3)$$

where T is the transmit power, A is sensor area, γ is the irradiance angle between the vector from light source to sensor and the normal vector to the source, ρ is the source-sensor distance and ψ is the AOA at the *sensor*. g is optical concentrator, which is a constant if ψ lies within the field-of-view of the sensor. m is the Lambertian order, which is 1 for common indoor LEDs. It follows that the light intensity varies inversely to distance, AOA and irradiance angle.

Problem Formulation: Fig. 2 depicts an AP at position (x, y, z) with respect to an iTrack client, where the reference frame is centered at the client's planar phased array, with *z-axis* orthogonal to the array. By geometry, angles θ_{cl} and ϕ_{cl} shown in the figure correspond to the azimuth and elevation components of the AOA from the AP to the client's array for the LOS path. Our objective is to estimate $(\hat{\theta}_{cl}, \hat{\phi}_{cl})$ as the il-AOA using the incoherent light from the AP's LED using off-the-shelf light sensors.

Sensor Array Design: The two components of the il-AOA cannot be estimated using a single sensor since the light intensity depends on both the position of and the AOA at the sensor. Moreover, since the sensor may have an arbitrary orientation, the AOA (ψ) at the sensor may not be the same as the il-AOA, but a projection of it along the sensor's axis. Our key technique is to exploit an array of multiple sensors with known angular separation to estimate θ_{cl} and ϕ_{cl}. When introducing more sensors, the entropy of measurements is maximized by placing sensors at right angles, since it gives maximum angular separation. Therefore, in our sensor array design, we use at least six sensors arranged mutually orthogonally on the six facets of a mobile device. For the rest of this section, we discuss this case of six-sensor array, but the formulation can easily be extended to larger array sizes.

Estimation Method: Fig. 2 depicts an iTrack client with $J = 6$ light sensors arranged mutually orthogonally. In this case, the light intensity from the AP's LED received at the jth sensor of the client is given as:

$$I_j = C \cdot cos(\psi_j) \cdot \frac{cos(\gamma_j)}{(\rho_j)^2} \quad (4)$$

where C is a constant parameter for sensors of same type, and ρ_j is the distance between the LED and the jth sensor. If $\overrightarrow{P} = [x, y, z]^T$ is the position vector to the AP's LED and $\overrightarrow{P_j}$ is that of the jth sensor (with unit normal vector $\overrightarrow{u_j}$), then angles γ_j and ψ_j can be computed as:

$$cos(\gamma_j) = \frac{\overrightarrow{z} \odot (\overrightarrow{P_j} - \overrightarrow{P})}{\rho_j} \quad (5)$$

$$cos(\psi_j) = \frac{\overrightarrow{u_j} \odot (\overrightarrow{P} - \overrightarrow{P_j})}{\rho_j} \quad (6)$$

Since the size of mobile devices is usually much smaller compared to the AP-client distance, our key technique is to approximate the irradiance angle and distance from the AP to be the same at all sensors ($\forall j, \gamma_j = \gamma, \rho_j = \rho$). With this approximation, the ratio of intensities at any two adjacent sensors is a function of their AOA only, independent of ρ and γ:

$$\frac{I_{j1}}{I_{j2}} \approx \frac{cos(\psi_{j1})}{cos(\psi_{j2})} \quad (7)$$

Since the arrangement of sensors is fixed and known at the client, we consider the ratio of intensities at adjacent sensors in three perpendicular planes to estimate the il-AOA component in that plane, without requiring client's position or orientation. For example, in the case when sensors are arranged mutually orthogonally, this difference in AOA is in fact 90°, such that we can make the substitution $cos(\psi_{j2}) = sin(90 - \psi_{j1}))$ in Eq.7 to estimate ψ_{j1} as follows:

$$\hat{\psi}_{j1} = tan^{-1}\left(\frac{I_{j2}}{I_{j1}}\right) \quad (8)$$

Note that it is not necessary that light sensor array and client's phased array are coplanar and aligned; only the mapping is required such that angles estimated using the light-sensor array can be rotated to find angles with respect to the mmWave phased array. However, for simplicity and without loss of generality, here we assume that the two arrays are aligned, so that the same reference frame defined in Fig. 2 can be used for the light sensor array as

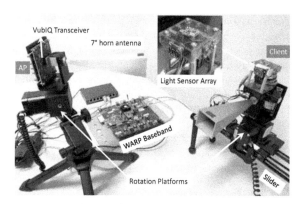

Figure 3: Dual-band hardware platform.

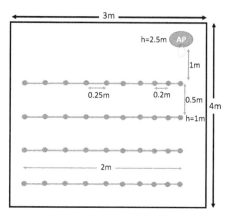

Figure 4: Testbed setup in the lab environment.

well. With this simplification, we can define $\overrightarrow{u_j}$ as unit vectors along +x,-x,+y,-y,+z,-z axes for the six mutually orthogonal sensors.

Moreover, by array geometry, at most three sensors on the array can have LOS path to the AP, one along each axis (I_x, I_y, I_z). Using the negligible array dimension approximation and solving for $cos(\psi_j)$ at adjacent sensors in the three perpendicular planes, we estimate θ_{cl} and ϕ_{cl} as follows:

$$\hat{\theta}_{cl} = tan^{-1}\left(\frac{I_y}{I_x}\right) \quad, \quad \hat{\phi}_{cl} = tan^{-1}\left(\frac{\sqrt{I_x^2 + I_y^2}}{I_z}\right) \quad (9)$$

3 IMPLEMENTATION AND EVALUATION

In this section, we first describe our implementation of iTrack on a custom dual-band hardware platform, and then discuss our preliminary experiments to evaluate key components of iTrack for indoor mmWave networks.

3.1 Dual-band Hardware Testbed

For our initial evaluation, we select 60 GHz transceivers for communication in the mmWave band, and develop a custom hardware testbed comprising of an AP and a client node, as depicted in Fig. 3. In particular, we develop programmable nodes using VubIQ transceiver system, operating in the 57-64 GHz unlicensed frequency band with 1.8 GHz bandwidth (compliant with 802.11ad) and WARP baseband (a software-defined radio platform). To achieve narrow sector widths, we use horn antennas with 7° beamwidth at both AP and client sides. To implement beam-steering and rotation, both nodes are mounted on Cine-Moco motion platform with a rotation precision of 0.01°. Using this platform, antennas are rotated in discrete steps to emulate discretized sectors (predefined by a codebook) to achieve sector sweeps and beam steering.

Further, we use an off-the-shelf Lumileds LED (1200 lm, 33V, 100° viewing angle) at the AP. For the client, we build a 7 × 7 × 3 cm array (emulating dimensions of a big smartphone or a tablet) with six sensors (Adafruit TSL-2591, 180° FoV).

3.2 Experimental Setup

We evaluate the accuracy of il-AOA estimation and client-side sector selection for both phases in iTrack (i.e., Beam Acquisition and Beam Steering). For beam steering, our initial experiments encompass various rotational mobility scenario, whereas we leave evaluation of translational mobility for future version of this paper.

For this, we setup the dual-band testbed in a lab within 4×3×5m space with the AP at 2.5m height in a corner. For the client, we consider 40 different locations along four rows at radial distances 1m, 1.5m, 2m and 2.5m respectively from the AP at 1m height, as shown in Fig. 4. This setup helps us evaluate iTrack performance under a broad set of AP-client distances and angular separations, which affect the light intensity measurements and beam steering. Further, at each client location, we rotate the client by 60° in steps of 1° and take measurements across both bands. As such, our experiments also encompass (61 × 40) different position-orientation combinations for evaluating beam acquisition accuracy in addition to rotation. Note that there is always a LOS path in the visible light and 60 GHz bands in these experiments; we leave evaluation of blockage scenario for future work.

3.3 Results

3.3.1 Beam Acquisition Phase. We first evaluate the accuracy of il-AOA estimation using light measurements. To identify various sources of estimation error, we also perform light channel model based simulations to analyze the performance of sensor arrays with various dimensions, and for comparison with our over-the-air experiments. Fig. 5a depicts the CDF of il-AOA estimation error. First, for simulation of an array of negligible dimensions (0.01cm), we observe an almost perfect il-AOA estimation accuracy, which validates our key technique. Second, simulation results for a 7cm array (same dimensions as our testbed array) show up to 2° estimation error, indicating that array dimension plays a key role in determining the accuracy of our method. Sensors can be placed close to device edges to further minimize this error and achieve better accuracy. However, for our tested, we develop a cubic shaped array with relatively large distance between sensors to test the viability of our method for arrays with relatively larger dimensions.

Next we analyze the performance in over-the-air experiments. The blue curve for measurement results indicates that the estimation error is within 4.5° of the true AOA even for our reasonably large cubic array. The error is also higher than the simulations due to the deviation of intensity measurements from the channel models, which we discover increases with distance between light source and sensors. To investigate this further, we compute the average il-AOA estimation error across all locations in the four rows of our setup, such that the average distance increases across the

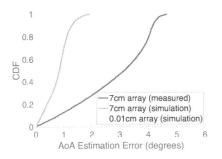

(a) CDF of il-AOA estimation error.

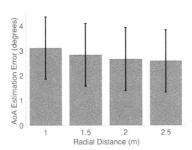

(b) il-AOA estimation vs. distance

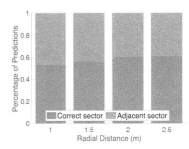

(c) Sector selection accuracy.

Figure 5: Client-side sector selection during beam acquisition via il-AOA estimation using light measurements.

rows. Fig. 5b shows that as the radial distance of the rows increases (plotted along the *x-axis*), the average il-AOA estimation error in fact decreases. This is because of an additional factor which impacts our il-AOA estimation accuracy; the validity of our negligible array dimensions approximation, which improves with an increase in distance. Results show that this factor is dominant in determining the il-AOA estimation accuracy.

Finally, we evaluate sector selection accuracy at the client in our experiments, by comparing sectors selected by iTrack to the ground truth by geometry. Fig. 5c depicts the client-side sector selection accuracy, averaged across locations and orientations for each of the four rows, with the radial distance of rows plotted along the *x-axis*. We observe that for all instances, the correct client-side sector is selected more than 50% of times, with selection accuracy improving slightly with distance. This is consistent with the improving il-AOA estimation accuracy with increasing AP-client distance. Further, the selected sector differs from the true maximal strength sector at most by 1 sector for all location, orientation combinations.

Findings: Even with an array of reasonably large edge-dimensions, iTrack estimates il-AOA within 4.5° of the ground truth. Higher accuracy can be realized by placing sensors close to device edges to further reduce inter-sensor distance, a key factor affecting the estimation accuracy. Further, iTrack acquires client beams to within 1 sector of the true highest strength sector in all cases without any in-band training. Thus our light based il-AOA estimation eliminates the need for exhaustive beam search at mobile clients.

3.3.2 Beam Steering Phase. Next we evaluate the beam steering capability of iTrack for various rotational mobility scenario in the aforementioned experiments. A key factor that impacts iTrack's beam steering accuracy is the frequency at which il-AOA estimates are computed. This is determined by multiple factors, such as sampling frequency of light sensors and computational resources of smart devices. Moreover, rotational speed of the client may also affect steering accuracy; the faster the speed, the harder the tracking since the client may rotate more for the same estimation frequency. Therefore, instead of evaluating all these factors separately, we normalize the estimation frequency to client's rotation, such that an il-AOA estimate is computed for every δ degrees of client's rotation. Here we present results for four δ values: $1°, 2°, 5°$ and $10°$.

First we analyze rotation estimation accuracy by computing the change in estimated il-AOA between the initial and final orientations of the client. Fig. 6a plots the CDF of rotation estimation error for the four δ values. We observe that when il-AOA estimates

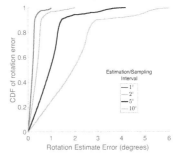

(a) CDF of rotation error.

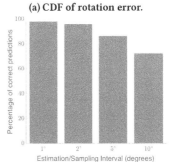

(b) Beam steering accuracy.

Figure 6: Rotation with various estimation intervals.

are computed most frequently (every 1° of client rotation), the estimation error is the lowest since we have the most light measurements to estimate the same rotation compared to the other cases. Further, we observe that the rotation estimates are within 0.5° of the true value for more than 90% of instances, which is much higher than absolute il-AOA estimation accuracy in Fig. 5a. This is because il-AOA estimation is affected by the AP-client relative angle and distance, which predominantly determines the deviation of measured results from the theoretical channel models. However, for estimating rotation, this il-AOA estimation error has the same location bias, and this component of error is cancelled out when computing the change in il-AOA to find client rotation. Moreover, the graph also shows that as the estimation interval (δ) increases, rotation estimation error also becomes large, since there is a greater change in client's orientation between two measurements.

Next we analyze the client-side sector steering accuracy in Fig. 6b for various values of δ plotted along the *x-axis*. Consistent with a high rotation estimation accuracy, we observe that iTrack is able to steer client sectors to the true highest strength sectors for more than 97% of the time with $\delta = 1°$. Although steering accuracy decreases with an increase in estimation interval, even with a high interval of $10°$, which represents very high rotational speeds or conversely very low sampling rate of sensors, iTrack computes the correct sectors more than 70% of the time.

Findings: By estimating changes in il-AOA from the AP's light source, iTrack is able to track rotation at even higher accuracy than it does absolute il-AOA, leading to almost 97% steering accuracy when il-AOA estimates are computed at a modest rate of every $1°$ of client rotation. Consequently, once a mmWave link is established, iTrack can maintain alignment at the narrowest beamwidth level despite device mobility solely by passive light sensing.

4 RELATED WORK

Visible Light Sensing: There are few existing works on AOA estimation using incoherent light. [9] uses model driven AOA calculation for localization from *multiple* light sources. In [24], non-linear intensity differences between two sensors of different fields of view was employed to estimate the AOA. However, it is limited to the azimuth plane due to 1-D AOA estimation and requires calibration of sensors.

mmWave Beam Training: *In-band* solutions to reduce training overhead include model-driven beam steering and channel profiling [20, 25], efficient beam searching [17, 23], sector switching and backup paths [7, 15, 18], and beamwidth adaptation [7]. These solutions help reduce steering overhead and maintain alignment in certain environments, however, they still incur training overhead when constructing channel profiles, searching for backup or redundant paths, or SNR degradation when switching to wider beams. In this work, we target to eliminate beam search at mobile devices by obtaining direction estimates from existing LEDs on APs. Nonetheless, prior solutions can be integrated to reduce training overhead for AP-side sweeps or when light measurements are not available.

Lastly, prior *out-of-band* solutions also address mobile clients in directional networks e.g., via session transfer to legacy bands [11, 16], AOA estimation in legacy bands to eliminate exhaustive search [12], and using sensors on mobile devices [4, 13, 23]. In contrast, we use passive light sensing which has much less power requirements than mechanical sensors, requires no communication in the sensing band, and is more resilient to multipath due to dominant LOS propagation of visible light.

5 CONCLUSION AND FUTURE WORK

In this paper, we present iTrack to steer mmWave beams at mobile devices by tracking the indicator LEDs on wireless APs to passively acquire direction estimates, and demonstrate that iTrack acquires and maintains beam alignment despite device mobility, without incurring any training overhead. We also implement our system on a custom dual-band platform for proof-of-concept. Our preliminary experiments show that iTrack estimates the incoherent-light AOA to within 4.5 degrees and steers beams correctly more than 97% of instances while in tracking mode, without incurring any in-band training or feedback.

Our next step is to extend the experimental setup to include our wide-band platform with phased array antennas [14] and THz transceivers [10], and using RGB photodiodes to track colored LEDs

on commercial APs. We also plan to explore further interesting applications of our work, especially LOS path blockage and self blockage detection using light sensing. In such cases, even if AOA estimate is not available, some steering directions can be eliminated in the beam-search space when performing beam training.

6 ACKNOWLEDGEMENTS

This research was supported by Cisco, Intel, the Keck Foundation, and by NSF grants CNS-1642929 and CNS-1514285.

REFERENCES

[1] ABARI, O., HASSANIEH, H., RODRIGUEZ, M., AND KATABI, D. Millimeter Wave Communications: From Point-to-Point Links to Agile Network Connections. In *Proc. of ACM HotNets* (2016).
[2] ALKHATEEB, A., EL AYACH, O., LEUS, G., AND HEATH, R. W. Channel Estimation and Hybrid Precoding for Millimeter Wave Cellular Systems. *IEEE JSTSP 8*, 5 (2014), 831–846.
[3] BARRY, J. R. *Wireless Infrared Communications*, vol. 280. Springer Science & Business Media, 2012.
[4] DOFF, A. W., CHANDRA, K., AND PRASAD, R. V. Sensor Assisted Movement Identification and Prediction for Beamformed 60 GHz Links. In *Proc. of IEEE CCNC* (2015).
[5] GHASEMPOUR, Y., DA SILVA, C. R., CORDEIRO, C., AND KNIGHTLY, E. W. IEEE 802.11 ay: Next-Generation 60 GHz Communication for 100 Gb/s Wi-Fi. *IEEE Communications Magazine 55*, 12 (2017), 186–192.
[6] GHASEMPOUR, Y., PRASAD, N., KHOJASTEPOUR, M., AND RANGARAJAN, S. Link Packing in mmWave Networks. In *Proc. of IEEE ICC* (2017).
[7] HAIDER, M. K., AND KNIGHTLY, E. W. Mobility Resilience and Overhead Constrained Adaptation in Directional 60 GHz WLANs: Protocol Design and System Implementation. In *Proc. of ACM MobiHoc* (2016).
[8] IEEE. 802.11ay task group. http://www.ieee802.org/11/Reports/tgay_update.htm.
[9] LEE, S., AND JUNG, S.-Y. Location Awareness using AoA based Circular-PD-Array for Visible Light Communication. In *Proc. of APCC* (2012).
[10] MA, J., WEIDENBACH, M., GUO, R., KOCH, M., AND MITTLEMAN, D. Communications with THz Waves: Switching Data Between Two Waveguides. *Journal of Infrared, Millimeter, and Terahertz Waves 38*, 11 (2017), 1316–1320.
[11] NITSCHE, T., CORDEIRO, C., FLORES, A., KNIGHTLY, E., PERAHIA, E., AND WIDMER, J. IEEE 802.11ad: Directional 60 GHz Communication for Multi-Gigabit-per-second Wi-Fi. *IEEE Communications Magazine 52*, 12 (2014), 132–141.
[12] NITSCHE, T., FLORES, A. B., KNIGHTLY, E. W., AND WIDMER, J. Steering with Eyes Closed: mm-Wave Beam Steering without In-Band Measurement. In *Proc. of IEEE INFOCOM* (2015).
[13] RAVINDRANATH, L., NEWPORT, C., BALAKRISHNAN, H., AND MADDEN, S. Improving Wireless Network Performance using Sensor Hints. In *Proc. of USENIX NSDI* (2011).
[14] SAHA, S. K., AND ET.AL. X60: A Programmable Testbed for Wideband 60 GHz WLANs with Phased Arrays. In *Proc. of ACM WinTech* (2017).
[15] SINGH, S., ZILIOTTO, F., MADHOW, U., BELDING, E. M., AND RODWELL, M. Blockage and Directivity in 60 GHz Wireless Personal Area Networks. *IEEE JSAC 27*, 8 (2009), 1400–1413.
[16] SUR, S., PEFKIANAKIS, I., ZHANG, X., AND KIM, K.-H. WiFi-Assisted 60 GHz Wireless Networks. In *Proc. of ACM MobiCom* (2017).
[17] SUR, S., VENKATESWARAN, V., ZHANG, X., AND RAMANATHAN, P. 60 GHz Indoor Networking through Flexible Beams: A Link-Level Profiling. In *Proc. of ACM SIGMETRICS* (2015).
[18] SUR, S., ZHANG, X., RAMANATHAN, P., AND CHANDRA, R. BeamSpy:Enabling Robust 60 GHz Links Under Blockage. In *Proc. of NSDI* (2016).
[19] TP-LINK. Talon ad7200 multi-band router. http://www.tp-link.com/en/products/details/AD7200.html.
[20] WEI, T., ZHOU, A., AND ZHANG, X. Facilitating Robust 60 GHz Network Deployment By Sensing Ambient Reflectors. In *Proc. of USENIX NSDI* (2017).
[21] XIONG, J., AND JAMIESON, K. ArrayTrack: A Fine-Grained Indoor Location System. In *Proc. of USENIX NSDI* (2013).
[22] XU, H., KUKSHYA, V., AND RAPPAPORT, T. S. Spatial and Temporal Characteristics of 60-GHz Indoor Channels. *IEEE Journal on Selected Areas in Communications 20*, 3 (2002), 620–630.
[23] YANG, Z., PATHAK, P. H., ZENG, Y., AND MOHAPATRA, P. Sensor-Assisted Codebook-Based Beamforming for Mobility Management in 60 GHz WLANs. In *Proc. of IEEE MASS* (2015).
[24] ZHANG, C., AND ZHANG, X. Pulsar: Towards Ubiquitous Visible Light Localization. In *Proc. of ACM MobiCom* (2017).
[25] ZHOU, A., ZHANG, X., AND MA, H. Beam-forecast: Facilitating Mobile 60 GHz Networks via Model-Driven Beam Steering. In *Proc. of IEEE INFOCOM* (2017).

Sensibility Testbed: Automated IRB Policy Enforcement in Mobile Research Apps

Yanyan Zhuang
University of Colorado, Colorado Springs

Albert Rafetseder
New York University

Yu Hu
New York University

Yuan Tian
University of Virginia

Justin Cappos
New York University

ABSTRACT

Due to their omnipresence, mobile devices such as smartphones could be tremendously valuable to researchers. However, since research projects can extract data about device owners that could be personal or sensitive, there are substantial privacy concerns. Currently, the only regulation to protect user privacy for research projects is through Institutional Review Boards (IRBs) from researchers' institutions. However, there is no guarantee that researchers will follow the IRB protocol. Even worse, researchers without security expertise might build apps that are vulnerable to attacks.

In this work, we present a platform, Sensibility Testbed, for automated enforcement of the privacy policies set by IRBs. Our platform enforces such policies when a researcher runs code on mobile devices. The enforcement mechanism is a set of obfuscation layers in a secure sandbox, that can be customized for any level of IRB compliance, and can be augmented by policies set by the device owner.

CCS CONCEPTS

• Security and privacy → Privacy protections;

KEYWORDS

Privacy protections, Policy enforcement

ACM Reference Format:
Yanyan Zhuang, Albert Rafetseder, Yu Hu, Yuan Tian, and Justin Cappos. 2018. Sensibility Testbed: Automated IRB Policy Enforcement in Mobile Research Apps. In *HotMobile '18: 19th International Workshop on Mobile Computing Systems & Applications, February 12–13, 2018, Tempe , AZ, USA.* ACM, New York, NY, USA, Article 4, 6 pages. https://doi.org/10.1145/3177102.3177120

1 INTRODUCTION

End-user mobile devices, such as smartphones, have become indispensable gadgets in people's everyday lives. As a result, the value of smart devices as data collection vehicles for research studies continues to grow. Since these devices have embedded GPS, accelerometers, cameras, and microphones, they can generate data for large-scale studies such as determining noise levels within an urban neighborhood [9], or studying traffic patterns [15].

However, for device owners, privacy threats to mobile devices have increased dramatically due to these sensors[1] and the sensitive data they generate. Potential attackers seek to take advantage of the rich functionality of sensors on mobile devices. Therefore, Institutional Review Boards (IRBs) review research protocols to evaluate whether researchers collect user data ethically. However, IRBs cannot ensure that a curious or erroneous researcher will follow the protocols for user data. Even worse, attackers might hack into an experiment to steal sensitive data from users [1]. For researchers without security expertise, it is particularly difficult to protect participants' privacy.

We introduce Sensibility Testbed, a testbed that streamlines the process of running IRB-compliant experiments on mobile devices. Sensibility Testbed simplifies the process of implementing IRB-compliant data access policies, without relying on the researcher to protect sensitive data. Instead, it technically enforces a series of policies that limit what information can be collected from end-user devices and how often. Researchers can establish a secure, direct connection with remote mobile devices to run experiments without any policy violation. Furthermore, they do not need to build their own app and deploy in an app store to collect data; they only need to configure IRB policy, and write about one line per sensor to collect data with our platform.

Sensibility Testbed uses policies to define the granularity of access for all sensors conforming to a researchers's IRB, such as identifying the city where they live, without revealing the exact address; accessing GPS every ten minutes, instead of continuously. In addition, Sensibility Testbed has a set of *baseline policies* that are always enforced on each research experiment. These policies address common attacks, and by default disable access to sensors of high risks, such as cameras and microphones. Sensibility Testbed's infrastructure applies the IRB policies specified by the researcher's institution, by implementing the policies on end-user devices. These policies can be customized according to the types of sensors accessed by an experiment. Finally, device owners can also adjust the privacy settings locally through configuring these policies.

All these policies are enforced through *obfuscation layers* in a secure sandbox. Each obfuscation layer is customized to limit the precision of data collected, the frequency with which the sensor can

---

[1] We broadly define sensors as hardware that can record phenomena about the physical world, e.g., the WiFi/cellular network, GPS location, movement acceleration, etc.

be accessed, or both. All obfuscation layers are programmable to meet each device owner's privacy preference, and each institution's IRB requirements.

The contributions of this work are as follows:

- We introduce Sensibility Testbed as a platform for experimentation on mobile devices that enables programmable enforcement of IRB policies.
- We develop and integrate a set of baseline privacy policies into the testbed design that respond to common attack techniques identified in the literature. These policies prevent attackers from accessing private data on personal devices.

2 OVERVIEW

In this section, we use an example to show how a researcher uses Sensibility Testbed to conduct an experiment. We assume that Alice, a device owner, participates in a research experiment, while a researcher, Rhonda, wants to run code using a number of devices, including Alice's.

Interaction among different parties. Alice decides to install the Sensibility Testbed app because she altruistically wants to help scientific progress. She may configure the privacy settings in her app, e.g., to block any possible access to her microphone. Once the app is started, an instance of the testbed sandbox (Section 4.1) will be created. At this point, her device is ready for researchers to use.

Rhonda wants to study different cellular technologies in her city. She wants to gather the network type (3G, 4G, LTE, etc.), provider, and signal strength from device owners. Rhonda registers her experiment with Sensibility Testbed (Section 3.3) and enters information about the types of data her experiment requires. Rhonda's IRB protocol specifies that she requires accurate carrier network information, such as cellular signal strength, network type, but randomized cell IDs in lieu of the cell ID that the device is associated with. She also configures that her experiment requires GPS data to be within 30 meters of accuracy for her measurements, and needs to update this information every 10 minutes.

If Rhonda's IRB protocol requests access to sensors in a manner that is equal to or at a coarser level than Sensibility Testbed's baseline policies, her experiment will be immediately approved. If not, Rhonda's experiment will be subject to an additional check at Sensibility Testbed. If approved, Rhonda can deploy her experiment on remote end-user devices (including Alice's), which she can request through Sensibility Testbed. She may start/stop her experiment at any time, and collect the results from the remote devices using an ssh-like console. Even if attacker Eve hacks into Rhonda's experiment, the sensor access will still be blocked except in the manner specified by the IRB and baseline policies.

Threat model. We assume that Rhonda may inadvertently access private data on Alice's devices. However, Rhonda's IRB cannot prevent this because IRB does not know Rhonda's implementation details. Furthermore, an attacker may maliciously compromise Rhonda's experiment to collect data. Sensibility Testbed provides protection against all these threats.

3 TESTBED DESIGN

In this section, we use the example in Section 2 to explain the design of Sensibility Testbed. We first present an overview of the requirements to build a smartphone testbed, and then describe the detailed design as Rhonda studies the cellular service quality using Alice's device.

3.1 Testbed Requirements

To design and implement a mobile testbed, we have to strike a balance between the security guarantee of code execution, the privacy of device owners, and usability including the programming interface and experiment setup. We summarize the main requirements as follows.

Security Guarantee of Code Execution. To responsibly provide access to smartphones, a smartphone testbed should provide security guarantee for the experiments running on the device. Any experiment should not affect a device owner's normal interaction with the other apps, and should never do any damage to the device's file system, slow down network connectivity, etc.

Privacy Protection and IRB Compliance. An equally important requirement is to provide privacy protections for device owners, and ensure that experiments comply to IRB policies that involve privacy. This prevents researchers from accidentally over gathering data, and further enables a wide range of research that were difficult to perform due to the overhead of IRB.

Informed Consent is one of the foundations of responsible research. It involves having participants understand the overarching goals, procedures, and risks of the research that will be performed on them (or using their data) and for them to indicate their willingness to participate. Appropriate materials must be provided in lay language so that participants can comprehend what they agree to.

Usability. Last but not least, it is crucial to make it easy for researchers to access the testbed and deploy experiments on a variety of devices. This requires a user-friendly interface, as well as a well-designed and well-managed infrastructure.

In the following, we present the design choices we made according to the requirements above.

3.2 Informed Consent

In designing Sensibility Testbed, we note that informed consent need not be done individually for every use of data. It is common in medical research, social sciences, economics, and other fields to simply have participants opt in for their data to be used for research purposes related to that field, especially in cases where the research involves low or no risk for participants. We have already obtained IRB approval for Sensibility Testbed to use a similar structure, where participants opt in to computer science research with low to no risk for participants. Therefore, Alice consents to provide access to researchers like Rhonda to run IRB-approved experiments on her devices. Meanwhile, Rhonda is bound to the IRB agreement of her institution, and is also bound by the policies of Sensibility Testbed.

3.2.1 Device Owner Policy. Also part of informed consent is that device owners can control how information is gathered from their devices. For example, Alice can opt out of individual experiments, disable or stop all experiments at any time. Furthermore, she can control, in a more precise manner, how sensors are accessed on her device, in a way she is comfortable with. The device owner's policies supersede any policies set by researcher's IRB. For example, if Alice disallows access to her microphone, then Rhonda's experiment

Privacy concerns	Sensor data	Baseline policies†
Low risk.	Battery status (charging/discharging), temperature, technology, health (good/overheat), battery level, voltage, plug-in type.	Full precision, round-up (if numeric), or constant.
	Bluetooth scan mode, state (enabled/disabled).	
	Cellular network roaming status, SIM card status (ready/absent), phone status (idle/busy), signal strength.	
	Location service provider.	
	WiFi link speed, association state, nearby routers' frequency, signal strength.	
	Vibrate mode, screen settings (on/off, brightness, timeout), media/ringer volume.	
Prevent keyloggers and activity tracking.	Motion sensors: accelerometer, gyroscope, magnetometer, orientation, ambient light, etc.	Full precision, round-up, random rotation, constant; restrict access frequency.
Prevent locating a device.	Latitude, longitude, altitude.	Approximate to the nearest zipcode region, or city/state/country center; restrict access frequency.
	Nearby Bluetooth device names.	Hashed device names; restrict access frequency.
	Cellular network cell ID, neighboring cell ID(s).	Randomized ID; restrict access frequency.
	Cellular network operator ID and name, country code, area code.	Hashed ID, names, and code; restrict access frequency.
	WiFi connection information (SSID and MAC address of currently connected router).	Hashed SSID, randomized MAC address; restricted access frequency.
	WiFi scan result (nearby WiFi routers' SSIDs and MAC addresses)	
Prevent identifying a device owner.	Bluetooth MAC address, local name.	Randomized MAC address, hashed device names.
	Cellular device ID, incoming number.	Randomized ID and number.
	WiFi connection information (device MAC address, IP address).	Randomized MAC address, hashed IP address.
Prevent video/audio recording.	Take pictures, record videos using a camera.	Disabled.
	Voice record using a microphone.	
Prevent actions for owner.	Scan barcode, search, etc., using an Intent.	
	Send/receive messages, delete messages, dial/pick up phone calls.	
Protect owner's contacts.	Contact list of the device owner in an address book.	

†This lists the policies at publication time. Policies need to be adjusted as new threats emerge.

Table 1: Sensibility Testbed's baseline policies for sensor data.

cannot get access to Alice's microphone, even if the IRB policy at Rhonda's institution allows the access.

3.3 Researcher Specifies IRB Policies

Before conducting any experiments, Rhonda first registers an account with Sensibility Testbed. The testbed sets up the relevant IRB policies that must be enforced on remote devices on behalf of Rhonda.

To register an experiment, Rhonda must indicate the precision and frequency at which Rhonda's IRB protocol allows her experiment to access each sensor. The list of sensors and their available policies defined by Sensibility Testbed are in Table 1. Each policy can be further customized. Rhonda sets the policies by specifying that her experiment can (1) read location information from devices with accuracy within 30 meters, (2) read accurate cellular signal strength and network type, but use randomized cell IDs, and (3) get location and cellular network updates every 10 minutes. Lastly, she specifies the experiment duration, after which the testbed deletes her experiment. All the information above is checked against the approved IRB certificate to ensure that the policies are consistent. This information is used to define obfuscation layers that enforce technical restrictions for her experiment. These obfuscation layers cannot be bypassed.

When an account is approved, Rhonda can request a number of mobile devices for her experiment through the testbed. If Alice's device (among other devices) is discovered by the testbed, Sensibility Testbed assigns a sandbox on her device to Rhonda's account, in which Rhonda's experiment will run. The testbed then creates access policies for Rhonda's experiment in accordance with her specified IRB policies, and deploys them on Alice's device.

3.3.1 Baseline Policies. Sensibility Testbed uses *baseline policies* to prevent common privacy and security attacks, as listed in Table 1. The baseline policies disable highly sensitive sensors, such as cameras and microphones. Additionally, the baseline policies disable intrusive actions such as making phone calls, scanning a barcode on behalf of the device owner, or accessing an address book, and so on.

Furthermore, the baseline policies obfuscate some common privacy risks: (1) identifying a device or its owner via, e.g., MAC address and device ID; (2) locating a device through cell IDs, WiFi SSIDs, etc.; and (3) inferring keys strokes and activities of a device owner using motion sensors such as accelerometers and gyroscopes. For example, the policies enforce randomized MAC addresses in a Bluetooth or WiFi network, and approximated location coordinates, as well as controlling the frequency of access to motion sensors. Note that keyloggers and activity trackers are more effective when the access frequency to motion sensors is high [10, 14].

Finally, there are low-entropy sensors like battery status and WiFi link speed whose privacy impact is small. Access to them still must be requested through the IRB process, as the goal is to minimize the privacy risk for device owners whenever possible.

Sensibility Testbed's baseline policies are set to appropriate levels to protect against known attacks today. However, these levels will need to change over time as new attacks emerge, making the baseline policies stronger over time.

3.3.2 Policy Hierarchy. Device owner's policies are always applied first. Following this, the baseline policies for the experiment are used. Then the experiment-specific IRB policies are put into place. The experiment code is subject to all policies. The ability to combine policies makes it easy to create complex policies. Next, we introduce how these policies are implemented.

4 IMPLEMENTATION

We describe the implementation details of Sensibility Testbed, including its secure sandbox, and the way to enforce privacy policies as described in Section 3.

4.1 Secure Sandbox

The sandbox in Sensibility Testbed provides a programming language interface equipped with system calls for networking, file system, threading, locking, logging, and most importantly, sensors. Every system call is strictly sanitized to preserve consistent behavior across different OSes, and to avoid exploitable vulnerabilities. Additionally, the sandbox can interpose on system calls that use resources, such as network, disk I/O, and sensors, and prevents or delays the execution of these calls if they exceed their configured quota. The details of the sandbox implementation can be found in our prior work [3].

4.2 Policy Enforcement

Rhonda's IRB policies are implemented as obfuscation layers, with each layer enforcing an access control policy over a sensor. The sandbox provides a list of system calls, such as `get_location()`, `get_accelerometer()`. The sandbox can also control the behavior of these calls using system call interposition [3]. Each obfuscation layer is thus implemented as template code, pre-loaded in each sandbox, and can be instantiated with parameters from Rhonda's policy specification to interject a system call. Each obfuscation layer defines one or two of the following categories of policies.

4.2.1 Reducing Data Precision. As an example, to obfuscate Alice's location to a nearest city, the obfuscation layer conceptually takes these steps:

```
define get_city_location():
  # call the full-precision get_location function
  exact_location = get_location()

  # look up city corresponding to the exact location
  city_location = find_closest_city(exact_location)

  return city_location
```

The function first retrieves the device location at full precision. It then returns the closest city as the obfuscated device location. In every sandbox that Rhonda can access, each function call to `get_location` is interposed and then replaced by a call to `get_city_location`. This is achieved in a transparent and non-bypassable way, much like a derived class can override its parent class's implementation of a method.

4.2.2 Restricting Data Access Frequency. When an experiment attempts to use a sensor more frequently than the given threshold allows, the obfuscation layer pauses the code for as long as required to bound it, on average, below the threshold. The code of a rate-limiting obfuscation layer for accessing an accelerometer is as follows.

```
define rate_limited_accelerometer(pause_time):
  # pause the code for a time threshold
```

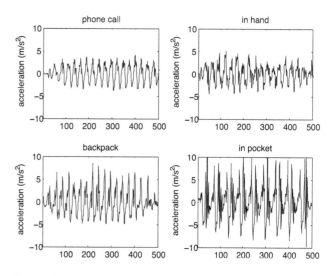

Figure 1: Accelerometer data based on different activities.

```
  lock.acquire()

  while (current_time < next_allowed_access_time):
    pause

  # update time threshold for next sensor access
  next_allowed_access_time = \
      current_time + pause_time
  lock.release()

  # call the original get_accelerometer function
  accelerometer = get_accelerometer()
  return accelerometer
```

The rate-limiting code ensures that enough time has elapsed before the accelerometer is accessed. Note that locking is necessary to prevent race conditions among different threads that try to access the sensor at the same time. Access frequency is controlled by `pause_time`, a parameter determined by Rhonda's IRB policies. After enough time has elapsed, the code accesses the accelerometer, and returns its reading. When this obfuscation layer is in place, all calls to `get_accelerometer()` will be replaced by `rate_limited_accelerometer(pause_time)`.

4.2.3 Policy Stack. Different sets of policies can be customized as a *policy stack*. In this stack, every layer inherits the policy defined by its ancestor layers, with the exception of the lowest layer (the sandbox kernel). The experiment runs at the top of the policy stack, inheriting all the policies defined by the lower layers. Each policy stack acts as a set of filters for different sensors, through which sensor calls must pass before being accessed by a sandboxed program.

5 EVALUATION

The mobile testbed in this work serves two purposes: providing resources for conducting research experiments, and protecting end-users' privacy. Since it is difficult to evaluate the Sensibility Testbed IRB workflow from a researcher's point of view, we discuss technical issues as well as the system's usability and practicality.

Q1: Do the proposed privacy policies effectively protect device owners in research experiments? Here we provide an example where an adversary uses an accelerometer to infer a device owner's everyday activities. We show that a Sensibility Testbed policy can effectively prohibit such activity tracking.

Activity tracking. A user's activities, such as reading text messages or emails, making a phone call, or carrying the phone in a backpack, are reflected by motion sensors. These sensors do not require permission from the device owner to access, therefore attacks using them are more difficult to detect and prevent. Figure 1 shows the accelerometer data patterns of a device owner when the access rate is 50 Hz. The x-axis is the number of samples, and the y-axis is the accelerometer data with the gravity removed. From this figure, a device owner's activities can be inferred by detecting periodic maxima in the magnitude of acceleration. These maxima can also be used to segment the data into individual steps, which provide a signature that is unique to each device owner and the specific activity. For example, when the device is placed in the owner's pants pocket, for each pair of steps, the data will show a large spike and a smaller spike due to leg swings. Nevertheless, when the signal is reduced to below 25 Hz, every pattern that we saw looks like the one when the device is held in hand.

Policy enforcement. To test the effectiveness of policy enforcement, we recruited 16 device owners and asked them to carry their phones in each of the four modes. The raw accelerometer data rate from their devices varied from 50 to 100 Hz. We subsampled the raw accelerometer data with rates from 20 to 50 Hz. Each activity's tracking accuracy with different access rates are shown in Figure 2.

There is a sharp decline in the tracking accuracy when the access rate drops below 25 Hz. At this rate, it is impossible to distinguish the activity of the device owner, as all patterns become similar to the reference pattern when the device is held in hand. Thus, in Figure 2 the accuracy when the phone is held in hand is always greater than zero. To prevent activity tracking, Sensibility Testbed sets a baseline policy to restrict motion sensor's frequency to below 25 Hz.

Q2: What utility does restricted data provide? We showed above that privacy policies effectively prohibit tracking a user's activities. However, the rate-limited data still suffices for many other applications, e.g., the accelerometer data reduced to 25 Hz can be used for pedometry, as one can still differentiate one step from another in the accelerometer data.

In another experiment, Sensibility Testbed was used by a high school student as part of a vehicle data collection project. The student connected his device to the on-board diagnostics (OBD) sensor interface in a car, and used Sensibility Testbed to capture data, such as fuel consumption, pressure, mileage, and engine RPMs. The student then drove around the NYC area and used this data to derive information about traffic patterns [13]. Even when the location was restricted to a ZIP code area, the data allowed him to make inferences about traffic conditions, when combined with information about the weather or large gatherings at entertainment venues, and to predict possibly hazardous road conditions.

While it is an open question that whether the policies using obfuscation may affect the accuracy of an experiment, we plan to carry out more studies like the ones above, to investigate such a privacy-functionality tradeoff.

Q3: Is Sensibility Testbed effective for developing sensor-enabled experiments? In the past, we have hosted hack-a-thons

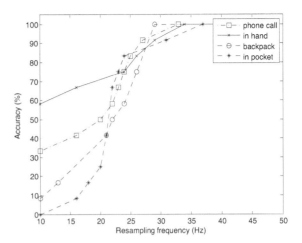

Figure 2: Accuracy at different resampling frequencies.

co-located with the IEEE Sensors Applications Symposium (SAS) [2]. This conference attracts a diverse community of researchers that use sensors in their research. The vast majority of participants come from other scientific disciplines than computer science. Each time we have had about twenty participants spend a day of the conference building applications using Sensibility Testbed. None of the participants had any prior experience with our platform.

Researchers implemented code that they tested in the same day. Despite only knowing about Sensibility Testbed for roughly six hours, many researchers built many interesting and complex applications. These included applications for navigating between conference rooms using WiFi connection information, and monitoring battery information and turning off WiFi and Bluetooth when battery level is low. Among all the 25 teams we had, only one group did not finish the application development.

6 CHALLENGES

During the implementation and evaluation of Sensibility Testbed, we observe the following research challenges, which we will leave to our future work.

6.1 Accessing Personal Data

Due to privacy considerations, Sensibility Testbed deliberately disallows access to personal data stored on the phone (such as performing research using the device owner's phone book), or introspection into the mobile OS. We consider the obfuscation techniques presented in this paper valid for these resources as well. However, interesting approaches for querying privacy-preserving database would be helpful to improve the utility of the testbed.

6.2 Technical Challenges

Sensibility Testbed is designed to minimize the privacy repercussions of smartphone research by limiting an experiment's access to sensors. However, this does not guarantee that the existing obfuscation layers and configurations will always be able to address adequately all possible privacy concerns. Therefore, we anticipate that the baseline policies will need to adapt over time. Additionally, bugs in the sandbox or obfuscation code might expose the device owner's privacy, thus requiring updates of the platform code.

6.3 Usability Challenges

Letting device owners choose and parametrize their own privacy policies also poses a usability challenge. There are many interesting problems to explore in this space. For example, how to help device owners configure the policies to make informed decisions about how their devices are used, whether device owners would want to have different policies to different researchers, and so on.

7 RELATED WORK

Sensibility Testbed is the first mobile testbed that supports automatic IRB policy enforcement. We compare our work with previous research in this section.

7.1 Data Anonymization

Some researchers employ a third-party anonymizing agent as a proxy between the data source and the service using the anonymized data [6, 11]. Sensibility Testbed's privacy preservation is carried out on the device, without using a third-party agent. The only data leaving the device is what researcher requests through the IRB policies.

7.2 Data Obfuscation

Data obfuscation has been suggested in [8] for privacy preservation. The authors demonstrate location and time obfuscation of reports. Sensibility Testbed built a systemic solution for data obfuscation, and enable purpose-based access control for the data (eg., the granularity of data-sharing depends on the utility), which is never studied systemically in previous papers. Besides, we add new schemes such as topological obfuscation (e.g. mapping exact locations to ZIP code areas), hashing, and randomization, and also applies them to other sensor types.

7.3 Detecting Privacy Violation

There has also been much work dedicated to detecting privacy violation from mobile apps [4, 5, 7, 16]. These approaches alert the user when sensitive data is exfiltrated from the device, either at runtime [4, 5] or install time [7]. Although these systems notify the user when there is a potential privacy breach, they leave the mitigation decision up to the user because they do not know whether the data sharing is legitimate or not. Sensibility Testbed, on the other hand, protects the user directly from exfiltration of sensitive data without requiring manual intervention at a critical time, because Sensibility Testbed conforms to the IRB protocol.

7.4 Other Smartphone Testbed

There are several smartphone testbeds with researcher purchased devices. For example, PhoneLab [12] is a smartphone testbed for research experimentation. It provides low-cost devices to students. However, it only requires researchers to submit their approved IRB protocols and the URLs to their apps in the Google Play Store. This model cannot enforce privacy policies as Sensibility Testbed does.

8 CONCLUSION

By enabling programmable enforcement of IRB-approved privacy policies through the control of sensor access, Sensibility Testbed is able to provide flexible policy implementation. As a result, not only researchers no longer need to have a "hands-on" role in policy enforcement, it also greatly reduces the risk of participation for device owners. Sensibility Testbed thus encourages the development of larger-scale experiments, protects the privacy of participants, and is easy for researchers to use.

REFERENCES

[1] [n. d.]. Hackers can attack your phone via 76 popular iOS apps. ([n. d.]). Accessed January 14, 2018, http://www.dailymail.co.uk/sciencetech/article-4203180/Hackers-attack-phone-76-popular-iOS-apps.html.
[2] [n. d.]. Sensors Applications Symposium. ([n. d.]). http://sensorapps.org/.
[3] Justin Cappos, Armon Dadgar, Jeff Rasley, Justin Samuel, Ivan Beschastnikh, Cosmin Barsan, Arvind Krishnamurthy, and Thomas Anderson. 2010. Retaining sandbox containment despite bugs in privileged memory-safe code. In *Proceedings of the 17th ACM conference on Computer and communications security*. ACM, 212–223.
[4] Supriyo Chakraborty, Chenguang Shen, Kasturi Rangan Raghavan, Yasser Shoukry, Matt Millar, and Mani Srivastava. 2014. ipShield: a framework for enforcing context-aware privacy. In *11th USENIX Symposium on Networked Systems Design and Implementation (NSDI 14)*. USENIX Association, 143–156.
[5] William Enck, Peter Gilbert, Seungyeop Han, Vasant Tendulkar, Byung-Gon Chun, Landon P Cox, Jaeyeon Jung, Patrick McDaniel, and Anmol N Sheth. 2014. TaintDroid: an information-flow tracking system for realtime privacy monitoring on smartphones. *ACM Transactions on Computer Systems (TOCS)* 32, 2 (2014), 5.
[6] Marco Gruteser and Dirk Grunwald. 2003. Anonymous usage of location-based services through spatial and temporal cloaking. In *Proceedings of the 1st international conference on Mobile systems, applications and services*. ACM, 31–42.
[7] Shashank Holavanalli, Don Manuel, Vishwas Nanjundaswamy, Brian Rosenberg, Feng Shen, Steven Y Ko, and Lukasz Ziarek. 2013. Flow permissions for android. In *Automated Software Engineering (ASE), 2013 IEEE/ACM 28th International Conference on*. IEEE, 652–657.
[8] Apu Kapadia, Nikos Triandopoulos, Cory Cornelius, Daniel Peebles, and David Kotz. 2008. AnonySense: Opportunistic and privacy-preserving context collection. In *Pervasive Computing*. Springer, 280–297.
[9] Chucri A Kardous and Peter B Shaw. 2014. Evaluation of smartphone sound measurement applicationsa). *The Journal of the Acoustical Society of America* 135, 4 (2014), EL186–EL192.
[10] Emiliano Miluzzo, Alexander Varshavsky, Suhrid Balakrishnan, and Romit Roy Choudhury. 2012. Tapprints: your finger taps have fingerprints. In *Proceedings of the 10th international conference on Mobile systems, applications, and services*. ACM, 323–336.
[11] Mohamed F Mokbel, Chi-Yin Chow, and Walid G Aref. 2006. The new Casper: query processing for location services without compromising privacy. In *Proceedings of the 32nd international conference on Very large data bases*. VLDB Endowment, 763–774.
[12] Anandatirtha Nandugudi, Anudipa Maiti, Taeyeon Ki, Fatih Bulut, Murat Demirbas, Tevfik Kosar, Chunming Qiao, Steven Y Ko, and Geoffrey Challen. 2013. Phonelab: A large programmable smartphone testbed. In *Proceedings of First International Workshop on Sensing and Big Data Mining*. ACM, 1–6.
[13] Michael Reininger, Seth Miller, Yanyan Zhuang, and Justin Cappos. 2015. A First Look at Vehicle Data Collection via Smartphone Sensors. In *Sensors Applications Symposium (SAS), 2015 IEEE*. IEEE.
[14] Zhi Xu, Kun Bai, and Sencun Zhu. 2012. Taplogger: Inferring user inputs on smartphone touchscreens using on-board motion sensors. In *Proceedings of the fifth ACM conference on Security and Privacy in Wireless and Mobile Networks*. ACM, 113–124.
[15] Yanyan Zhuang, Jianping Pan, Yuanqian Luo, and Lin Cai. 2011. Time and location-critical emergency message dissemination for vehicular ad-hoc networks. *Selected Areas in Communications, IEEE Journal on* 29, 1 (2011), 187–196.
[16] Sebastian Zimmeck, Ziqi Wang, Lieyong Zou, Roger Iyengar, Bin Liu, Florian Schaub, Shomir Wilson, Norman Sadeh, Steven M Bellovin, and Joel Reidenberg. 2017. Automated analysis of privacy requirements for mobile apps. In *Proceedings of the Network and Distributed System Security (NDSS) Symposium*, Vol. 2017.

Author Index